MAYORS IN THE MIDDLE

MAYORS IN THE MIDDLE

POLITICS, RACE, AND MAYORAL CONTROL OF URBAN SCHOOLS

Edited by

Jeffrey R. Henig and Wilbur C. Rich

14/05

PRINCETON UNIVERSITY PRESS   PRINCETON AND OXFORD

Library of Congress Cataloging-in-Publication Data

Mayors in the middle : politics, race, and mayoral control of urban
schools / edited by Jeffrey R. Henig and Wilbur C. Rich.
p. cm.
Includes bibliographical references and index.
ISBN 0-691-11506-0 (cloth : alk.paper) — ISBN 0-691-11507-9
(pbk. : alk. paper)
1. Education, Urban — Political aspects — United States — Case
studies.   2. Urban policy — United States — Case studies.
3. Mayors — United States — Case studies.   4. Education and
state — United States — Case studies.   I. Henig, Jeffrey R., 1951–
II. Rich, Wilbur C.
LC5131.M39 2004
370'.9173'2 — dc22   2003054450

British Library Cataloging-in-Publication Data is available

This book has been composed in Sabon

Printed on acid-free paper. ∞

www.pupress.princeton.edu

Printed in the United States of America

10   9   8   7   6   5   4   3   2   1

Contents

Acknowledgments

THIS BOOK began as a workshop organized while we were both visiting scholars at The Russell Sage Foundation (RSF). We are extremely grateful to RSF president Eric Wanner and his staff for providing the funds, encouragement, staff support, and space for the workshop. A special thanks is due to Marian Manichaikul, a former RSF staff member who arranged the logistics for the meeting participants.

We also would like to thank all the participants in the workshop, not only those who wrote papers but also those who provided thoughtful commentary and helped lead the project toward a higher level of insight. Chuck Myers, of Princeton University Press, also deserves a lot of gratitude for expressing interest early on and then overseeing this project through to its end.

For ourselves, and on behalf of the other contributors, we want to thank the individuals interviewed for the case studies. Many of those we talked to dropped public poses and talked honestly about some of the sensitive and not always heroic sides of the story of urban school reform.

Finally, we thank all the outside readers for their insightful comments and suggestions. Of course, we take full responsibility for the final product.

List of Contributors ———————————————

About the Editors

Jeffrey R. Henig is Professor of Political Science & Education at Teachers College and Professor of Political Science at Columbia University. Recent books of which he is the author or co-author include *Rethinking School Choice: Limits of the Market Metaphor* (1994); *Shrinking the State: The Political Underpinnings of Privatization* (1998); *The Color of School Reform: Race, Politics and the Challenge of Urban Education* (1999); which the Urban Politics Section of the American Political Science Association named the best book written on urban politics in 1999; and *Building Civic Capacity: The Politics of Reforming Urban Schools* (2001), which the Urban Politics Section of the American Political Science Association named the best book written on urban politics in 2001.

Wilbur C. Rich is professor of political science at Wellesley College. He is the author of *The Politics of Urban Personnel Policy: Reformers, Politicians and Bureaucrats* (1982), *Coleman Young and Detroit Politics: From Social Activist to Power Broker* (1989), and *Black Mayors and School Politics* (1996). He has also edited three books: *The Politics of Minority Coalition* (1996); *The Economics and Politics of Sports Stadiums* (2000); and with James Bowers *Mayoral Leadership in Middle-Sized Cities* (2000). In addition, he has published several articles and reports concerning local government administrative problems.

About the Other Contributors

Stefanie Chambers is an assistant professor at Trinity College in Hartford, Connecticut. She earned her Ph.D. from Ohio State University in 1999. Her research interests include urban politics, urban public policy, and racial and ethnic politics.

Kenneth J. Meier is the Charles Puryear Professor of Liberal Arts and Professor of Political Science at Texas A&M University. He also holds the Sara Lindsey Chair in Government in the George Bush School of Government and Public Service at Texas A&M. He is pursuing two major research agendas. One is a national study of Latino and African American education policy in 1,800 school districts. The second is building and testing an empirical theory of public management.

Jeffrey Mirel is Associate Dean for Academic Affairs in the School of Education at the University of Michigan. He is also Professor of Educational Studies, Professor of History, and Faculty Associate in the Center for Russian and East European Studies. Mirel is the author of *The Rise and Fall of an Urban School System: Detroit, 1907–81*, Second Edition (1999), and co-author of *The Failed Promise of the American High School, 1890–1995* (1999).

Marion Orr is a Professor of Political Science at Brown University. His book, *Black Social Capital: The Politics of School Reform in Baltimore, 1986–1998* (1999), won the Policy Studies Organization's 2000 Aaron Wildavsky Best Book Award. He is co-author of the *Color of School Reform: Race, Politics, and the Challenge of Urban Education* (1999). He is currently engaged in a study of the organizing experiences of the Industrial Areas Foundation (IAF) in various U.S. cities.

John Portz is a Professor in the Department of Political Science and the School of Education at Northeastern University. He has written several articles on education policy and was the lead author on a recent study of school politics in three cities, titled *City Schools and City Politics: Institutions and Leadership in Pittsburgh, Boston, and St. Louis* (1999). Focusing on governance, he authored a related article in *Urban Education*, "Supporting Education Reform: Mayoral and Corporate Paths" (November 2000). Currently, he is the principal investigator for a Northeastern/Harvard University team that is under a three-year contract with the Boston Public Schools to evaluate its Transition Services Program for academically at-risk students in grades 3, 6, and 9.

Dorothy Shipps is Assistant Professor of Education at Teachers College, Columbia University. She is a Carnegie Scholar for 2000–2001, an award that supports the research and writing of *School Reform, Corporate Style: The Nexus of Politics, Business and Education Change in Twentieth Century Chicago* (forthcoming). She is co-editor, with Larry Cuban, of *Reconstructing the Common Good in Public Education: Coping with Intractable American Dilemmas* (2000) and author of several articles, chapters and reports on school reform in Chicago. Her research interests include business involvement in education and the historical and political analysis of urban schooling.

Clarence N. Stone is Research Professor of Public Policy and Political Science at the George Washington University. His most recent books include *Changing Urban Education* (1998) and *Building Civic Capacity: The Politics of Reforming Urban Schools* (2001), co-authored with Jeffrey Henig, Bryan Jones and Carol Pierannunzi. Stone's current research interests include urban school reform, urban regimes, and the politics of local agenda-setting.

Part 1

INTRODUCTION

Chapter One

Mayor-centrism in Context

JEFFREY R. HENIG AND WILBUR C. RICH

SCHOOLS in many of our inner city school districts are failing. Children who attend them are at risk. The risk is not just short-term for it puts in jeopardy the learning careers of many minority students. Students in non-urban school districts are more than fifty percent more likely than urban students to score at or above the "basic" level in reading, mathematics, and science. Much of this performance gap is attributable to social and economic problems, such as poverty and racial discrimination, which fall especially hard on inner city children and are largely outside the schools' ability to control. But the poor performance of inner city schools is not solely attributable to the low incomes and minority status of the populations they serve. Although white students in large central cities perform as well as their white counterparts nationally on SAT scores, for example, African American students in large cities score substantially worse than their national counterparts.[1] Forty-six percent of nonurban students in high poverty schools reach the basic level in reading, for example, compared to only 23 percent in high poverty urban schools; in math the comparable rates are 61 percent to 33 percent achieving basic level, and in science they are 56 percent to 31 percent (Olson and Jerald 1998; Stone, Henig, et al. 2001).

America has not been blind to the problem of poorly performing schools. Over the past two decades the need to improve the nation's public schools has consistently been high on the public agenda. Public attention escalated in 1983, when the National Commission on Excellence in Education announced "a crisis in confidence," and nearly two decades later education issues continued to be a prominent factor in the presidential platforms of both Al Gore and George W. Bush. In a 2000 Gallup poll, only 36 percent of Americans said they were satisfied with the quality of K–12 education in the nation (Chambers 2000). Such sustained agenda status is unusual in a country where a fickle media and citizens with a limited span of attention have been known to shuttle issues in and out of the limelight with surprising rapidity (Downs 1972). While much of the language of this broad school reform movement has been framed in more general terms, it is the special case of urban schools that has provided much of the imagery of failure and near despair.[2]

Despite glimmers of success and incremental signs of progress, the results of this sustained attention have been disappointing.[3] Hot new reforms and celebrated school reformers cycle through urban school systems in quick succession, raising high hopes that are soon deflated. This pattern, variously labeled "policy churn," "spinning wheels," "reform *du jour*," has engendered a deeper sense of fatalism among some and a desperation-driven readiness to adopt radical solutions among others (Farkas 1992; Hess 1998; Henig, Hula, et al. 1999; Stone, Henig, et al. 2001).

Out of this context has emerged a new approach. Rather than focusing on a particular pedagogical philosophy or way to organize schools — indeed, rather than focusing on any specific vision of schools, teachers, classrooms, and the ways they interact — this model emphasizes a straightforward change in the formal structure of governance. But unlike a rival model that seeks to stimulate reform by turning sharply away from government and relying instead on market forces and consumer choice (Chubb and Moe 1990), this approach locates responsibility squarely on elected leaders and traditional institutions of local democracy.

Traditionally, Americans have endeavored to keep elected municipal politicians out of their school administration. Now that approach is being turned on its head (Mahtesian 1996; Stanfield 1997; Kirst and Bulkley 2000). Drawing on theories of public administration, analogies to corporate practice, and what has been heralded as a proven success led by Chicago's Mayor Richard M. Daley, more and more school reformers are looking to mayors for leadership. While some believe mayors already have enough formal and informal power to fill this role if they can be convinced to do so, the more serious efforts have involved a wholesale transfer of formal decision-making authority to mayors, usually at the expense of elected school boards. While this "mayor-centric" approach is sometimes promoted and adopted by local interests, more often it has involved intervention by governors and state legislators who claim that they must take extraordinary steps in order to rescue a faltering system unable to heal itself. While the theories and rationales for this reform are framed in universal terms that should apply to any community struggling with disjointed educational initiatives and ineffective schools, actual cases to date nearly always involve central city school districts with predominantly Black students and school leadership.

This book examines the movement to put mayors in the middle of urban school reform through the window of six cities that have chosen, or been forced, to give mayors a strong formal role in school governance. While similar in many respects, the case cities — Baltimore, Boston, Chicago, Cleveland, Detroit, and the District of Columbia — vary in the route they have taken to mayor-centrism, the particular form they have adopted, and the lessons they seem to present. Through the case studies and the wide-ranging essays that follow and build upon them, we hope to raise and at least begin the process of answering some questions that are critical to the future of inner city children, the prospects for urban revitalization, and the shape of American education in the years to come.

- Is the movement toward mayor-centrism the kind of bold institutional change that can build strong civic capacity and break the cycle of ephemeral reform initiatives, or is it just the latest entry in the copycat world of American school reform *du jour*?
- Does giving city hall the authority to select school board members, dictate budget priorities, and manage the day-to-day operations of the educational system give central city residents a clearer target at which to direct their hopes and frustrations and break the reactionary hold of an educational bureaucracy that has acted as a "public school cartel" (Rich 1996), or is it better understood as a power grab by corporate leaders and state legislators with their own visions of urban revitalization and a belief that they can pursue those visions more effectively if power is moved into venues in which their access and influence is more assured?
- Are the racially defined battle lines that frequently form around proposals to put mayors in charge of schools epiphenomena fueled by misunderstandings and misplaced loyalties deliberately stirred by entrenched groups seeking to maintain their privileged status, or is race-based politics rooted in real and deep conflicts of interest that are central to understanding this serious effort to reshape the formal structure of urban governance?

It is a mark of the complexity of the challenge — and indication of the naïveté of some of the prominent solutions commonly offered — that this book's analyses of these questions point to mixed motives, multiple dimensions, complex consequences, and context-specific answers.

A Break with American Tradition

Public school districts have enjoyed structural autonomy, if not political independence from city halls, for generations. We are seeing that autonomy threatened. Why? Despite their frustrations, Americans still have abiding faith in public schools (Moe 2001). They are losing faith, though, in the governance structures in which public schools are embedded. In groping for a rational response to the urban public school crisis it was perhaps predictable that mayors would volunteer, or allow themselves to be drafted by state legislatures, to rescue the school system. It represents, nonetheless, a sharp break with the past.

The notion that changing the formal structure of governance can lead to better schools has deep roots in American political and intellectual history. The current shape of public education governance owes much to the Progressive Era reformers who, early in the twentieth century, sought to improve public education by buffering it from political interference. Establishing school districts as relatively autonomous governments, with dedicated revenue streams and nonpartisan modes of selecting school boards, was seen as a way to grasp authority out of the hands of urban machines (Tyack 1974). Beginning in the 1960s in some cities, and developing considerably later in others, a second wave of school reformers set out to undo some of these changes. Believing that the Progressive Era reforms had led to an overly centralized and bureaucratic system, they sought to alter the formal structures of school governance in order to put more decision-making authority at the neighborhood or school level (Gittell, Hoffacker et al. 1980).

While the current reform movement shares with both the *professionalizers* and the *decentralizers* a strong confidence that formal governance structure matters, the substantive thrust of its proposals is to reverse many of the changes introduced by its predecessors in school reform. Like the professionalizers, they believe it is important to centralize decision-making authority in order to pursue citywide objectives and to have a clear pathway to accountability. But like the decentralizers, they believe that authority and accountability should run directly through electoral politics, with the education bureaucracy implementing democratically defined policies, rather than effectively setting policy on its own.

More specifically, the current school takeovers by big city mayors represent the melding of school and municipal politics. Public acquiescence to this fundamental change in the way schools are governed may be testimony to widespread frustration with poor performance on achievement tests, fiscal mismanagement, or violence in the public schools. An alternative explanation is that this may be yet another state-legislature-driven reform aimed at undermining minority control of big city schools. In any case, the changes will tell us much about how public demands to *do something* are translated into political action.

This *do something* imperative, found in public opinion surveys, also reflects a loss of confidence in elected boards, superintendents, and other traditional school decision makers. The new trends toward mayoral appointed school boards, chief executive officers (CEOs), and the hiring of "nontraditional" superintendents from business and the military also reveal an envy of corporate management structures. Long-standing notions of representative boards and pluralistic policymaking have been tossed aside.

In the 1980s and into the 1990s, critics of public schools were particularly harsh (Chubb and Moe 1990; Lieberman 1993; Rich 1996). Some claimed that public school professionals were unwitting contributors to the current organizational malaise and pedagogic bankruptcy. Even defenders of the public school system raised questions about the efficacy of school management, curriculum trends, and the continuing doldrums of student achievement scores. Conversely, neither critics nor supporters during that era looked to city halls as the solution to the public school crisis. Mayors, then, were still seen as part of the problem and not the solution.

Today, though, some of the same individuals and organizations that looked askance at local politicians favor giving unprecedented appointment powers given to mayors; some believe that such a radical structural change maybe the best or only way to stimulate "real" school reform. Proponents of a mayor-centric approach to school reform argue that it promotes efficiency, comprehensive rationality, accountability, and democratic participation. Mayoral control, it is asserted, is likely to promote efficiency because it puts decisions about spending in the hands of the same actors who must make decisions about taxation and other forms of revenue, a linkage that is severed by the formal structures in many cities.[4] Mayoral control is designed to promote comprehensive planning by putting decisions about schools in the hands of a leader in position to steer decisions about child welfare, safety, public health, recreation, job training, and economic development—issue areas that bear heavily on the tasks that schools are expected to perform but which typically are outside the sphere of influence of superintendents and school boards. Mayoral control promotes accountability and democracy, at least in theory, by placing responsibility in the hands of an easily identifiable actor who is subject to election in high visibility, high-turnout campaigns.

This mayor-centric strategy raises two broad kinds of questions. One set of questions addresses issues relating to the emergence of mayor-centrism on the school reform agenda and its prospects for success. Why have mayors come back into favor as instruments of school governance, why at this particular time, and why in the particular places that it has? Is the emergence of mayor-centrism a response to objective indicators of school failure? Has it emerged through a learning process during which other approaches were first tried and found wanting? Do local, indigenous movements for mayor-centrism differ in important ways from those that are externally developed and forcefully imposed? What types of organizations and interest groups promote (and oppose) this approach and what are their motivations for doing so? When such proposals are resisted, what determines who wins and who loses?

The second set of questions involves the consequences in districts that put such formal changes into place, and the conditions and strategies that make effective reform a more or less likely outcome. Do appointed school boards become rubber stamps for mayors? Do mayors come to use their direct and indirect appointment power as new sources of patronage? Does city hall micro-manage the school budget? Placed more clearly in competition with other demands that mayors must attend to, have schools held their own as far as budgetary commitments? What organizational changes flow from mayoral involvement? Are the performance problems that are so often pointed to in order to justify radical reforms in fact ameliorated as a result? What have been the distributional consequences of these changes? How, if at all, have governance changes affected patterns of political access? And how have they affected popular conception of the ideals of publicly provided education and of the legitimacy of the institutions through which we pursue those ideals?

These questions about the origin and consequences of the mayor-centric movement draw this book's investigations into the orbit of broader intellectual endeavors having to do with the general politics of policy making and the prospects for effective governmental intervention to improve social well-being. The research and conclusions that the separate articles present are deeply informed by theories that have emerged in the literatures of political science and public policy that are not limited to the education sphere. In return for that illumination, we frame our answers in ways that we hope may shed some light on the broader questions as well.

We are not looking to declare with finality that mayor-centrism either is—or is not—the key to urban school reform. One of the contributing factors to the fruitless and frustrating churning among reform notions that has characterized efforts in most American school systems is the misguided pursuit of a self-executing panacea. Structural changes such as the introduction of mayor-centrism can be counted upon to alter the relationships among key stakeholders. But whether that alteration ultimately does good or ill—or nothing at all—will depend upon a series of subsequent choices, only some of which will be influenced by the formal institutions of governance.

Cities and Schools in Context

Broad societal changes are forcing changes in the ways in which we understand schools and cities. Throughout much of the last century, education decision making and city politics were conceptualized as both discrete and self-contained, separate from one another, and from the broader metropolitan, state, and national institutions in which they were contained. This was always an overly simplistic vision, and is much more so today.

To understand the problems confronting urban schools and the range of solutions open to them it is increasingly necessary to regard school systems and local politics as intertwined and irretrievably linked to forces outside their boundaries. Those currently advocating a move toward greater mayoral authority recognize the fallacy of treating school systems as self-contained, but for the most part they continue to portray cities that way. Among the background themes that emerge from the case studies in this volume, three that illustrate the need to put both schools and cities into context involve cities and schools as elements in a regional and global economy; cities and schools as elements within a federal system; and cities and schools as leverage points in enduring conflicts over power and race.

Regional and Global Economic Transformation

The observation that we live in an era of a globalizing economy has become so familiar as to seem a bit trite, but it is no less true or important for being so. Urbanists with a nose for political economy began noting more than three decades ago that the flow of jobs and capital from the cities to the suburbs was having profound effects on physical and social developments within the city walls (Kirp, Dwyer and Rosenthal 1997; Long 1972; Sternlieb 1971; Banfield 1974). It did not take long for analysts to realize that there were analogous but broader shifts — from the Northeast and Midwest to the Southwest (Sale 1975) and from the United States to other nations with lower taxes and less expensive labor (Bluestone and Harrison 1984) — with similar consequences. Older cities, it was realized with alarm, might become technologically obsolete; left with the unhappy task of warehousing the least economically productive populations, while a declining tax base left them less and less maneuvering room to address their residents' needs (Sternlieb 1971). Reflecting on the structural dilemma facing central cities, Paul Peterson (1981) concluded that local leaders had no choice but to orient their policies around economic development and growth, with redistributive initiatives taken off the table out of deference to above average taxpayers who might exercise their exit option.

The advantages that allowed the older cities once to flourish (location on rivers and ports; concentration of diverse, complementary economic activities; public infrastructure) became less relevant, or in some in-

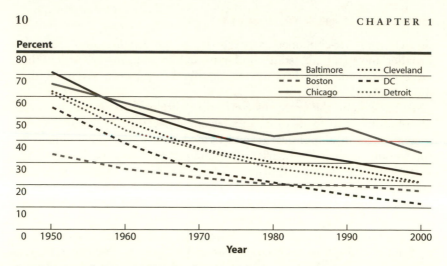

1.1 City population as percent of metropolitan area population. (U.S. Census Bureau, Statistical Abstract of the United States. Washington, D.C.: U.S. Department of Commerce. Various years.)

stances liabilities, as the economy made the transition from manufacturing to services and as capital could more fluidly relocate to respond to changing opportunities. Figures 1.1 and 1.2 illustrate two dimensions of the changes induced by these forces as manifested in the six cities that are the focus of the case studies. From 1950–2000, the population of each of the cities declined substantially relative to its surrounding metropolitan area; in a political system such as the United States, in which representation in state and national legislatures reflects population, declining populations translates almost directly into declining political clout (Stephens 1996; Weir 1996). As indicated, moreover, the decline was not merely in numbers, but also in the relative economic status of residents. In 1950, the six central cities had median family incomes averaging just under 95 percent of those for the entire metropolitan areas in which they were housed. By 1990, they averaged just over 65 percent, with Detroit showing the steepest decline, and only three cities (D.C., Boston, and Chicago) showing some sign the flow was beginning to be stemmed.

Older cities like these face, as a result, what Clarence Stone (this volume) characterizes as a "modernization challenge," not wholly unlike that confronted in many less developed countries. That affects what schools need to do. Manufacturing jobs once provided a viable career path for young people with no more than basic literacy, but the demands on today's education system are greater. Traditional school board recruitment patterns tend to draw disproportionately on those

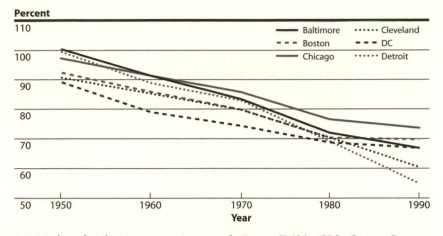

1.2 Median family income, ratio central city to SMSA. (U.S. Census Bureau, *Statistical Abstract of the United States*. Washington, D.C.: U.S. Department of Commerce. Various years.)

familiar with and invested in the "old way" of doing things. During a more insular period and one of slower change, the continuity, familiarity, and deep commitment they offered have often been more than sufficient to compensate for a dash of parochialism and conservatism, but perhaps that is no longer the case. Not only schools themselves, but also the institutions governing them might have to change to meet this modernization challenge. During the first half of the twentieth century, mayors were themselves often parochial in vision; many ignored education or focused on schools primarily as sources of patronage.

Contemporary mayors present a different profile. Compared to both traditional school boards and the earlier generations of mayors, today's generation of locally elected executives by training, orientation, and stronger links to the corporate sector may be better able to open up the education decision-making process so that it incorporates and responds to signals from the global economy.

Federalism, External Intervention, and Indigenous Reform

Just as some mayors historically found it politically safer to steer clear of the "hot potato" of school politics, so for many decades did national and state level officials find it convenient to delegate tough decisions about schooling to the local level.[5] How and why state and national politics have increasingly infused the education policy arena are complex stories with various twists and turns and involving legal, fiscal, and regulatory changes with relatively independent dynamics. Overviews of that story can be found elsewhere (Gittell 1998); the case studies in this volume provide microversions.

The role of the state and national government in feeding the current emphasis on mayors can be understood in large measure as an extension of a familiar paradox confronting central authorities in complex federal systems. Various economic and social transformations have made it increasingly hard for state and national leaders to ignore their responsibilities to improve the effectiveness and equity of urban education. But tough lessons with the experience of intervention have confirmed that simply articulating goals, enacting policies, and sending money are not enough. Central authorities need local partners, with local knowledge and indigenous constituencies, if their policies are to be implemented and if their reforms are to be sustained once their own attention is drawn elsewhere, as it invariably is.

State and federal interests have inserted their way into the traditionally local school decision-making arena through two basic routes. One involves the courts; the other involves electoral politics and democratic responsibility. Federal courts became involved most dramatically, of course, in relation to school desegregation. In recent years, state courts have been the more visible forces, especially through their adjudication of cases concerning school funding inequities. More recently, some state courts are being drawn into cases concerning the quality of education, as lawyers reframe challenges to move beyond student racial composition and funding equity to questions of outcomes (Id). When courts historically have found constitutional violations that require broad remedies, their actions and experiences have been mixed, but several generalities seem to hold. First, when local actors (school boards; mayors; civic leaders) have accepted the legitimacy of the court's decision and pragmatically sought to respond, the outcomes were much more favorable than when they resisted (Crain 1969; Hochschild 1984; Lukas 1985). Second, when courts have found themselves forced to institute their own implementation regimes — relying on special masters, precise guidelines to reluctant legislators or direct judicial oversight — their successes in forcing adherence to their orders have come at substantial costs (Dentler 1981; Lukas 1985; Formisano 1991). The most visible of those costs are financial and near-term, but at least as important may be longer-term costs. These include feeding political backlash movements that change laws so courts no longer have a justification to intervene or change the composition of the courts by steering the selection of judges in a less activist direction (Rosenberg 1991). They also appear to include a subtler erosion of local reform capacity, as local interests become accustomed to decisions being handed down from a higher level (Fraga, Erlichson, et al. 1998; Stone, Henig, et al. 2001).

While state governors and legislators often had to be dragged kicking and screaming into the thickets of school integration and funding equity, they have become much more proactive as the agenda has shifted toward education performance. New Jersey led the way in the late 1980s, when Governor Tom Keane initiated legislation allowing the state to take over local districts that consistently failed to perform; subsequently, the state used that authority to unseat and replace the local school boards in Jersey City, Patterson, and Newark. Other states followed suit, although initially with some tentativeness. As more and more states have turned to high-stakes testing (Ladd 1996; Heubert and Hauser 1999), however, takeover provisions of one kind or another have become standard fare as the ultimate sanction for schools and districts that fail to raise scores sufficiently.

Like the courts, however, state governors and legislators gradually are learning that their direct intervention exposes them to high financial and political costs. Where states have directly taken over districts, they have tended to find that the challenge of turning a system around is more daunting than initially imagined and have had little substantive change to show for their efforts.[6] One attractive alternative is to hand the ball of implementing reform to someone else. One model for doing so involves granting contracts or school charters to private corporations that promise to a better job. Another is to shift the burden to city hall, along with greater power and an initial injection of new resources.

Although the national government remains a bit player as far as its contribution to K–12 educational spending is concerned, occupants of the White House from Reagan onward have been quite aggressive about using their office to advance particular visions of education reform. For Presidents Reagan and George H. W. Bush, a primary emphasis was on promoting a school choice agenda; for Clinton and George W. Bush, greater attention has focused on standards and accountability. For the most part, these presidents — three of them former governors — have focused on the states as their primary partners. But the tendency of states to use mayors as their point of local leverage has been embraced as well at the national level. During the 1960s, a Democratic-controlled national government pioneered in this pattern of partnering with city hall through programs like Model Cities.[7] Conservative Republicans, at that time, saw this as a partisan effort to buck up an urban voting bloc firmly in the liberal camp. That the Republican leadership today sees urban mayors as reliable partners represents a genuine sea change. The explanation has more to do with changes that have made even Democratic mayors sound and act like fiscal conservatives than with any fundamental ideological evolution in Republican thought.

While state and federal actors traditionally have been more likely to view mayors as obstacles than partners, at least three factors may contribute to this new top-down constituency for stronger mayoral involvement. As the case chapters in this volume reveal, there has been a new wave of mayors elected in many large central cities. This new generation is seen as more pragmatic, technocratic, and managerial and less partisan, ideological, and beholden to racial, ethnic, and public employee constituencies than its predecessors. State and federal actors in the courts, legislatures, and executive branches seem to find these individuals more congenial and reliable partners than their more populist precursors. Moreover, even when state and federal interests feel no particular tie to these new mayors, they often feel a need to work with corporate interests; local business leaders who feel they have the ear of the mayor are among those promoting to state and federal actors the notion that mayors can be the linchpin for change. So too there may be a collective learning process involved, comparable to that which ensued after what some considered to be the failure of War on Poverty programs that had been designed to bypass the mayors.[8] As interpreted by Moynihan (1970) and others, Congress, President Johnson, and the broader policy community learned that funneling their efforts through city hall might necessitate some compromises in expectations but would also reduce the risks of high profile failures. This learned lesson was manifested in the Model Cities program, which put the mayors back in the driver's seat (Frieden and Kaplan 1977).

One way that intergovernmental influence traditionally has been judged is through the flow of revenues from one level to another. As indicated in Table 1.1, the six case cities differ much more in this respect than they do in the population and economic trends discussed earlier. Detroit raises only about thirteen cents of every dollar available for elementary and secondary education. Washington, D.C., which is in the unique position of lacking a state to which to turn, is at the other extreme, raising about 90 cents out of every dollar from local sources. State fiscal responsibility is substantially higher in Detroit, Baltimore, and Cleveland than in the other cities.

Racial Dimensions of Institutional Reforms

One of the most important stakeholders in central city school systems is the large and typically growing minority community. Figure 1.3 illus-

TABLE 1.1
Financial Attributes of School Systems, FY 1997

| City | | Financial Attributes of School System, FY 1997 | | |
	Expenditure per Student	Percent Revenue Local	Percent Revenue State	Percent Revenue Federal
Baltimore	$6,702	28.0	59.0	13.0
Boston	$9,537	60.5	32.9	6.6
Chicago	$5,784	53.6	33.7	12.7
Cleveland	$7,297	36.6	51.0	12.4
DC	$8,048	89.7	NA	10.3
Detroit	$6,934	13.4	76.0	10.6

Source: U.S. Department of Education, National Center for Education Statistics, Common Core of Data, Public Elementary/Secondary School Universe Survey, 1998–1999, and Local Education Agency Universe Survey, 1998–1999.

trates the decline in the white population that affected all six case study cities during the last half of the twentieth century. All six had majority white populations in 1950; by 2000, all but Boston were predominantly nonwhite. Table 1.2 provides a more precise categorization of racial and ethnic composition. When one distinguishes Hispanics as separate group, all six of the cities now have a "majority-minority" population; with Hispanics and Asians having a substantial presence in Boston and Chicago. Table 1.3 makes it clear that the racial transition has affected the public school enrollment even more dramatically than that of the population at large. In all six cities, 80 percent or more of the enrollment is Black, Hispanic, or Asian.

If urban schools fail to provide students the environment and teaching they need to become fully functional workers and citizens, it is these minority populations that will most directly bear the human costs. While the racial pattern of impact is clear, proponents of school reform in general and mayor-centric reform in particular have shied away from race when discussing their ideas. They believe either that race is incidental to the organizational, institutional, and systemic dynamics that are the source of the challenge, or they have made a tactical decision that discussion about race is so sensitive and polarizing that acknowledging its relevance risks stirring up political hornets' nests that will make reform even more unlikely.

Despite the race-neutral terms in which the arguments typically are framed, however, racial patterns are evident in the political configuration of support and opposition that emerges at least in the initial battles over these new governance proposals. While the movement to shift

Percent White

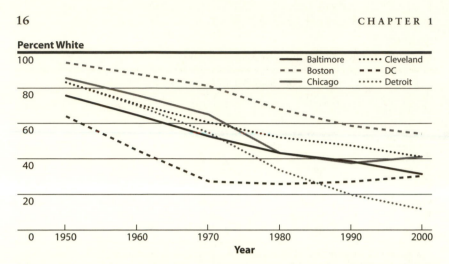

1.3 Racial change percent White, 1950–2000. (U.S. Census Bureau, Statistical Abstract of the United States. Washington, D.C.: U.S. Department of Commerce. Various years.)

power to the mayors is almost exclusively limited to large central cities with substantial proportions of minorities in the public schools, resistance has often centered in the minority communities, with the primary impetus behind the reform proposals coming from the business sector, state legislatures, and some foundations and "good government" groups. Ironically, the movement to put mayors in charge tends to be portrayed in some cities as a "white" initiative even when the mayor in question is Black.

TABLE 1.2
Racial Composition of Case Cities

City	Population 2000	Percent White, Not Hispanic	Percent Black, Not Hispanic	Percent Hispanic, any Race	Percent Asian
		Racial Composition of Case Cities			
Baltimore	651,154	31.0	64.3	1.7	1.5
Boston	589,141	49.5	25.3	14.4	7.5
Chicago	2,896,016	31.3	36.8	26.0	4.3
Cleveland	478,403	38.8	51.0	7.3	1.3
DC	572,059	27.8	60.0	7.9	2.7
Detroit	951,270	10.5	81.6	5.0	1.0

Source: U.S. Census Bureau, Census 2000 Redistricting Data.

TABLE 1.3
Student Race and Ethnicity

City	Enrollment Fall 98	Student characteristics, Fall 1998			
		Percent White, Not Hispanic	Percent Black, Not Hispanic	Percent Hispanic any Race	Percent Asian
Baltimore	106,540	12.2	86.4	0.5	0.6
Boston	63,043	15.6	48.8	26.2	9.0
Chicago	430,914	10.1	53.1	33.4	3.2
Cleveland	76,500	19.5	71.3	8.0	0.9
DC	71,889	4.3	85.9	8.3	1.6
Detroit	173,557	4.3	91.3	3.3	1.0

Source: U.S. Department of Education, National Center for Education Statistics, Common Core of Data, Public Elementary/Secondary School Universe Survey, 1998–1999, and Local Education Agency Universe Survey, 1998–1999.

What insights, in particular, can be gained by examining this phenomenon through a racial lens? Proposals to reallocate educational decision-making authority potentially intersect with race in at least three ways.

The first involves the material interest of the many minorities employed by the public school system. Principals, teachers, cafeteria workers, bus drivers, and others may expect that a mayor-centric regime is more likely to pursue cost-savings tactics involving school closures, teacher-testing, tough bargaining over contracts, and privatization of selective school functions, all of which could compromise their job security or hit them in the pocket book. What gives such material interest a racial configuration is the historical fact that public school systems have tended to hire minorities, particularly college educated ones, for a longer time and more aggressively than many other local government agencies or the local private sector.

The second intersection with race has to do with collective experience and racial symbolism. The important historical roles that educators and public schools have played in minority, and especially African American, communities, has given them an emotional and psychological meaning that transcends their direct economic impact. Teachers, along with preachers, for many decades served as key institutional leaders in black society; their higher level of education and accomplishment made them a source of pride, and the contribution many made in promoting the idea and cause of civil rights earned them a deep loyalty and respect (Henig, Hula, et al. 1999; Orr 2000). Beyond their function as an employment bureau, the public school system came to represent an institutional niche that Black Americans could thrive within. In the historic war for integration and justice it was the most visible front, and the site of some of the greatest victories. Against this backdrop, some within the minority community see efforts to put mayors in charge as an assault upon a valued institution and therefore rally around the status quo even if they are disappointed in the objective performance of the schools.

Finally, restructuring proposals may engage racial issues because of the differing demographic characteristics of the electoral constituencies that are empowered within the alternative institutional arrangements. In most central cities minorities comprise a much smaller proportion of the general voting age public than they do of the public school population. While all citizens are entitled to vote for school boards, where such boards are elected, turnout often is considerably lower than in general elections and disproportionately constituted by those with direct and current interest in the schools. Often, too, urban school boards are elected on a ward basis, an arrangement generally proven to advantage minority candidates and those with more grassroots support. Moving formal decision-making authority from a school board elected largely by parents, and often by ward, to a mayor elected by a city-wide electorate that includes many singles, older households, and families whose children attend private schools may have a direct effect on the racial distribution of political power.

Overview

These issues were discussed in a May 2001 conference, sponsored by the Russell Sage Foundation, on "Mayors, Minorities and Urban School Reform." Six papers were presented, each focusing on a particular city's experience. Some of these cities have had a relatively long experience with mayor-centrism, while others have moved in that directly more recently. In some cities, the decision to put mayors in the middle was the result of local debate and action; in others, the initiative came from above. Through a wide-ranging discussion including the authors, three discussants, and an audience comprising other scholars with relevant interests, the conference identified similarities and differences across the cases. We used those as the foundation to develop broad themes and questions for further analysis. These, in turn, guided the authors in revising their chapters, and gave birth to the analytical overview chapters that follow the case studies.

Some of the case cities have had considerably longer experience working within mayor-centric frameworks than the others. We lead with Baltimore and Chicago, which have the longest track records, and conclude with the District of Columbia, which did not install its restructured, partially mayor-appointed board until January 2001.

Marion Orr's study of Baltimore schools, a mayor-centric model of long-standing, reviews the leadership styles and contrasting stances toward educational issues of the city's last three mayors. William Donald Schaefer, a colorful politician of the old school, focused his energies on downtown development. Racial politics in the city made Schaefer reticent to use all the formal education policy powers at his disposal, except as a source of patronage through which to strengthen his political base. His successor, Kurt Schmoke, a highly visible African American mayor, made major efforts to reform the schools. Aside from making it a priority of his administration, he also handpicked the superintendent and hired a private company to manage a few of the city schools. Despite his formal power and strong personal commitment, Schmoke was unable to make headway in the battle to improve Baltimore schools. Ironically, while states have been key actors in promoting mayor-centrism elsewhere, in Maryland the state legislature responded by intervening in ways that arguably left the mayor less power than before. Although some observers argue that contemporary mayors have no choice but to make education reform a central part of their agendas, Orr shows that Baltimore's current mayor, Martin O'Malley, seems to be adopting some of Schaefer's reticence, with his primary emphases instead being modernizing basic service delivery and reducing violent crime.

Dorothy Shipps' analysis of the Chicago school reform effort illustrates how one reform (decentralization) was upstaged by a more centralized mayor-centric system. In Chicago's case, the business community played a critical role in getting the state legislature to pass the law that gave the mayor power to appoint trustees and a CEO. The result has been a corporate model that other cities find appealing. Both New York City, which handed the reins of the school system to a mayor, Michael Bloomberg, whose prior career had been centered on the corporate world, and Philadelphia, which imported a key architect of the Chicago reforms, Paul Vallas, to run its school system, have self-consciously copied elements of the Chicago model. But, as Shipps explains, the impact of the Chicago reforms for minority stakeholder groups, and minority children only now are becoming clear. And, by the summer of 2001, a dramatic change in the leadership of the teachers union led to a wholesale reconfiguration in the mayor's hand-picked management team, raising issues in labor/management relations under the corporate governance model. Chicago has a large and rapidly growing Latino population, and Shipps' analysis highlights ways in which Latino and African American advocates part company on the issue of mayor-centric reform.

Most of the recent moves toward mayor-centrism have been initiated or received critical support from external forces, such as the state legislature, governor, or, in the case of Washington, D.C., Congress and its appointed financial control board. John Portz's chapter on Boston follows a case in which the switch to a stronger mayoral role grew out of local experience and indigenous political forces. Since 1992, Boston mayors have appointed the school committee (board). The superintendent is a member of the mayor's cabinet. Portz illustrates how, under this new governance regime, the schools have slowly risen to the top of the mayoral agenda. Mayor Tom Menino has taken a high profile in school reform including asking the electorate to judge him by how well he does with school reform. Portz includes careful analysis of mayoral speeches and budgets to test the extent to which mayor-centrism affects local priorities and finds evidence of improvements in educational performance.

Jeffrey Mirel provides a historical analysis of the struggle for school reform in Detroit. Detroit, the Motor City, is a near-prototype of a strong-union city. Yet, despite teacher union opposition, the Republican governor and the state legislature were able to pass a law that eliminated the elected board and gave the mayor the power to appoint the school board. This transition has not gone smoothly, and in April 2001 Mayor Dennis Archer — the seeming beneficiary of the state's action — made the surprise announcement that he would not seek reelection. Mirel shows that the roots of Detroit's problems run deeper, perhaps, than could be reached by a simple reallocation of formal authority.

Wilbur Rich and Stefanie Chambers analyze the history of the high profile mayoral takeover of the Cleveland Public Schools and why that transition seems to be going well. In the early nineties, Mayor Michael White organized a citywide summit to debate school policy. But his effort to mobilize local capacity coexisted with external intervention on the part of the state legislature, which handed White the opportunity to appoint the school board and its chief executive officer. Later in his administration, White adopted a lower profile on school issues and his approach is an example of both mayoral confrontation and cooperation with the school establishment. His surprise decision not to seek reelection, announced in May 2001, hints at the high personal cost to mayors who attempt to battle for their cities on every front.

Jeffrey Henig examines the nexus of race and interest group interest in Washington, D. C. In the place of a state government, the federal government plays the key role as overseer in a federal structure. Working through a Financial Control Board it established, Congress helped to introduce a proposal to give the new reform mayor, Anthony Williams, power to appoint a substantial proportion of the school board. Despite powerful backers, the referendum to restructure the school board nearly failed, and the vote on the issue revealed a sharp racial cleavage. Henig explains how racial perceptions affected the vote in D.C., and draws implications relevant to other cities as well.

Following the six case studies are three chapters that offer a broader theoretical, political and policy framework for interpreting the lessons to be drawn. Kenneth Meier examines the six case studies from the viewpoint of structural change. He presents the formal *a priori* logic in support of greater mayoral control over the public school system, that is, how and why it should work. He then notes the types of biases that greater mayoral control are likely to engender and uses the case studies to demonstrate why structural reforms might produce different outcomes in practice that they do in theory. The chapter concludes by probing the relationship between structural reform and the performance of urban educational systems.

As elected big-city mayors join the move to improve schools, they confront strong crosscurrents. Although in principle everyone wants high-performance schools, in practice substantial barriers are posed by entrenched practices, skepticism about reform, and anxiety about jobs. Clarence Stone, in his chapter, suggests that one way to see the problem is as a modernization challenge. Children in inner city public schools often come from families that are on the margins of the contemporary economy; their parents' skills, education, work history, and social networks give them almost no chance to find well-paying jobs in the expanding sectors of the national economy. Stereotypes of race, ethnicity, and class help perpetuate urban backwaters and preserve them as places where pessimism reigns. Those who take on the task of improving city schools therefore cannot simply launch a new initiative. They face practices that have grown up around a long history of social and economic inequality, practices that are embedded in a past not easily discarded. The promise of a new order, teeming with possibility, holds little appeal to those who have experienced the world as an ungenerous and inhospitable place. To those accustomed to life on the margins, interpersonal networks of mutual protection have strong appeal, and such protection is not easily abandoned for the uncertain promise of reform and modernization.

In our concluding chapter, we return to some of the issues raised here, and reflect on broad implications for the understanding of urban politics and education, as well as for public policy in the coming decades.

Notes

1. An analysis of SAT 1 scores among members of the Council of Great City Schools (CGS) found that African American test-takers in their member districts

averaged 411 (Verbal) and 422 (Math), compared to 422 and 434, respectively, for African Americans nationally; at the same time, white students in those cities scored virtually the same as white students nationwide (531 verbal and 527 math for white CGS students versus 529 and 528, respectively, for whites nationally) (Council of Great City Schools 2001).

2. Commentators and the public are often too glib in generalizing between the special case of inner city schools and the more general challenge of public education. See Cuban 2001.

3. The Council of Great City Schools (2001) provides a somewhat more upbeat view of the situation in large urban school systems. Note, too, that some of the horror stories about American educational performance overall have been exaggerated (Berliner 1995; Rothstein 1998).

4. Mayors, it must be noted, do not make such revenue decisions autonomously. They are constrained, to varying degrees but always substantially, by city councils, state legislatures, and state and federal laws.

5. "Convenience" and political wariness are not the only forces that historically have buttressed local control in American education. Ideology and norms have also played a role in creating a sense in the United States—unusual compared to other industrialized nations—that state and especially national involvement in education represents an "intrusion." See McDermott 1999.

6. For example, in the spring of 1995, about six years after the state's takeover in Jersey City and four years after its takeover of the Paterson schools, New Jersey's commissioner of education told a state senate committee that the improvement in test scores in Jersey City and Paterson "is not as high as we hoped." F. Sullivan, "Improvement Lags after School Takeovers, State Says," *New York Times*, 25 April 1995. Also, N. MacFarquhar, "Better Finances, but Not Better Test Scores," *New York Times*, 9 July 1995. Test scores apparently did show some improvement in 1996, although it is not clear whether those improvements could be attributed to the intervention. See, too, Firestone 1997.

7. For a discussion of the Demonstration Cities Act of 1966, which gave birth to the Model Cities program, see Frieden and Kaplan 1997.

8. The War on Poverty comprised a number of distinct programs, such as Vista, Head Start, and the Community Action Program, launched by the Economic Opportunity Act of 1964.

References

Banfield, E. 1974. *The Unheavenly City Revisited*. Boston: Little, Brown & Company.

Berliner, D. C., and B. J. Biddle. 1995. *The Manufactured Crisis*. New York: Longman.

Bluestone, B., and B. Harrison. 1984. *The Deindustrialization of America*. New York: Basic Books.

Chambers, C. 2000. "Americans Dissatisfied with U.S. Education in General, but Parents Satisfied with Their Kids' School." Gallup News Service: 1.

Chubb, J. E., and T. M. Moe. 1990. *Politics, Markets, and America's Schools.* Washington, D.C.: Brookings Institution Press.

Council of Great City Schools and The College Board. 2001. *Making the Grade: A Report on SAT Results in the Nation's Urban Schools.* Washington, D.C.: Council of Great City Schools.

Crain, R. L. 1969. *The Politics of School Desegregation.* Garden City, N.Y.: Anchor Books.

Cuban, L. 2001. "How Systemic Reform Harms Urban Schools." *Education Week,* 30 May.

Dentler, R. A. 1981. *Schools on Trial: An Inside Account of the Boston Desegregation Case.* Cambridge: Abt Associates.

Downs, A. 1972. "Up and Down with the Ecology: The Issue Attention Cycle." *The Public Interest* 28:28–50.

Farkas, S. 1992. *Educational Reform: The Players and the Politics.* New York: The Public Agenda Foundation.

Firestone, W. A., M. E. Goertz, et al. 1997. *From Cashbox to Classroom: The Struggle for Fiscal Reform and Educational Change in New Jersey.* New York: Teachers College Press.

Formisano, R. P. 1991. *Boston against Busing: Race, Class, and Ethnicity in the 1960s and 1970s.* Chapel Hill: University of North Carolina Press.

Fraga, L. R., and B. A. Erlichson. 1998. "Consensus Building and School Reform: The Role of the Courts in San Francisco." In *Changing Urban Education,* ed. C. Stone. Lawrence: University Press of Kansas.

Frieden, B. J., and M. Kaplan. 1977. *The Politics of Neglect.* Cambridge: MIT Press.

Gitell, M. 1980. *Limits to Citizen Participation.* Berkeley: Sage Publications.

———, ed. 1998. *Strategies for School Equity: Creating Productive Schools in a Just Society.* New Haven: Yale University Press.

Henig, J. R., R. C. Hula, M. Orr, and D. S. Pedescleaux. 1999. *The Color of School Reform.* Princeton, N.J.: Princeton University Press.

Hess, F. M. 1998. *Spinning Wheels: The Politics of Urban School Reform.* Washington, D.C.: Brookings Institution Press.

Heubert, J. P., and R. M. Hauser, eds. 1999. *High Stakes: Testing for Tracking, Promotion and Graduation.* Washington, D.C.: National Academy Press.

Hochschild, J. L. 1984. *The New American Dilemma: Liberal Democracy and School Desegregation.* New Haven: Yale University Press.

Kirp, D. L., J. P. Dwyer, and L. Rosenthal. 1997. *Our Town: Race, Housing, and the Soul of Suburbia.* New Brunswick, N.J.: Rutgers University Press.

Kirst, M., and K. Bulkley. 2000. " 'New, Improved' Mayors Take Over City Schools." *Phi Delta Kappan* 81 (March): 538–46.

Ladd, H. F., ed. 1996. *Holding Schools Acountable.* Washington, D.C.: Brookings Institution Press.

Lieberman, M. 1993. *Public Education: An Autopsy.* Cambridge: Harvard University Press.

Long, N. E. 1972. *The Unwalled City: Reconstituting the Urban Community.* New York: Basic Books.

Lukas, J. A. 1985. *Common Ground: A Turbulent Decade in the Lives of Three American Families.* New York: Alfred Knopf.

Mahtesian, C. 1996. "Handing the Schools to City Hall." *Governing* 10(1):36–40.

McDermott, K. 1999. *Controlling Public Education: Localism versus Equity*. Lawrence: University Press of Kansas.

Moe, T. M. 2001. *Schools, Vouchers, and the American Public*. Washington, D.C.: Brookings Institution Press.

Moynihan, D. P. 1970. *Maximum Feasible Misunderstanding*. New York: The Free Press.

Olson, L., and C. Jerald. 1998. "Quality Counts '98: The Urban Challenge." *Education Week (special report)* 17 (17 January): 8.

Peterson, P. E. 1981. *City Limits*. Chicago: University of Chicago Press.

Rich, W. 1996. *Black Mayors and School Politics*. New York: Garland Press.

Rosenberg, G. 1991. *The Hollow Hope: Can Courts Bring About Social Change?* Chicago: University of Chicago Press.

Rothstein, R. 1998. *The Way We Were?* New York: The Century Foundation.

Sale, K. 1975. *Power Shift: The Rise of the Southern Rim and Its Challenge to the Eastern Establishment*. New York: Random House.

Stanfield, R. 1997. "Bossing City Schools." *National Journal* 28 (8 February): 272–74.

Stephens, G. R. 1996. "Urban Underrepresentation in the U.S. Senate." *Urban Affairs Review* 31(3):404–18.

Sternlieb, G. 1971. "The City as Sandbox." *The Public Interest* 25 (fall).

Stone, C., J. R. Henig, and C. Pierannunzi. 2001. *Building Civic Capacity: Toward a New Politics of Urban School Reform*. Lawrence: University Press of Kansas.

Tyack, D. 1974. *The One Best System*. Cambridge: Harvard University Press.

Weir, M. 1996. "Central Cities' Loss of Power in State Politics." *Cityscape*, May, 23–40.

Part 2

CASE STUDIES

Chapter Two

Baltimore: The Limits of Mayoral Control

MARION ORR

UNTIL 1997, Baltimore had in place the kind of mayor-dominated school structure many reformers and state level officials advocate. Baltimore's 1899 City Charter provided that the mayor appoint all nine members of the Board of School Commissioners, giving the mayor considerable formal authority over the operation and direction of the public schools. Theoretically, Baltimore's school superintendent reported to the school board. In reality, a superintendent's appointment and continued tenure in office were based largely on the level of mayoral support. Baltimore's mayor also wielded considerable budgetary control over the Baltimore City Public School system (BCPS). The school system's budget was subjected to the same mayoral review as any department of city government. All spending above $300 by the BCPS, the school board, or the superintendent required the approval of the five-member Board of Estimates (Hunter 1997, 227–28). The mayor controlled the board, appointing two of its members and holding a seat himself.

In 1997, however, Maryland officials moved away from relying on Baltimore's mayor as the primary public official overseeing public education in the state's largest city. Frustrated with Baltimore's school reform efforts, Maryland's governor and legislature reshaped the political relationship between the mayor and the BCPS, intervening in a way that reduced the mayor's direct authority over the schools. Maryland's structural reform of the BCPS moved in the opposite direction from the mayor-dominated approach established in Boston, Chicago, Cleveland, Detroit, and New York City. Ironically, the central advocates of Maryland's effort to take Baltimore's mayor out of the middle of school affairs were virtually the same constituency advocating the same approach in the other cities.

Electoral and Governing Coalitions

My examination of the mayoralties of William Donald Schaefer (1971–1986), Kurt L. Schmoke (1987–1998), and Martin O'Malley (1999–

present) highlights the connection between schools and city politics. As Henig and Rich (this volume) note, urban school systems are intertwined with local politics. Mayors are concerned about gaining, maintaining, and expanding their support among the electorate in order to win elections. The appropriate electoral appeal is often a function of the political opportunities available to a mayoral candidate and the local political context. Thus, mayors have built winning electoral coalitions around racial and ethnic divisions, improving police and community relations, fighting government corruption, and a litany of other concerns. Similarly, all Baltimore's recent mayors staked out issues designed to build a winning electoral coalition.

An electoral coalition, even when successful, is not the same as a governing coalition (Ferman 1985). The literature on urban political economy (Swanstrom 1985) and urban political regimes (Stone 1989; Elkin 1987) recognizes that governance involves more than the public sector alone. Business organizations, for example, play a crucial role in local governing coalitions or urban regimes. Because business organizations command significant resources and have fixed assets located within the city, their prerogatives often help shape the scope and nature of city governance. "A business presence is always part of the urban political scene" (Stone 1989, 7). Black voters, for example, played a significant role in William Donald Schaefer's electoral coalition. But the city's corporate structure dominated Schaefer's governing coalition; downtown redevelopment became the focus of Schaefer's fifteen-year reign as mayor.

Under some circumstances the interests of both the electoral coalition and governing coalition align and point in the direction of, say, a systemic school reform effort. In this situation, experimentation and a departure from the normal way of doing things are likely to occur. However, as the discussion of Mayor Schmoke's tenure shows, even when there is alignment and general agreement between the electoral and governing coalitions, tensions can arise about the nature and design of reform favored by corporate players, as compared to the vision and material interests of key constituents in the mayor's electoral base.

Advocates for vesting more power over urban school districts in the mayor's office assume that contemporary mayors cannot build sustainable regimes without emphasizing education. The public school system, they argue, is such a critical element in the overall health of the city, that mayors simply can no longer be disengaged from school affairs. To the contrary, in the age of globalization and competition, all successful mayors must put themselves in the middle. Kirst and Bulkley (2000, 538) report that mayors in Los Angeles, CA, Milwaukee, WI and Philadelphia, PA have tried to exert influence over school policy, even with-

out any substantial formal structural changes in the relationship between city hall and the school district. However, my examination of
Martin O'Malley's electoral campaign and tenure illustrates that contemporary mayors do not necessarily have to construct a school-focused
electoral coalition or governing coalition. In O'Malley's first two years
as mayor, he focused on more tractable local issues: public works,
neighborhood blight, efficient city services, and public safety.

Background

To understand the role Baltimore's most recent mayors have played in
school affairs, it is important to consider how race and racial politics
have shaped city politics. Baltimore's location makes it unique among
other large northeastern industrial cities. Situated just below the Ma-
son-Dixon line, Baltimore has many traditions that are characteristic of
the Deep South. Historian Joseph Arnold (1990) described Baltimore as
a city with a "southern culture and a northern economy." Supreme
Court Justice Thurgood Marshall often described his native city as "up-
South Baltimore" (Watson 1990, 81).

Like those in many Deep South cities, white residents in Baltimore
kept African American residents firmly "in their place" through a system of legal and social segregation. White citizens' desire to avoid race
mixing led to the creation of two educational systems: one Black, one
white. The Black schools were typically overcrowded; textbooks and
other educational materials were dated and typically secondhand.

In the 1950s and 1960s, however, the city underwent a profound
transformation. First, the Supreme Court's 1954 decision in *Brown v.
Board of Education of Topeka*, 347 U.S. 483 (1954) gave hope to Blacks
that, at last, their quest for educational justice had the sanction of law.
Although city officials in Baltimore desegregated quickly without huge
disruption, systemwide desegregation never occurred (Crain 1968). In
the early 1960s, faculty and staff in the BCPS remained racially segregated. Second, the shift of Baltimore's white population to the suburbs
triggered the numerical dominance of the city by African American residents. By the late 1970s, Black residents were the majority; by 2000,
African Americans were sixty-four percent of the total population.
These demographic trends are reflected in enrollment trends in the
schools. In 1955, the year after *Brown*, only forty percent of the students in the BCPS were Black. By 1960, fifty-one percent of the students
were African American; by 1974, seventy percent were. In 2000, the
student population was eighty-seven percent Black. Third, the Civil
Rights movement altered the way white politicians related to the Black

community and brought about the rise to power of African American elected officials, changing the social and political life of the city. Fourth and finally, the economic structure of the city changed profoundly: Baltimore was no longer a manufacturing center. From 1950 to 1990, the number of manufacturing jobs declined by sixty-five percent. Growth in the economy took place primarily in the service sector, with much of it centered in the Inner Harbor redevelopment area and downtown. The suburbanization of middle-class whites (and, increasingly, middle-class Blacks) has left behind many poor residents. The exodus of retail and wholesale trade and manufacturing jobs contributed to high unemployment and weakened tax base (Rusk 1996).

These powerful forces shaped local politics and school affairs. And given their formal authority over the BCPS, Baltimore's mayors were pulled into "school politics." Thomas D'Alesandro III was the first modern mayor to directly confront the challenge of race and school politics. He was elected in 1967, at the height of African American political mobilization. As city council president, D'Alesandro had worked closely with his predecessor, Theodore Roosevelt McKeldin, in passing civil rights and community action legislation. D'Alesandro was considered a liberal and received overwhelming support from African American voters. As mayor, D'Alesandro vowed to address Black leaders' call for a more active role in local government. He continued McKeldin's policy of hiring roughly equal numbers of Black and white applicants for municipal jobs, supported passage of a 1968 bond referendum to help finance construction of new school buildings in the city's Black neighborhoods, and appointed more Blacks to the school board. D'Alesandro also directed school administrators to hire "neighborhood people" as teacher aides through Title I of the federal Elementary and Secondary Education Act of 1965, thus providing employment for hundreds of Black residents (Bowler 1991, 12).

African American disenchantment, however, grew. Like many major cities, Baltimore erupted in flames after the assassination of the Rev. Dr. Martin Luther King in 1968. The riots deeply wounded the city, exacerbating racial tensions. The racial tensions spilled over into the schools. "Board meetings were so raucous in those days that . . . D'Alesandro called the [school] commissioners to a private meeting and threatened to fire them all if the 'name calling, picayune bickering and discourtesies' didn't stop" (24).

In July 1971, racial tensions between the white and Black members of the school board forced the resignation of Superintendent Thomas Sheldon. He was replaced by Roland Patterson, an assistant superintendent from Seattle, Washington, becoming the city's first Black school superintendent. The racial strife, however, continued. As a city councilor recalled years later: "The school board was a battleground. I would go to the board meetings; they would put on a show each week. Tommy D'Alesandro really wanted justice for the school system. He wanted to help the system but couldn't because of the conflict" (Orr 1992, 181). Concerned about the enormous strain the job of mayor was putting on himself and his family, D'Alesandro decided to retire from public life after only one term in office.

During the 1971 mayoral election, with African Americans representing forty-six percent of the city's population, there was considerable speculation that Baltimore would follow Newark, New Jersey; Gary, Indiana; and Cleveland, Ohio, by electing its first Black mayor. William Donald Schaefer, a white former city council president, however, won. Schaefer, closely connected to the city's Democratic clubs, had developed a following across the city. He defeated two African American candidates, winning citywide backing, including support in the city's black precincts. As council president, Schaefer did nothing to alarm the Black community: he supported all of the civil rights legislation that came before the city council and lived with his mother in a predominantly African American neighborhood. Verda Welcome, an African American legislator during the 1960s and 1970s, explained that "If kitchen tables could talk, there would probably be several thousand in Baltimore with tales of Schaefer's visits" (Welcome 1991, 208). During the 1971 campaign a young Black woman, asked why she was supporting Schaefer, replied, "I just remember all those times when my grandmother asked him to get something done in our block, and it was always done" (Fleming 1972, 5). Schaefer also vowed to build on his predecessors' efforts of giving African Americans greater access to city government.

Mayor Schaefer and School Politics: Maintaining an Electoral Coalition

Schaefer assumed the mayor's office in December 1971, a few months after the appointment of Superintendent Roland Patterson, an assertive educator whose willingness to develop close ties to Black critics of Schaefer and militant black leaders did not endear him to the new mayor (Scott 1980). Patterson and Schaefer clashed immediately. Observers noted that "City Hall" seemed "to scrutinize" Patterson "much more assiduously than it had his predecessors" (Bowler 1991, 14). At one point, the mayoral-controlled Board of Estimates denied Patterson funds to take a business trip to Denver, an action viewed by many as a symbolic slap in the face. The superintendent's administrative reorganization plan also concerned Mayor Schaefer. First, the plan reassigned many high-ranking white administrators, replacing many of them with African Americans. Second, Patterson's insistence that "good people from outside the system" be considered for top school department posts collided with Schaefer's strategy of relying on the school system to give African American leaders a greater a voice in city governance and jobs in the school system (Scott 1980, 112).

Among Baltimore's political movers and shakers—the men and women connected to the city's Democratic clubs—it was well known that patronage flourished in the school system. Businessman Walter Sondheim recalled that after he became school board president in the 1950s, he "was told that a principal's post could be purchased from the bosses for $150, a vice principal for $100" (Smith 1999, 70). According to Verda Welcome, a former Baltimore teacher, "The political connection between the mayor's office and the school system had long been a well-kept secret. The thousands of jobs available at city schools naturally made them a magnet for patronage, and mayors had traditionally taken full advantage of this" (Welcome 1991, 235).[1]

In August 1974, chaos broke out when hundreds of Patterson's supporters packed a school board meeting after they learned that a majority of the board (its white members) planned to dismiss the superintendent. As the *Baltimore Sun* reported, "An angry crowd briefly surged onto the stage, ripping out microphone cords and slamming papers and books about the meeting table." One black school board member reportedly "leapt from his seat" and "nose-to-nose" screamed at one of his white colleagues: "There ain't gonna be no vote. You don't get no vote tonight" (Cramer and Pietella 1974). Black Congressman Parren Mitchell, an ardent supporter of Patterson, angrily denounced the attempt to oust him, saying: "Never have I seen the racist scum come through as it has tonight" (Id).

A lawsuit filed by Patterson delayed his removal. However, by 1975 Mayor Schaefer had appointed four new school board members, three of whom were Black, to replace members whose terms had expired. With the extension of Schaefer's authority over the school board, it voted in July 1975 to fire Patterson. A federal court judge upheld the board's action. The controversy surrounding Patterson's removal challenged the city's civic leadership. For Mayor Schaefer, the Patterson controversy reminded him of the volatile and racial nature of school politics.

I have argued elsewhere that in the early 1970s, Mayor Schaefer and other city elites forged a tacit agreement that made the school system the "Black agency" of Baltimore municipal government (Orr 1999, 57).[2]

As Schaefer biographer Smith (1999, 136) observed: "Control of the schools was given over to African Americans as their inviolate patronage pool, recognition no doubt that black voters were many and might, in time, be a force in city elections."

The Black community was a major beneficiary of many of the jobs in the BCPS during Schaefer's term in office. After Patterson's dismissal, two veteran African American educators from within the BCPS—John Crew and Alice Pinderhughes—served as superintendent. In 1980, "two of the four deputy superintendents, thirteen of the sixteen assistant superintendents, and three of the six regional superintendents were blacks" (Wong 1990, 88). Demographic data on the BCPS faculty suggest how city politics shaped decisions regarding hiring in the BCPS. The data in Figure 2.1 show a steady climb in the number and percentage of African American faculty during the Schaefer years, peaking at 6,284, or 71 percent of the total BCPS faculty in 1984. From 1972 to 1986 the BCPS faculty increased by nearly 11 percent; the number of Black faculty rose 32 percent.[3] Meanwhile, during the same period, total student enrollment in the BCPS fell by 42 percent, with Black student enrollment dropping by 32 percent. Ken Wong (1990, 115) accurately captured the linkage between city politics and education policy during Schaefer's tenure: "Increasingly, the school district resembled a patronage base. Personnel that orchestrated mayoral activities were put on the school system's payroll. Central office school administrators critical of the administration were either demoted or transferred. Not infrequently, school resources were allocated in a politicized manner to serve as a warning to dissenters at the school building level."

Schaefer's efforts to address the material interests of African Americans through patronage in the BCPS were rewarded at the voting booth. Schaefer won reelection easily in 1975, 1979, or 1983, winning 71, 80, and 73 percent of the Democratic primary vote, respectively. In each election he received the majority of the African American votes cast (O'Keefe 1986, 9).

Data from the 1983 Democratic mayoral primary help illuminate the extent to which African American voters were a major component of Schaefer's electoral coalition. The 1983 race is instructive because it was the first mayoral primary in which African Americans held absolute registration and voting majorities, and because it was the first time Schaefer faced a credible African American challenger.

William H. Murphy Jr., a well-known attorney, was a successful judicial candidate in 1980, and a member of the prominent African American family who owned the newspaper *Afro-American*. Murphy attacked Schaefer, citing the deteriorating conditions of the city's Black

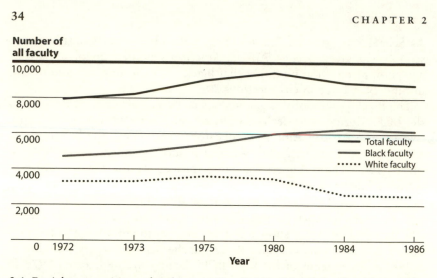

2.1 Racial composition of Baltimore City Public School faculty 1972–1986. (Baltimore City Public Schools)

neighborhoods, rising Black youth unemployment, and the failing schools. He criticized Schaefer for building a glittering downtown area while ignoring these persistent problems (Id; Orr 1999).

Table 2.1 shows a breakdown of the 1983 Democratic mayoral primary vote for all six city council districts. Schaefer won easily in all the districts, including the majority African American districts. In the city's Second District, where Blacks were 69 percent of the population, Schaefer won 63 percent of the total vote. In the Fourth District, where Blacks were 96 percent of the population, Schaefer won 51 percent of the votes cast. Similarly, in the 63 percent Black Fifth District, Schaefer won nearly 70 percent of the vote.

The data in Table 2.2, which show an analysis of all 144 voting precincts with Black populations of 90 percent or more, confirm the district-level results. In 1983, Schaefer won nearly 66 percent of the votes cast in these so-called "supermajority" Black precincts. Though he was a white mayor in a predominantly African American city, Schaefer was able to defeat his Black mayoral opponent, outpolling him with voters of both races.

Throughout most of his tenure as mayor, Schaefer distanced himself from significant education issues. From Schaefer's perspective, heavy involvement in school affairs was like walking into a minefield, where one wrong move could cripple his electoral coalition. School policy was thus left to trusted associates on the school board and Black administrators who owed their appointments to city hall. One of Schaefer's last school

TABLE 2.1
1983 Baltimore Mayoral Primary Results, City Council Districts

Council District	Percent African American	Percent of Votes for Schaefer	Percent of Votes for Murphy	Percent of Votes for Others
First	27	86	12	2
Second	69	63	34	3
Third	32	82	17	1
Fourth	96	51	46	3
Fifth	63	69	29	2
Sixth	42	77	21	2

Source: Board of Supervisors of Elections of Baltimore City, 1983.

board presidents, developer Mark K. Joseph, recalled that Schaefer "saw it [school affairs] as a divider" (Smith 1999, 138). As historian Edward Berkowitz (1997, 423) rather gently stated in his examination of Baltimore's schools during the early 1970s, "the mayor attempted to take the schools out of the spotlight and to highlight the urban renaissance instead."

Mayor Schaefer and the Downtown Regime

Schaefer won the 1971 mayoral election and was reelected three times, both because he carefully worked to gain and hold on to Black voter support *and* because he strenuously supported the downtown redevelopment plans created by the city's corporate elites and embraced by its two previous mayors. In the early 1950s, under the direction of the Greater Baltimore Committee (GBC), the city's principal business orga-

TABLE 2.2
1983 Baltimore Mayoral Primary Results, Super-Majority Black Precincts

Candidate	Total Votes Received	Percent of Votes Cast
William Donald Schaefer	81,730	65.7
William Murphy, Jr.	40,230	32.3
Other	2,370	2.0
Total	124,330	100

Source: Board of Supervisors of Elections of Baltimore City, 1983.
Note: The data presented are vote totals for all 144 Baltimore City precincts that had an African American population of 90 percent or more in 1983.

nization, corporate leaders devised a center city revitalization plan to increase property values and retail sales revenues and reverse downtown blight. The central component of the plan, conceived in 1964, focused on what is now known as the Inner Harbor redevelopment area (Levine 1987). The city's business elites believed downtown redevelopment, in particular the revitalization of the Inner Harbor redevelopment area, was the cornerstone to making Baltimore a "renaissance city." Former Mayor D'Alesandro recalled years later, "McKeldin and I left a legacy that Schaefer has to deal with. He couldn't come out and retrench on the [downtown] renaissance" (Goldberg 1984, 160).

Mayor Schaefer was always clear about his pro-business orientation, assuring corporate leaders that his administration endeavored to create a good business climate. The Schaefer administration earmarked a significant amount of public sector funds to support redevelopment plans and established quasi-governmental organizations to help facilitate developers' efforts to revitalize downtown. Between 1971 and 1985, when millions of dollars in public subsidies were provided to developers, municipal spending on public education, in inflation-adjusted terms, was slashed by more than 25 percent (Levine 1987). Schaefer provided corporate leaders with a dominant role in the city's governing coalition by creating quasi-public corporations that coordinated and supervised all downtown redevelopment projects. The quasi-public development corporations — dubbed the "shadow government" by critics — allowed "extra-governmental officials" to control Baltimore's downtown redevelopment efforts (Stoker 1987). In other words, Schaefer's governing coalition was different from his electoral coalition: the former was centered on white corporate leaders; the latter, on African Americans.[4]

It was during Schaefer's long tenure that the major components of Baltimore's downtown revitalization efforts were completed: the Maryland Science Center (1976); the World Trade Center (1977); the Baltimore Convention Center (1979); the National Aquarium (1981); and Harborplace (1981), a waterfront "festival marketplace" designed by the Rouse Company. The priority of Schaefer's governing coalition was the fervent promotion of downtown economic development.

By contrast, the public schools were not high on either the corporate community's or Schaefer's action agenda. An official of the GBC conceded that during the 1970s and 1980s, the business community "abandoned the school system and gave it to a segment of the black community" (Orr 1992, 178). The influential *Baltimore 2000* report, commissioned to examine Baltimore's future, was issued in 1986, shortly before Schaefer resigned to become governor. The report was critical of the quality of Baltimore's schools and Schaefer's leadership of the BCPS. "The [school] system," the report concluded, "is now widely condemned as

ineffective, undisciplined and dangerous" (Szanton 1986, 10). Even in
the report's diplomatic language, the fact that Schaefer did little to help
improve the public schools is clear. Future mayors, the report argued,
should play a more substantial role. "The mayor appoints the school
board and can set its course. No substantial renovation of the school
system can be accomplished without his deep interest, steady pressure,
and willingness to apply the political weight of his office to insure results" (Szanton 1986, 41). Schaefer's biographer stated the matter
bluntly: "Schaefer's stewardship of the schools . . . would be regarded
as weak and ineffective, his greatest failure" (Smith 1999, 138).

The Election of Kurt L. Schmoke

In the 1987 mayoral election, one thing was certain: Baltimore would
elect a Black mayor. The Democratic primary was the first mayoral primary in Baltimore history to pit one African American candidate
against another. The two candidates, however, represented radically different generations and backgrounds.

Clarence "Du" Burns — sixty-eight years old, largely self-educated,
and outgoing — had worked for twenty-two years as a high school jani-
tor (a patronage appointment), formed his own political club, and been
elected to the city council in 1971 (Arnold 1990, 31). In 1983, he ran
citywide and became the first Black to win election as president of the
city council. As president, Burns automatically became mayor when
Schaefer resigned before his term ended to become governor in 1986.

Nearly thirty years younger than Burns, Kurt L. Schmoke grew up on
Baltimore's west side, as the son of college-educated parents. Schmoke
was a high school and college sports star. A graduate of Yale University
and Harvard Law School, he was also a Rhodes Scholar. In 1982, in
his first bid for elected office, Schmoke was elected state's attorney
(O'Keeffe 1986). Schmoke was able to unite the black community behind his candidacy and also received considerable support from liberal
whites and many of the city's prominent civic leaders (O'Keeffe 1986,
63–90).

Among the several issues dominating the 1987 mayoral campaign,
downtown redevelopment and education were, perhaps, the most important. Schmoke expressed the view that Baltimore's economic goals
had not balanced neighborhood improvement with downtown development. He also embraced the *Baltimore 2000* report's call for an emphasis on improving public education. Candidate Schmoke vowed to
make Baltimore "the city that reads." If elected, Schmoke stated, he
would focus on public education.

TABLE 2.3
1987 Baltimore Mayoral Primary Results, City Council Districts

Council District	Percent African American	Percent of Votes for Schmoke	Percent of Votes for Burns	Percent of Votes for Others
First	27	33	65	2
Second	69	51	44	4
Third	32	48	50	2
Fourth	96	63	35	2
Fifth	63	60	39	1
Sixth	42	43	55	2

Source: Board of Supervisors of Elections of Baltimore City, 1987.

During the campaign, Baltimoreans United for Leadership Development (BUILD) — a coalition comprising about fifty African American churches; the Baltimore Teachers Union (BTU); the Public School Administrators and Supervisors Association (PSASA); and the Hospital and Health Workers Union; and affiliated with the Industrial Areas Foundation, a national community-organizing network — sought to shape public debate. It launched a petition drive to show support for its antipoverty program, which included a school compact program; site-based (school) management; reduction in class sizes; creation of more low-income housing; and improvement in municipal services (Orr 1992; Orr 2000). After collecting more than 70,000 voter signatures BUILD asked each candidate to endorse its antipoverty agenda. Schmoke did so without reluctance; Burns initially rejected it as "unrealistic," but later changed his mind and confirmed his commitment to the BUILD agenda.

Governor Schaefer and many of the white-led Democratic clubs supported Burns. Schaefer's support helped Burns in Baltimore's white workingclass communities, strongholds of old-line club politics. Schmoke was supported by the city's influential African American clergy (many of them affiliated with BUILD), the predominantly African American BTU, Black fraternities and sororities, and many of the city's leading African American politicians. Schmoke also received broad support among liberal white voters and civic and business leaders. Although Schmoke's Ivy League credentials were a cause for distrust among Baltimore's white, blue-collar voters, they were important to the city's corporate community.

Schmoke won the 1987 Democratic primary with 51 percent of the vote. As Table 2.3 shows, African Americans anchored Schmoke's electoral coalition. Burns won all of the majority-white districts but Schmoke won the majority of votes in the predominantly black city council districts. The support African American voters gave Schaefer in

TABLE 2.4
1987 Baltimore Mayoral Primary Results, "Super-Majority" Black Precincts

Candidate	Total Votes Received	Percent of Votes Cast
Kurt L. Schmoke	80,114	76
Clarence "Du" Burns	23,908	23
Other	1,221	1

Source: Board of Supervisors of Elections of Baltimore City, 1987.
Note: The data presented are vote totals for all 149 Baltimore City precincts that had an African American population of 90 percent or more in 1987.

1983, did not transfer to Burns, the candidate more closely identified with the former mayor. A precinct-by-precinct analysis shows that Schmoke received 76 percent of the votes in the 149 precincts where African American were at least ninety percent of the population (see Table 2.4). Schmoke's extensive support among Black voters suggests that they responded positively to his campaign's emphasis on improving public education. Schmoke was easily reelected in 1991 and 1995, with education remaining a top agenda item.

Schmoke and Schools: From Electoral to Governing Coalition

In his first inaugural address, Schmoke vowed to improve the city's public schools, stating: "Of all the things I might be able to accomplish as mayor of our city, it would make me proudest if one day it could simply be said of Baltimore that this is the city that reads. This is the city that waged war on illiteracy. This is the city that recognized brainpower as it most precious resource. And this is the city whose citizens, businesses, industries, and institutions joined together to make education work for all who were willing to work for an education" (Schmoke 1987, 7–8).

Once in office, Schmoke sought to use his formal authority to influence education policy. For example, after ushering in the retirement of Superintendent Pinderhughes, Schmoke played an active role in the national search for a replacement. In the summer of 1988, he rejected the school board's initial choice, asking that Richard C. Hunter, an education professor at the University of North Carolina and former superintendent of the Richmond, Virginia, schools, be named the new superintendent. Later, in December 1990, after it became clear that Hunter was not as strong a supporter of Schmoke's education vision as the mayor had initially thought, the school board — under orders from Schmoke — voted not to renew Hunter's three-year contract.

Because he controlled the Board of Estimates, the agency charged with formulating, determining, and executing the city's fiscal policy,

TABLE 2.5
Local Revenues Allocated for Education in Baltimore, 1983–1991

Fiscal Year	Amount ($ millions)	Percent Change
1991	$181.1	9.0
1990	166.1	9.9
1989	151.1	11.0
1988	136.1	7.7
1987	126.4	4.1
1986	121.4	3.2
1985	117.6	4.1
1984	113.0	6.1
1983	106.5	N/A

Source: City of Baltimore Finance Department 1991.

Schmoke was able to use his formal authority to increase the amount of local revenues allocated to education. As Table 2.5 indicates, the actual share of local revenues spent on education increased each year during Schmoke's first term. The annual percentage increase of local funds to the BCPS during Schmoke's first term was often double the yearly increases in 1984, 1985, and 1986, the last years Schaefer presented a municipal budget. These budget data suggest that the change in mayoral leadership impacted the city's financial priorities, as they related to the schools.

Schmoke sought to incorporate a broad array of education stakeholders into his governing coalition, including the leaders of BUILD. "I had it in my mind," Schmoke recalled, "even before BUILD detailed their agenda, to make BUILD an ally with me as mayor . . . mainly because, for the most part, their agenda and my agenda overlapped" (Schmoke 2001). A BUILD organizer recalled that after Schmoke was sworn in as mayor, "he took members of BUILD to his cabinet and told them that we are part of the cabinet too" (Orr 1992, 185). BUILD was regularly briefed on education policy by Schmoke or by his top advisers. Schmoke kept his campaign promise to involve city government in the Baltimore Commonwealth (common wealth), a school compact program formed by BUILD with support from the business community. Schaefer had refused to support the Commonwealth, but in 1990, under Schmoke, BUILD became the only community group involved in planning the school system's site-based management pilot program. When Schmoke was deliberating on the future of his hand-picked superintendent (Richard C. Hunter), he consulted BUILD leaders.

Schmoke's governing coalition also included key sectors of the corporate community that now embraced school reform. The GBC began to show more interest in school affairs after the 1983 mayoral election, releasing a study of the school system's management recommending that the BCPS adopt "school-based budgeting" (Bowler 1991, 37). The GBC's involvement became more active after 1985, when it hired a full-time education staff member and began helping fund the search for new superintendents. During Schmoke's mayoralty, the GBC was customarily consulted whenever a new superintendent was appointed. The corporate community was no longer satisfied with downtown development initiatives only. Because schools were a major electoral theme of Kurt Schmoke, members of the corporate community were drawn to him.

Marilyn Gittell's (1994) study of school reform in New York City and Chicago highlighted the vital function played by the leaders of local nonprofit foundations. Local foundations can provide important start-up funds, encourage innovation, and generate analyses and reports on schools. During most of Schmoke's tenure, the most active local foundation interested in schools was the Abell Foundation (Abell) (Orr 1996, 329–331).

Abell's interest in schools reflected the preoccupation of its president, Robert C. Embry Jr. Embry, a Baltimore native and graduate of Harvard Law School, had served a brief stint on the city council in the 1950s. In the 1960s, he was the city's first housing commissioner, and also served as an assistant secretary in the federal Department of Housing and Urban Development during the Carter administration. Embry was also one of the chief architects of the city's downtown revitalization strategy. A close associate of William Donald Schaefer, Embry was Baltimore's school board president from 1985 to 1986. When he became governor, Schaefer appointed Embry to the Maryland State Board of Education, with Embry serving as its president from 1990 to 1994.

Abell supported and funded the successful Barclay-Calvert collaboration in which the curriculum of an elite private school was adopted by an inner city public school. Embry was instrumental in convincing Mayor Schmoke and city health officials to make Norplant, the surgically implanted contraceptive, available to high school students. Abell provided the funds for the contraceptive. The city also joined with the Abell Foundation on a project to send troubled middle school boys to the Baraka School in Kenya. The idea was to change the environment of the youths to prepare them for success in high school. Embry's political connections made him a key player in Baltimore and state politics. As president of a foundation principally concerned with public education, he was an especially influential member of Schmoke's governing coalition.

This is not to suggest that BUILD, key leaders in the GBC, and Ab-

ell's Robert Embry were the only members of Schmoke's governing coalition. Leaders of the Citizen Planning and Housing Association, an
organization formed in 1941 to address the problems of slum housing
and urban blight, added education to its portfolio in the late 1980s and
helped shape school issues. Key ministers affiliated with the Interde-
nominational Ministerial Alliance (IMA), comprised of Black ministers
from more than one hundred and sixty Baltimore churches, were also
part of the governing coalition. However, BUILD, the GBC, and Robert
Embry were more influential than the others.

A Clash of Ideas and Interests: Governance and School Reform

In 1991, a school board member commented on Schmoke's education
effort: "There is so much emphasis on education because it's the
mayor's major theme . . . He has tried to make it a household word.
He's been successful. Everybody is talking about education" (Quoted in
Orr 1992, 182). Momentum to reform the BCPS, however, became
more difficult to sustain as policy was turned into action, and ideas and
interests clashed. Two episodes help illustrate this point: the failed effort
to implement site-based management (SBM), and Baltimore's experience
with private management of nine public schools.
    In the middle and late 1980s, SBM was a popular reform method in
school districts across the country. SBM moves decision-making authority from the district's central administration to local schools. The basic
idea is simply to give principals, teachers, parents, and other community
members more authority to make management decisions concerning the
operation of their individual schools.
    SBM and the creation of neighborhood school autonomy were key
components of BUILD's 1987 "municipal agenda." Schmoke campaigned in support of SBM. The city's corporate sector also favored
SBM, viewing it as consistent with the GBC's call for "school-based
budgeting." In addition, in the early 1980s, corporate leaders had experienced the successful transfer of authority to their own site-level
managers.
    Early in his first administration, Schmoke appointed a committee of
central office administrators, teachers, and representatives from BUILD
to develop an SBM plan. The committee eventually developed a pilot
SBM plan for twenty schools. However, unlike some other cities' SBM
plans, Baltimore's did not give school-level committees the authority to
hire or fire staff. In addition, the school-level committees established
by the SBM plan had only limited representation of parents; educators
would dominate the committees. When the school board held hearings

on the proposal, many school activists opposed it. Parent groups complained that the proposed school-level committees were stacked with educators, diminishing the voice of parents. School activists criticized the proposal for not creating parent and community boards, giving unprecedented power to teachers and parents. GBC leaders, on the other hand, declared the plan too vague and timid, complaining because the school-based committees could not terminate underperforming teachers and other staff. For many years, business leaders had criticized school officials for failing to hold teachers accountable or terminate incompetent instructors. The SBM proposal, business leaders maintained, did little to remedy this situation. The proposal, they argued failed to allow individual schools to govern themselves.

BUILD leaders responded that they preferred to plot a moderate course in order to gain the support of school administrators. To those who criticized the plan for not giving the school-level committees authority to fire underperforming teachers, the president of BUILD responded that the plan's proponents decided against proposing policies "just for the dramatics" (Englund 1990). And responding to criticism that parents would not have a stronger voice in school governance, the president of the BTU declared that "educators still need to run schools, but the parents are going to be . . . invited into the educational process" (Englund 1990). The head of PSASA asserted that "the principal is still ultimately responsible" for the management of schools (Id).

The school board eventually modified the SBM proposal by removing the requirement that all teachers on the school-level committees be union members, while also insisting that parents or community representatives constitute at least forty percent of the committee's members. The final proposal stipulated that a school's principal and ninety percent of its faculty had to agree to participation in the pilot program.

In September 1991, only 27 of the city's 177 schools submitted SBM proposals; only fourteen were approved. Tight deadlines and a climate of uncertainty contributed to the low level of participation. Teachers at many schools voted against the pilot program because they believed it would be too demanding. Many principals, concerned that they did not possess adequate training as facility managers, were also reluctant to participate. Top central administrators also displayed little support for SBM. For example, the BCPS' director of instructional support commented that SBM is "mythological. How are you going to manage curriculum and finance at the school level? You're simply not going to be able to do it. . . . This doesn't mean that there shouldn't be input from community folk, or from the corporate community, but to argue that you're going to do away with [central office] bureaucrats is nonsense" (Bowler 1991, 37). Even Superintendent Hunter was reluctant to relinquish control over budgeting, hiring, curriculum, and procurement to principals, teachers, parents, and other school constituents.[5]

In the end, SBM was never fully implemented in the BCPS. In those schools where SBM was supposed to be operating, little changed. Principals reported that they had no greater authority over budget or personnel than they had before. On the other hand, parents complained the principal and teachers dominated decision making.

Baltimore's experience with another pilot project—contracting out the management of nine schools to Education Alternatives, Inc. (EAI)— also illustrates that even when a mayor's electoral and governing coalitions align to point in the direction of school reform, the particular form of school reform favored by some components of the governing coalition can run counter to the vision and interests of a mayor's electoral base.

The idea to contract out the operation of some of the city's schools to EAI came from Robert Embry. In 1991, Embry invited the president of EAI, John Golle, to Baltimore. Golle sold the idea to Embry, who later informed Schmoke about EAI. A Baltimore delegation of school administrators and union officials visited EAI-operated schools in Minnesota and Florida; the trips were funded by the Abell Foundation. The delegation returned impressed. Although soon to turn hostile, the BTU president appeared in public session before the school board, endorsing the experiment as "good for kids" (Asayesh 1991). Business leaders, who had long advocated implementing private management techniques in the operation of schools, liked the idea of having a business firm operating public schools. Schmoke, who was frustrated by the SBM experience, asserted that EAI would show that public personnel using private management techniques could improve school performance.

In the spring of 1992, shortly after Mayor Schmoke authorized his new superintendent, Walter Amprey, who succeeded Hunter, to contract with EAI, BUILD announced that it opposed the pilot program. Underlying BUILD's worries was the impact private management would have on the job security of school employees. The school system was the city's largest employer with over seventy percent of the jobs in the system held by African Americans. From BUILD's perspective, private management of the schools collided with the material interests of the African American community. Similarly, Black ministers' concerns about potential job loss were linked to the fact that many teachers, principals, administrators, and other personnel were prominent members of their congregations.

To allay concerns about job security, EAI's five-year contract specified that teachers and principals in the nine schools could stay where they were or transfer to other positions in the BCPS. However, when EAI transferred unionized teacher aides out of the nine schools and replaced them with non-union interns, the BTU's apprehensions about job security heightened. What was initially characterized as "good for kids" was now perceived as threatening.

BUILD leaders publicly opposed Schmoke on the EAI experiment. At a BUILD forum attended by over six hundred residents, with Mayor Schmoke in attendance, a BUILD leader declared, "We will fight you on this because the whole thing is contrary to public education" (Fletcher 1992). Union officials organized huge rallies on the steps of city hall and school headquarters, calling for the end of EAI and the resignation of Superintendent Amprey. The city council, led by president Mary Pat Clarke, a vocal critic of the Schmoke administration, voted to urge Schmoke to defer any expansion of EAI until an independent evaluation of the experiment could be completed. With mounting opposition from city council members, union leaders, and BUILD, Schmoke was forced to announce that EAI's fate depended primarily on student test scores and the results of an independent evaluation.

EAI was successful at quickly transforming the nine schools' physical plants, but it was unable to deliver on its promise to dramatically raise student performance on standardized tests. In August 1995, the first outside evaluation of the EAI experiment was completed. The evaluation found that student scores on standardized tests were about the same in 1995 as they were in 1992 for the EAI schools, the control schools, and the school system as a whole. Financial analyses showed that, despite EAI's initial claims, the nine EAI schools were receiving more money per pupil than other schools in the system. The independent evaluation found that Baltimore was spending about eleven percent more per student (approximately $628), in the EAI schools than in the control schools (see Richards, Shore, and Sawicky 1996).

In September 1995, Schmoke defeated city council president Mary Pat Clarke in the Democratic primary for mayor of Baltimore. Clarke, a white liberal, used the opposition to EAI to fuel what local observers viewed as a long-shot campaign. Although newspaper polls showed the race close, it was not to be. "Many black political and religious leaders who had not endorsed Schmoke or hadn't shown much enthusiasm for his campaign were pleading the mayor's case to voters, emphasizing that the black community could not relinquish a position that it had work so hard to get" (McCraven, 1995). The result was an unexpectedly large African American voter turnout and a huge Schmoke victory margin. Even though the dissension caused by EAI had divided Schmoke's governing coalition, it did not destroy his electoral coalition. In late November 1995, the school board unanimously voted to end the private management contract.

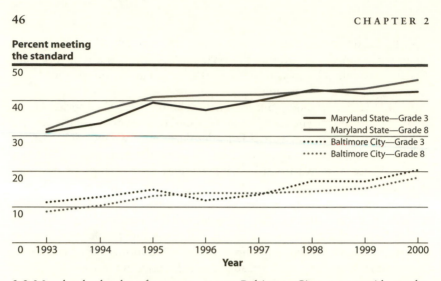

Percent meeting the standard

Legend:
- Maryland State—Grade 3
- Maryland State—Grade 8
- Baltimore City—Grade 3
- Baltimore City—Grade 8

2.2 Maryland school performance reports: Baltimore City vs. statewide results. (Maryland School Performance Report, July 2001)

Throughout Schmoke's tenure, state officials increasingly prodded BCPS and city officials to do something significant to improve the quality of public education. As he entered his third term in office, Schmoke admitted that the public schools "still have serious problems" (Hunter 1996). Figure 2.2 shows only modest performance increases among Baltimore's school children on the state-administered Maryland School Performance Assessment Program (MSPAP) examination. Baltimore's third–, fifth–, and eighth-grade students lagged far behind the rest of the state and the gap was not narrowing. By the middle of Schmoke's third four-year term, state officials intervened.[6]

State Intervention and the Weakening of the Mayor's Role in School Affairs

In 1994, the Maryland chapter of the American Civil Liberties Union sued the State of Maryland, charging that the state had failed to meet its constitutional responsibility to fund the BCPS at the level necessary for its students to receive an adequate education. One year later, the City of Baltimore filed a similar lawsuit. State officials quickly countersued, noting that over 60 percent of the BCPS budget was supported by state funds. The State also maintained that the BCPS suffered not from a lack of funds, but from mismanagement and a bureaucratic culture that resisted reform.

After months of intense and often heated negotiations, the lawsuits were settled out-of-court. A consent decree linked increased state aid to the city schools to expanded state involvement in the management and operation of the BCPS. The resulting "city-state partnership" called for an additional $254 million to the BCPS over five years — $30 million in 1998, $50 million per year in 1999 and 2000, at least $50 million in 2001 and 2002, and an additional $24 million for capital improvements. The mayoral-appointed school board would be replaced by a new nine-member board appointed by the mayor and the governor from a list compiled by the state board of education. The mayor and the governor would have to agree on all nine candidates. The new school board would also have a specified number of members with management experience in business and education. The appointment, tenure, and compensation of non-teaching personnel in the school system would shift from city hall to the new school board. School procurement and contracts would move from the mayor-dominated Board of Estimates to the new school board. The city's labor commissioner (a mayoral appointee) would relinquish authority to negotiate union contracts to the new school board. The superintendent would be replaced by a chief executive officer who reports to the new school board.

Initially, Mayor Schmoke was reluctant to support the city-state partnership. He believed that the state's offer of an additional $254 million was insufficient, falling short of the $500 million a governor's commission had concluded was necessary to help improve the performance of the BCPS. Moreover, a number of prominent Black leaders vigorously opposed the partnership, seeing it as an attack on local control. The most vocal opposition came from the powerful Black clergy, especially those in BUILD and the IMA, who jealously guarded Black administrative-control of the BCPS. The BTU and other municipal employee unions, the Baltimore school board, and various parent groups all denounced the proposal as a usurpation of local autonomy.

Schmoke, however, decided that it was the best deal he could strike for the city's school children. At a news conference, reportedly near tears and his voice cracking with emotion, Mayor Schmoke announced the partnership with the state. "When I came into office, I said it was my goal to make this the city that reads. It became clearer and clearer to me that our community could not achieve that goal without a partnership with the state" (Thompson and Siegal 1996). Schmoke noted that the partnership was the best thing for the children of the city. "I can tell you from the bottom of my heart, everything tells me this is the right thing to do" (Id). The plan was adopted by the Maryland legislature and signed into law by Democratic Governor Paris Glendening in April 1997. The partnership encroached on the mayor's authority over the BCPS, pushing Baltimore's mayor out of the middle of school affairs.

The Election of Martin O'Malley

Kurt Schmoke did not seek reelection in 1999. Although he remained extremely popular and polls showed him having a 60 percent approval rating among city residents, Schmoke declared that "right now, my gut tells me it's the right time" to move on (Penn and Shields 1998). His successor, Martin O'Malley, a 36-year-old white city councilman representing a majority Black district, announced his candidacy on a street corner widely known for illegal drug sales. O'Malley stated that city leaders must address Baltimore's high murder rate, much of it linked to illegal drugs. He declared that he would make "fighting crime" his top priority and that if elected he would implement a "zero tolerance" crime-fighting strategy (O'Malley 1999). "When we make fighting crime and closing down open-air drug markets the top priority of Baltimore City government, then, and only then, will we be able to build a stable and growing City tax base. Then, and only then, will we dramatically improve schools; then, and only then, will the new jobs created by increased private investment be things of our City's present and future. We will create jobs and improve schools by first improving public safety (Id)." O'Malley, by most accounts, ran a nearly flawless campaign, which he took across the city, including the city's African American neighborhoods. He won the endorsement of a number of Black elected officials and civic leaders, including State Representative Howard "Pete" Rawlings, chairman of the House of Delegates Appropriations Committee. Rawlings, a Baltimore legislator, was the chief sponsor of the 1997 legislation that increased the state's role in the BCPS, and the most politically powerful African American in the state. Rawlings reportedly helped O'Malley win the support of the Reverend Frank M. Reid, pastor of Baltimore's largest African American congregation, who broke with the IMA to endorse O'Malley. Reid's endorsement signaled to African American voters (and liberal white voters) that they could support O'Malley.

O'Malley's emphasis on public safety resonated with Baltimore's voters. While the crime rate had declined in New York, Boston, and other major cities in the United States, the number of murders in Baltimore had soared, reaching more than three hundred per year during the 1990s. In the pivotal Democratic primary, O'Malley outpolled a field of seventeen candidates — including two African American front-runners — winning 53 percent of the vote, including 30 percent of the black vote.[7] O'Malley's strongest support in the African American community came from voters in the precincts most affected by crime. O'Malley built his electoral coalition in Baltimore's white neighborhoods (90 percent of whites voters voted for him), but it was thousands of African Americans who crossed over to vote for him that sealed his victory.

The O'Malley Regime: Crime, Grime, and Bureaucracy

During his first two years in office, O'Malley focused on reducing crime and increasing public safety, improving the delivery and efficiency of city services, and cleaning the city's streets and neighborhoods of trash and abandoned vehicles. Reducing violent crime, however, was O'Malley's top priority. O'Malley appointed Edward T. Norris, who had played a critical part in New York's efforts to lower that city's crime rate, as the new police chief. Norris replicated ComStat, New York's computer-driven crime analysis and management system. Throughout his first two years in office, O'Malley regularly announced his administration's crime-fighting efforts and successes. For example, six months after he was sworn in, O'Malley — joined by community leaders and police officers — returned to the street corner where he had announced his candidacy to declare that ten open-air drug corners had been closed. O'Malley argued that safe streets were the foundation for healthy neighborhoods, improved schools, and economic growth. "You can't have a healthy city for very long if you can't protect the lives of your people, including the children," he explained (O'Malley 2001).

Mayors often use their visibility to promote their agendas. For example, in an effort to publicize the opening of the Baltimore National Aquarium, a major addition to the Inner Harbor redevelopment project, Mayor Schaefer climbed into an 1890-era swimsuit, clasped a rubber duck, and jumped into the seal pool. Mayor Schmoke would often be seen wearing a crossing guard's vest while escorting a group of kindergartners across a city street. Similarly, Mayor O'Malley donned the traditional orange jumpsuit worn by the city's garbage collectors to pick up trash from the back of a city garbage truck. After his first year in office, O'Malley proudly announced that the city had collected over 5,000 tons of trash off streets, alleys, and empty lots.

Providing efficient and responsive city services has also been a top agenda item for O'Malley (Siegel and Smith 2001). Shortly after taking office, O'Malley asked volunteers from the GBC to examine the effectiveness and efficiency of the fire, health, public works, recreation and parks, citywide management, information technology, and housing departments. O'Malley implemented a new computer mapping and accountability system ("CitiStat") — modeled after the police department's computer program — for all city departments (except the BCPS) to improve performance.

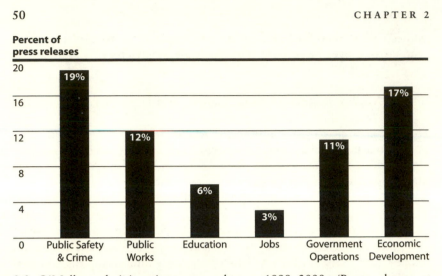

2.3 O'Malley administration press releases, 1999–2000. (Press releases at City of Baltimore website, compiled and categorized by author: <www.ci. baltimore.md.us/news/press/index.html>)

On the other hand, O'Malley has paid considerably less attention to education than his predecessor, Kurt Schmoke. In an effort to quantitatively determine the policy emphasis of the O'Malley administration, I reviewed the content of all press releases issued by O'Malley's press office from December 1999 through July 2002. Mayors use press releases to grab the attention of the media and bring visibility to an issue, so policy matters important to a mayor are likely to be promoted and highlighted by the mayor's press office. Figure 2.3 shows the percentage of press advisories issued by the mayor's press office for six policy areas: crime and public safety; public works; education; job creation; city services; and economic development.[8] O'Malley's emphasis on public safety and making Baltimore a cleaner city is apparent: of the six policy areas, crime and public safety was covered most frequently (nineteen percent) in O'Malley's press releases. Economic development issues, public works, and city management were next. Education is near the bottom. Six percent of the press releases were devoted to schools or school affairs.

O'Malley sees his role in school affairs as an "advocate," lobbying in Annapolis (the state capital) for additional funds, publicizing successes in the schools, and holding schools publicly accountable by making unannounced visits to schools. As he explained in an interview: "I am the leading advocate in Annapolis for the school system. I spend a lot of time in Annapolis lobbying for money, pointing to the successes of our school system; doing a mailing from my office to all the legislators in the state bragging about what great math scores [we have]. I work those state legislators real hard in terms of turning around their image of Baltimore City (O'Malley 2001)."

O'Malley played a limited role in the selection of Carmen Russo as the school system's first CEO. Russo is a member of O'Malley's cabinet, a designation mandated by the 1998 city-state partnership. Jeanne Hitchcock, deputy mayor for intergovernmental relations, monitors the operation of the BCPS for city hall. Mayor O'Malley has left school affairs to the schools system's CEO and school board. "I am not really that involved" in school affairs, O'Malley (2001) admitted. When Kurt Schmoke was mayor, he talked daily with Superintendents Hunter and Amprey. During his first two years in office, Mayor O'Malley's contact with the school system's CEO was limited. "I talk daily to my police commissioner," O'Malley (Id.) emphasized. O'Malley's limited role in school affairs and his heavy emphasis on public safety do not (at least at this time) appear to concern the African American community.[9]

Summary and Conclusion

The experiences of Baltimore's mayors in school affairs remind us that politics matter on at least two levels. First, mayors are political actors who must be concerned with winning elections. Second, governing is characterized by an accommodation between public power and private resources. Proponents of lodging more authority over urban school systems into the mayor's office have tactically avoided or downplayed a central political reality: mayors must be concerned with building and sustaining an electoral coalition. Becoming mayor necessitates constructing a viable electoral coalition; getting reelected requires sustaining the coalition. Mayors, like other elected officials, seek to build a strong electoral base by appealing to voters around salient issues. The extent to which they embrace improving public education or streamlining the operation of city services as an electoral appeal depends on the local political environment and the composition and nature of the candidate's electoral constituencies. Even mayors who have principled goals and a desire to address issues like public education find themselves forced to weigh electoral concerns heavily.

Throughout his long tenure, Mayor Schaefer's electoral coalition was comprised largely of African American voters. Schaefer's tenure occurred in a context that made it politically difficult for him to manage school affairs, except through the arms-length and relatively easy route of dispensing jobs. The racial change in the city and school system complicated matters. As a white mayor, Schaefer did not wish to alienate his African American electoral constituency by interfering in the one area in which African Americans had gained administrative control and to which their material interests were closely connected. As an African American, and with BUILD's support, Kurt L. Schmoke built an electoral coalition behind an emphasis on education. Because his crusade to shape up the BCPS had Black indigenous roots, his initial efforts did not create a tremendous amount of political backlash. His emphasis on schools appealed to his electoral constituency.

An electoral coalition plays a significant role in determining who holds public office and what kind of policy issues are likely to be high on the mayoral agenda. But it is not the same as a governing coalition. For example, the business community is likely to be a significant actor in a governing coalition. Its resources and economic role are too important to be left out. During the Schaefer era, Baltimore's corporate community conceptualized economic development in fairly narrow terms (i.e., physical restructuring) and rewarded Schaefer for emphasizing the Inner Harbor and other downtown projects. The racial change in the city was perhaps also intimidating enough to business elites that they too were willing (perhaps anxious) to "cede" public education to African-American leadership in return for being left in control of an area that they considered most important. Consequently, Schaefer's governing coalition was indifferent to school issues.

Kurt Schmoke's tenure illustrates that sometimes an electoral and governing coalition can align behind a policy agenda. By the time Schmoke was elected, the corporate community (with some encouragement from BUILD) had begun to view schools as the missing link in Baltimore's downtown "renaissance." As a popular African American mayor who had the support of the city's influential Black clergy and majority population behind him and who possessed the credentials, demeanor, and policy agenda attractive to the corporate community, Schmoke drew many business elites into his electoral coalition. The key members of Schmoke's governing coalition, however, seldom reached the level of accommodation required to move school reform forward. Dissension within Schmoke's governing coalition occurred when policy was turned into action, especially when that action was perceived as a threat to the material interests of Schmoke's electoral constituency. Schmoke's failure to fully implement SBM and the upheaval caused by the private management experiment are manifestations of the structural weaknesses within the mayor-dominated approach to school reform. Schmoke struggled to shake-up the school system bureaucracy and to shape a progressive vision of education reform, while at same time embracing the reform initiatives favored by his corporate governance partners. When Schmoke embraced private management of public schools, racial tensions within his governing coalition surfaced: his white corporate partners applauded; his African American electoral constituency challenged him.

In 1997, the governance of Baltimore's schools was changed dramatically. The city-state partnership put considerable limits on the mayor's formal authority over the BCPS. Although the mayor and the governor jointly appoint the nine-member school board, school policy is no longer directed by city hall. Beginning in 1997, the school board played the dominant role in determining and formulating school policy (Westat 2001). An evaluation of the changed school structure applauded the requirements for board membership established through the 1997 restructuring legislation. The evaluation found that the new board members "have provided a cadre of professionals with outstanding experience to guide reform" and "played a unique role in the redirection" of the BCPS (Westat 2001, xxiii). Second, the new structure changed the dynamics and relationship between the school board and the superintendent. Prior to 1997, Baltimore's school superintendent took directions from the mayor (Hunter 1997). The new structure encourages the superintendent to work closely with the school board. Third, the city-state partnership struck a major blow to the patronage system embedded in the relationship between the mayor and the BCPS. All hiring and procurement matters shifted from city hall to the school district and its individual schools. Before 1997, all BCPS spending above $300 required city hall approval. Under the system established after 1997, any purchase under $5,000 can be authorized at the school level; purchases between $5,000 and $15,000 must be approved by the BCPS procurement office, and those above $15,000 must be authorized by the school board and put-out for bid. Finally, state education officials and BCPS leaders—the central players in the city-state partnership—have developed closer linkages.

BCPS leaders and Mayor O'Malley view the partnership as beneficial. Evaluators reached a similar conclusion, noting that they found "no basis on which to argue that BCPS should return to its previous status of being controlled by the City of Baltimore" (Westat 2001, xiii). Nevertheless, those advocating for greater mayoral control over public schools argue that schools are so vital for cities operating in the twenty-first century's global economy that mayors must play an active role in school affairs.

Martin O'Malley, Baltimore's first mayor of the twenty-first century, played a limited role in school affairs during his first two years in office, focusing instead on issues that offered more opportunities to generate visible results, such as street cleaning, economic development, efficient

management, and public safety. To be sure, O'Malley's election came
after state legislation decreased the mayor's role in school affairs. Baltimore's current structure, however, still allows for more formal mayoral involvement than Los Angeles and other cities. O'Malley, however,
did not take advantage of this opening, deciding that he was comfortable being out of the middle of school issues.

If there is an obvious conclusion to be drawn from this review it is
that the mayor's office provides neither a panacea nor a quick fix for
urban school districts. The case of Baltimore makes it clear that, even
when there is significant mayoral control, electoral concerns can con-
strain mayoral leadership in school affairs. The case material also seems
to support the view that a mayor, using the informal power and visibility of the position, can shape the local agenda. While Mayor Schmoke
had little success in transforming the city's schools, his consistent attention to the schools no doubt helped to elevate and keep school concerns
at the top of Baltimore's (and the state's) action agenda. Mayor O'Malley's focus on education has been limited. His attention in his first years
in office was focused on public safety, public works, and economic development, raising the question of whether school reform is just too
bruising an area for mayors to survive in.

Notes

1. The exact number of patronage positions available through the school system is not clear. The school system has over 170 schools, and has long been one
of Baltimore's largest employers. In 2000, over eleven thousand employees were
on the payroll of BCPS.

2. This type of "distributional" arrangement is familiar to students of American urban politics. Steve Erie (1988), in his study of Irish political machines,
discussed how machine bosses extended their political longevity by distributing
a variety of public sector jobs to their fellow Irishmen, who typically got positions in the police and fire departments. Teaching jobs went to Jews. The Ital-
ians dominated positions in sanitation. Pinderhughes (1987) provides a similar
discussion in her work on machine politics in Chicago.

3. Middle-class African Americans were also discriminated against in Baltimore's private sector economy, leaving the public sector as their only avenue
for economic and social advancement. Several studies have documented private
sector racial discrimination in Baltimore. See Joint Center for Political and Economic Studies 1991 and Wickman 1987.

4. In November 1981, the U.S. Commission on Civil Rights held hearings in
Baltimore to examine the level of minority participation in the economic development and revitalization of the city. In its final report, "Greater Baltimore
Commitment: A Study of Urban Minority Economic Development" (U.S. Commission on Civil Rights, 1983), the commission lambasted the Schaefer administration and the city's corporate leaders for their "dismal" record in this area,

concluding that "minority economic development has not been a priority in Baltimore City."

5. When Kurt Schmoke sought to remove Superintendent Hunter before his contract expired, this too challenged the governing coalition. Several educational stakeholders, especially key business leaders, quietly encouraged Schmoke to ask the school board to fire Hunter. Many African American leaders, including the powerful Black clergy aligned with BUILD, stood behind Hunter. They argued that Hunter had not been given enough time to turn around the struggling school system. And Schmoke faced pressure from prominent Black leaders who complained that the "white establishment" was out to get Hunter. Privately, the ministers told Schmoke they did not like the idea of the city's African American mayor publicly berating a fellow African American leader and urged him to keep Hunter in the interest of African American unity. Fearful of a bloody and public fight, Schmoke sought to cool the tensions by announcing the appointment of a deputy superintendent to manage the day-to-day affairs of the school system. Superintendent Hunter was allowed to stay but his three-year contract was not renewed when it expired in July 1991.

6. A thorough discussion of the state's role in Baltimore's school reform efforts can be found in Orr (1999, 165–84).

7. O'Malley's candidacy was aided by the fact that both Black candidates, Carl Stokes and Lawrence Bell, ran ineffective campaigns and received a barrage of unflattering media coverage. For example, during the campaign the media reported that Bell spent more than $4,000 from his campaign donations for new clothes. In addition, two of Bell's campaign supporters were forced to acknowledge making thousands of copies of white supremacist literature endorsing O'Malley and distributing them in Baltimore's Black neighborhoods. Stokes, while picking up critical endorsements from Black ministers and the *Baltimore Sun*, was also forced to address miscues, including driving with a suspended license, being served with a four-year federal tax lien during his council tenure, and falsely claiming a college degree on his campaign literature. Stokes' troubles cost him support among the city's white liberal community.

8. There were a total of 102 press releases. The other 33 percent of the press releases could not be categorized into any of the six policy areas. They included such matters as the Baltimore Ravens' Super Bowl appearance, visits by foreign dignitaries, and the unveiling of former mayor Schmoke's portrait in city hall.

9. A public opinion poll of Baltimore residents released in June 2000 showed that 61 percent believed that crime was "the most important issue facing Baltimore today." Sixty-nine percent of African American residents believed that O'Malley had been successful "in shutting down many of Baltimore's 'drug corners'" (Gonzales/Arscott Research 2000).

References

Arnold, J. L. 1990. "Baltimore: Southern Culture and a Northern Economy." In *Snowbelt Cities*, ed. R. M. Bernard. Bloomington: Indiana University Press.

Asayesh, G. 1991. "Baltimore Board Weighs Private School Operation." *Baltimore Sun*, 17 May.

Associated Black Charities. 1992. *A Report of a Management Study of the Baltimore City Public Schools*. Baltimore: Associated Black Charities.

Berkowitz, E. 1997 "Baltimore's Public Schools in a Time of Transition." *Maryland Historical Magazine* 92(4):413–32.

Bowler, M. 1991. *Lessons of Change: Baltimore Schools in the Modern Era*. Baltimore: Fund for Educational Excellence.

———. 1995. "Other Areas Have Dropped School Boards." *Baltimore Sun*, 11 November.

———. 1996. "Board Stands Up to Be Counted." *Baltimore Sun*, 21 February.

Crain, R. L. 1968. *The Politics of School Desegregation*. Chicago: Aldine.

Cramer, R., and A. Pietilla. 1974. "Board's Whites Try to Fire Patterson." *Baltimore Sun*, 9 August.

Elkin, S. L. 1987. *City and Regime in the American Republic*. Chicago: University of Chicago Press.

Englund, W. 1990a. "Home Rule Plan Draws Fire from Parents, Groups." *Baltimore Sun*, 17 September.

———. 1990b. "Hunter Tells Official He Will Stay despite Those 'Out to Get Him.'" *Baltimore Sun*, 19 January.

Erie, S. 1988. *Rainbow's End: Irish Americans and the Dilemmas of Urban Machine Politics, 1840–1985*. Berkeley: University of California Press.

Ferman, B. 1985. *Governing the Ungovernable City*. Philadelphia: Temple University Press.

Fleming, G. J. 1972. *Baltimore's Failure to Elect a Black Mayor in 1971*. Washington, D.C.: Joint Center for Political Studies.

Fletcher, M. 1992. "Schmoke: No School Moratorium." *Baltimore Sun*, 21 July.

Gittell, M. 1994. "School Reform in New York and Chicago: Revisiting the Ecology of Local Games." *Urban Affairs Quarterly* 30:136–51.

Goldberg, R. M. "Party Competition and Black Politics in Baltimore and Philadelphia." Ph.D. diss., Brandeis University.

Gonzales/Arscott Research. 2000. "Baltimore Residential Poll." 10–15 June. <www.baltimorecity.gov/news/press/000607.html>.

Henig, J., R. Hula, M. Orr, and D. Pedescleaux. 1999. *The Color of School Reform*. Princeton, N.J.: Princeton University Press.

Hunter, F. 1996. "Mayor Says Schools' Woes Still 'Serious.'" *Baltimore Sun*, 20 October.

Hunter, R. 1997. "The Mayor versus the Superintendent." *Education and Urban Society* 29:217–32.

Kirst, M., and K. Bulkley. 2000. "'New, Improved' Mayors Take Over City Schools." *Phi Delta Kappan* 81 (March): 538–46.

Levine, M. 1987. "Downtown Redevelopment as an Urban Growth Strategy." *Journal of Urban Affairs* 9:103–23.

Mahtesian, C. 1996. "Hand Schools to City Hall." *Governing: The Magazine of States and Localities* 73 (October): 37–40.

McCraven, M. 1995. "Black Voters Sensed a 'Crisis' and Turned Out." *Baltimore Sun*, 17 September.

McDougall, H. A. 1993. *Black Baltimore: A New Theory of Community*. Philadelphia: Temple University Press

O'Keefe, K. 1986. *Baltimore Politics 1971–1986: The Schaefer Years and the Struggle for Succession*. Washington D.C.: Georgetown University Press.

O'Malley, M. 1999. "Announcement Speech: Corner of Harford Road and The Alemeda." <www.cibaltimore.md.us/mayor/speeches/sp990622.html>.

———. 2001. Interview with the author. Baltimore. 1 August.

Orr, M. 1992. "Urban Regimes and Human Capital Policies: A Study of Baltimore." *Journal of Urban Affairs* 14:173–87.

———. 1996. "Urban Politics and School Reform: The Case of Baltimore." *Urban Affairs Review* 31:315–45.

———. 1998. "The Challenge of School Reform in Baltimore: Race, Jobs, and Politics." In *Changing Urban Education*, ed. C. N. Stone. Lawrence: University Press of Kansas.

———. 1999. *Black Social Capital: The Politics of School Reform in Baltimore*. Lawrence: University Press of Kansas.

Penn, I, and G. Shields. 1998. "Schmoke Calls This 'the Right Time,' Mayor Says Officially He Won't Seek Fourth Term." *Baltimore Sun*, 4 December.

Pinderhughes, D. 1987. *Race and Ethnicity in Chicago Politics*. Urbana-Champaign: University of Illinois Press.

Rich, W. C. 1996. *Black Mayors and School Politics*. New York: Garland Press.

Richards, C., R. Shore, and M. B. Sawicky. 1996. *Risky Business: Private Management of Public Schools*. Washington, D.C.: Economic Policy Institute.

Rusk, D. 1996. *Baltimore Unbound: A Strategy for Regional Renewal*. Baltimore: Abell Foundation.

Schmoke, K. 1987. Inaugural Address. Baltimore. 8 December. Recorded in author's files.

———. 2000. Interview with author. Baltimore. 23 August. Scott, H. 1980. *The Black Superintendent: Messiah or Scapegoat?* Washington, D.C.: Howard University Press.

Siegel, F., and V. Smith. 2001. "Can Mayor O'Malley Save Ailing Baltimore." *City Journal* 2 (winter): 64–75.

Smith, C. F. 1999. *William Donald Schaefer: A Political Biography*. Baltimore: The Johns Hopkins University Press.

Stoker, R. 1987. "Baltimore: The Self-Evaluating City." In *The Politics of Urban Development*, ed. C. N. Stone and H. T. Sanders. Lawrence: University Press of Kansas.

Stone, C. N. 1989. *Regime Politics: Governing Atlanta, 1946–1988*. Lawrence: University Press of Kansas.

Stone, C. N., J. Henig, B. Jones, and C. Pierannunzi. 2001. *Building Civic Capacity: The Politics of Reforming Urban Schools*. Lawrence: University Press of Kansas.

Swanstrom, T. 1985. *The Crisis of Growth Politics*. Philadelphia: Temple University Press.

Szanton, P. 1986. *Baltimore 2000: A Choice of Futures*. Baltimore: Goldseker Foundation.

Thompson, J., and E. Siegel. 1996. "City, State Sign Deal for Schools." *Baltimore Sun*, 7 November.

Watson, D. L. 1990. *Lion in the Lobby: Clarence Mitchell, Jr.'s Struggle for the Passage of Civil Rights Laws*. New York: William Morrow and Company.

Welcome, V. 1991. *My Life and Times*. Englewood Cliffs, N.J.: Henry House Publishers.

Westat. 2001. "Report on the Final Evaluation of the City-State Partnership." Presented to the New Baltimore City Board of School Commissioners and the Maryland State Department of Education. 3 December.

Wong, K. 1990. *City Choices: Education and Housing*. Albany: SUNY Press.

Chapter Three

Chicago: The National "Model" Reexamined

DOROTHY SHIPPS

CHICAGO HAS BEEN reforming its public school governance structure for more than twenty years. In 1995, the process led to an unprecedented assertion of mayoral control in this city famous for strong mayors. Shortly thereafter, the "Chicago model," became a national exemplar, lauded by President Clinton who promised "to help other communities follow Chicago's lead" (*Chicago Tribune* 1977, President 1998). The president's remarks referred to a governance structure in which Mayor Richard M. Daley was given personal authority to select the school board and the system's chief executive officer. At the same time, the State of Illinois deregulated the Chicago Public Schools, giving the mayor more fiscal, labor, and management discretion than any recent Chicago school board.

Balanced budgets, labor peace, student test score improvements, and an influx of middle-class residents to the city have been attributed to these new governing arrangements (Vallas 1998). In contrast to the previous era's near-continuous fiscal and labor disputes, since 1995 there has been little public discussion of budget shortfalls or strike threats, and two back-to-back four-year labor contracts have been signed (Forte 1995; Hinz 1998). Elementary school test scores have shown positive trends for most years (CPS 2002a). Failing schools are recognized as such and targeted for increasingly severe sanctions (CPS 2000b; CPS 2000c). Ancient buildings are being renovated, and new ones built (CPS 2002b). Gentrification of the central city housing stock and increased land values are much-discussed consequences of new middle-class professionals being lured back to the city, at least in part it is said, by better schools (Daley 1997).

The conventional explanation for these effects begins with a bold step taken by the Illinois State Legislature, one that shifted accountability from an array of competing authorities (including the school bureaucracy) to the mayor's office (Wong et al. 1997; Education Commission of the States 1999). Their decisive action, we are told, broke the cycle of ephemeral and superficial reform. It also created conditions for the growth of civic capacity that would be needed to sustain change into

the future. However, this explanation fundamentally mischaracterizes
the causal relationship between structural reform and the civic capacity
needed to undertake and sustain it. As far-reaching as the new governance structure appears, it is only the latest of three attempts to rees-
tablish the legitimacy of the city's public schools by breaking up the
bureaucracy and shifting authority, all three initiated by a coalition of
local civic actors in Chicago. Collectively, these efforts amount to one
ongoing process that begins with local reform initiative, seeks state legislative sanction, is implemented by a cross-section of civic actors, and
produces positive, but inadequate, results. The process, in turn, encourages a portion of the city's large civic community to contemplate further
governance change. Over a period of twenty years, this incrementalism
discredited an old school governing regime and replaced it with a new
one. Chicago's adoption of strong mayoral control is one of several
outcomes of building civic capacity for reform, not itself a cause of civic
capacity or reform.

Moreover, when the positive consequences of these governing arrangements have been reported the differential effects on Chicago's
heavily segregated racial and ethnic communities are rarely noted. Reports of student success are largely based on aggregate data that do not
take into account the large gaps between low-income and middle-class
students, or the unchanged disparities between Black or Latino students, and white students. Nor has identification of academically failing
schools, particularly Chicago's troubled high schools, done much to
help the worst of them. In the city's famously segregated neighborhoods, this too carries strong racial overtones. Labor peace has been
purchased with steady union raises, and with agreements to bargain
back nearly all of the union prerogatives struck from the 1995 law, but
these pacts are currently being challenged now that the union leadership
has passed from machine-savvy Blacks to reform-minded whites. Construction and renovation of schools has pitted middle-class and low-
income communities against one another for the new facilities. And
symbolic representation among the system's leadership team continues
to be watched for political signals about their motives and intentions.
Race, as it turns out, has been of consequence, despite a rhetoric of
school reform that ignores race in favor of a color-blind version of
merit.

In the remainder of this chapter I briefly describe the Chicago Public
Schools (CPS), and for context, sketch the city's current political economy. I then clarify how regime analysis helps conceptualize the school
system's structural and relationship transformations. Next, I compare
the system's old governing regime with its new one, providing historical
detail on the incremental and informal development of the school board's

new role as one example of the changes. Finally, I summarize the consequences for different civic sectors in Chicago, paying particular attention to the material interests, symbolic benefits and political incorporation of Chicago's Black and Latino majority.

An Uncommon System with Typical Problems

With 433,000 students the Chicago Public Schools (CPS) is larger than all but the school systems in New York City and Los Angeles. Although larger in scale, Chicago resembles the other cases considered in this volume in many critical respects. Chicago has high proportions of low-income families who suffer racial discrimination and the dislocations of immigrant status. Black and Latino students currently make up more than four-fifths of the school system, and the proportion of those from low-income families has been steadily rising, from 47 percent in 1983 to 85 percent in 2001. CPS also has a long-standing record of relatively poor performance, with periodic, but small, improvements. The current four-year dropout rate of about 43 percent remains unchanged from the 1980s (Allensworth and Easton 2001; Hinz 2001). Average student performance remains well below national norms on the Iowa Test of Basic Skills (ITBS), although there have been two waves of test score rises in the last twenty years. Between 1980 and 1985, upper elementary reading test scores rose in the majority of schools, but white students, especially those in magnet schools, showed most gains (Hess 1988). After dipping, average ITBS reading and math test scores rose again between 1991 and 1997, especially in the upper elementary grades. Since then, aggregate scores seem to have leveled off. As before, the recent rise shows no evidence that the Black–white achievement gap is closing, and a Latino gap is a growing source of concern (Easton et al. 2001).

Underlying this gradually improving, but still low, performance has been large and relatively rapid demographic and economic change. Chicago has both a sizeable white ethnic population that dates to nineteenth century immigration, and a large Black population that came up from the south in two waves of the Great Migration. Latinos — overwhelmingly from Mexico, but also from Puerto Rico and, more recently, from about half a dozen Central and Latin American countries — became a substantial presence in the city during the 1990s, after having been virtually ignored little more than a decade earlier (Attinasi 1991; Latino Institute 1994). In 1980, when the first school reform law went into effect, whites constituted almost half of the city's population; Blacks nearly 40 percent; and Latinos 14 percent. Black children occupied about 61 percent of the public school seats, while black adults held

48 percent of the teaching jobs, slightly less than 33 percent of the principalships and 39 percent of the central office administrator positions. Even then, Latino children occupied about one sixth of the seats in public school classrooms, while the Latino proportion of the school's professional employees was tiny (about 4 percent). There was no Latino equivalent to the Black professional middle class working in the public schools. Racial politics were most often negotiated bilaterally, between Blacks and whites.

By the mid-1990s, when the latest reform law was enacted, whites and Blacks each represented about 39 percent of the city's population. The proportion of Black children in the public schools had leveled off to about 55 percent and the black middle class held on to a stable half of the professional positions in the school system, even though that workforce had been reduced by three thousand administrators. Continuing, steady growth in the city's Latino population to over 20 percent in mid-decade (26 percent by 2000) magnified some of the challenges Chicago educators have always faced, but others are new. Latino children became nearly one-third of the public school enrollment. In 1990, a fifth of these newcomers lived in poverty; a quarter of the 16–19-year-olds were not in school. More than half reported they did not speak English well and 35 percent were linguistically isolated in Spanish-speaking households (Latino Institute 1994). More surprisingly, the proportions of Latino principals (12 percent) and central office administrators (16 percent) had grown exponentially, far outstripping their representation in the entry-level position of teacher (8 percent).

Paralleling these demographic changes has been a shift from Chicago's industrial base to a service economy dependent on central business district office work and tourism. In 1967, manufacturing provided forty-one percent of all city jobs; by 1990 that had shrunk to eighteen percent, representing a loss of over 330,000 blue-collar positions, including those traditionally attracting immigrants. During the transformation Black wages held steady at about sixty-six percent of white wages while average Latino wages fell, as a proportion of white wages, from sixty-one percent to fifty percent (Betancur and Gills 2000, 25–6).

The nationwide urban boom of the 1990s further increased Chicago's service sector employment, especially the hospitality businesses. In 1998, Chicago ranked first in the nation as a convention site. City Hall encouraged the economic growth by vastly increasing spending on infrastructure improvement. Not only were schools renovated, but so were all the city's firehouses and police stations. Branch libraries and "El" stations were rebuilt or refurbished, streets repaved, and flowers planted, all in an effort to insure that the central business district (CBD) remain a competitive global business headquarters and tourist destination. Downtown rental apartments and condominums soared in value. Toward the end of the millenium, some of this development even spilled over into the traditionally Black and Latino South Side and West Side neighborhoods nearest the downtown "Loop" city center (Simpson et al. 2002).

Despite clear evidence of affluence in the CBD, the neighborhoods where low income Black and immigrant Latino students live have not fared as well, and Chicagoans recognized this. A 1994 poll of municipal program delivery found that while residents of middle-class neighborhoods that were 85 percent or more white were pleased with their services, most Black and Latino neighborhood residents rated theirs "poor or very poor" (Alexander 2000 197). A 2002 poll discovered that residents believed the city's biggest problem (36%) remained "poverty and unemployment" (Simpson et al. 2002, 15). Some of the disparity is caused by an imbalance in budget priorities. Locally collected business and property taxes were cut in 1996, and replaced by regressive sales and entertainment taxes, fees and forfeitures. Most of the locally-raised budget not already dedicated to basic services was earmarked for rebuilding downtown and institutional infrastructure. Low-income services (e.g., housing, health, or jobs) were "almost exclusively" funded through federal, state, and private grants (Alexander 2000, 207).

Since the recession in 2001, Chicago, like most cities, has lost jobs and faced cutbacks in both state and federal aid. A stock market decline has diminished the capacity of private foundations to pick up the slack. Because low-income Black and Latino residents had only recently begun to benefit economically from the city's investments in infrastructure, and their children remained well behind their white counterparts on measures of school performance, political incorporation and symbolic benefits may be among the more lasting effects of reform. Improvements in the city's poorly performing schools may have reached another low plateau. Whether contrasts between the long-deferred material interests of low-income Black students and their families and those of the largely immigrant and rapidly-growing Latino communities can be reconciled remains an open question.

Using Regime Analysis

Regime analysis is especially helpful in clarifying how the politics of schooling in Chicago link its mayors to reform. The structural link needs little clarification. Chicago mayors have always had direct influence on school policy because every mayor since the founding of the city has selected the school board. Yet the quality of the mayor's influence has varied, depending on the informal governance arrangements each established, and the larger political agendas each embraced. Most Chicago mayors either supported the tradition of school governance by educational experts or used the schools as a patronage hiring hall. Few actively sought any reform, certainly no transformation of the governing regime of the schools;[1] nor did Mayor Richard M. Daley seek regime change. Instead, he was the recipient of a structural novelty that put him in control of the schools, and a local reform movement that forced his hand. The open question in May 1995 was whether the mayor would adjust the informal arrangements of his governing style to accept political accountability for the schools and take advantage of the opportunities that deregulation gave him to establish new governing patterns. I argue that on most, but not all, accounts he has seized the opportunities to solidify and extend regime change in the schools. The resulting new school-governing regime has affected the city's black community differently from its Latinos, partly reflecting their disparate levels of participation in the civic coalitions that set the stage for mayoral control.

Regime analysis is useful precisely because regime change is theorized as more than a change in leadership, or the reorganization of governmental functions. While regime analysis involves alteration of the formal institutions of governance, it also requires a change in the "informal arrangements that surround and complement the formal workings of government authority" (Stone 1989, 3). The theory of urban regime change, as developed by Clarence Stone and his colleagues, recognizes that transforming well-established patterns of governance requires a coalition of forces both within and outside of government. It requires involvement from private sector organizations that are willing to dedicate their own resources and "a significant degree of loyalty to the effort to see it realized" (p. 263). The composition of the coalition shapes its agenda for change, as different parties bring their values, expertise, and resources to the table. When they have the will and the resources to implement their goals, private sector actors gain special prominence because they do not require, as politicians do, broad political support or government funding. Although political leadership is indispensable at crucial points to mobilize and maintain a cross-sector coalition, the stimulus for change can be external to the system (Stone 1993; Stone et al. 2001). As the Chicago case demonstrates, the political leadership required to change an urban school governance regime need not be consistent throughout the re-forming process. Daley inherited a process begun long before he won a mayor's race. If mayoral control is not causal, the Chicago case also demonstrates that building civic capacity for reform is a critical and contingent process that can not be skipped.

The Old and New Regimes

Some things have not changed. Chief among them is the city's century-old relationship with the state. CPS operates under a separate school law, originally written into the 1870 State Constitution as applying only to cities over one hundred thousand in population. Wide political gaps exist — between the white, conservative, Republican, and heavily rural "downstate" and the multiracial, liberal, machine-oriented Democratic city of corporate headquarters — which have long provided reasons for the state legislature to avoid Chicago's troubled schools. In practice, this has meant that Illinois provides one of the nation's lowest proportion of funding to its city schools. It has also discouraged the state from tackling Chicago's school corruption scandals, fiscal crises, and desegregation battles unless the remedies were initiated in Chicago itself. Just such a locally induced process brought about the recent changes in the formal institutions of school governance.

Chicago's Old School-Governing Regime

For the thirty-three years before 1980, CPS was governed by a mayor-appointed school board that had responsibility for selecting a general superintendent, whose educational qualifications were spelled out by law.[2] Until 1980, the mayor also approved the system's total budget allocation. The general superintendent managed both the system's business and educational functions. Teachers boasted a long record of union activism including frequent strikes after Mayor Richard J. Daley (Daley Sr.) granted Chicago Teachers Union (CTU) bargaining rights in 1966. In addition, twelve other ancillary unions bargained with the board.

Despite structural ties between city hall and the CPS, most Chicago mayors avoided public school debates and disavowed any responsibility for their problems. Daley Sr., the mayor for most of this period, is famous for claiming he was not in control of the schools and for waffling on desegregation, even as it tore the city apart. When mayors did take on the school system's problems it was usually after key constituents asked for assistance. Decisions were made in private and the mayor acted indirectly, using the power of the office to bolster the formal authority of the board (Peterson 1981). Daley Sr. is known to have settled every strike during his mayoralty, much to the chagrin of community activists, but he did so quietly by working through sympathetic board members. Except for his kitchen cabinet of business advisors, few in the city knew about the unorthodox bookkeeping that accompanied Daley

Sr.'s budget-busting settlements until after his death (Grimshaw 1979; Shipps 1995). School board meetings were lively, contentious affairs. Community members used them to raise broad political issues, such as lack of progress on desegregation or resource inequities, but also to complain about topics as mundane as a single personnel decision or bus route. While the general superintendent typically attended board meetings, the body functioned as a buffer for the education professionals in the system, absorbing or deflecting criticism of teachers, principals and the central office (Meyer and Rowan 1978).

The CTU gained power under these circumstances. In addition to striking for almost biannual raises, workplace issues like class size, seniority privileges, the length of the school day, and "prep period" rights were bargained, then codified in Chicago's school law. Several of the system's noninstructional unions were firmly ensconced for different reasons; they were patronage employees, hired from city hall (Grimshaw 1979).

Thus, the old governing regime combined formal structures and informal patterns of interaction into a system that put the mayor in charge of negotiations with the unions and linked other school employment to the Democratic machine. In deference to the rhetoric of professional control of the schools, the old governing regime also permitted the mayor to avoid responsibility for budget deficits, crumbling schools, inequitable services, overpaid service employees, and inadequate teaching. One symbol of this informal arms-length relationship was the voluntary adoption by Chicago's mayors of an Advisory Commission on School Board Nominations to guide the selections of board candidates.[3] This group helped institutionalize the custom of board members being selected as representatives of different labor, management, and civic sectors of the city.

The general superintendent was the system's publicly accountable decision maker, despite the lack of formal authority to make most decisions. By law, that authority rested with the school board. Yet, partly because reform groups had discredited the school board as corrupt and guilty of nepotism, and partly because board members' allegiances had been divided in the Civil Rights Movement and remained so until the 1980s, the superintendent ruled supreme. Nearly all ran the system as chief bureaucrats, functionaries who tightly held information, dismissed questions by the press and parents, and saw themselves as accountable only to their superiors. They were wedded to the separation of professional control from the free-wheeling community politics of school board debates. The separation was taken for granted, and underscored by business leaders' near-constant efforts to upgrade the superintendent's managerial skills (Pois 1964; Cuban 1976).

Principals in the old regime were low-level (but tenured) managers in a steep hierarchy; subordinates were expected to "toe the line" in exchange for advancement to higher office, usually meaning to a larger school with higher grade levels, or perhaps to a (sub)district office. "As a principal, I felt accountable to the state of Illinois because of the chain of command . . . from me to the district superintendent, to the superintendent, to the state of Illinois." Their responsibilities to parents and community members were minimal. "Keep the community from complaining and the kids from killing each other" was the way one high-profile principal described her responsibilities to parents and other Chicagoans (Personal Interviews 1994). Teachers, in turn, answered to principals, and expected their union to protect them from unreasonable demands.

The New School-Governing Regime

Many structural changes have been formally codified since 1980. Most obviously, the mayor now selects a small school board of trustees—five members from 1995 to 1999; after 1999, seven—and designates its president and chief executive officer (CEO). Not one of these senior leaders is required to have educational credentials. The mayor and his management team have final budgetary authority, enhanced through the consolidation of fifteen separate local school tax levies into the general fund, and the combination of twenty-five formerly separate state categorical programs (e.g., bilingual education, drivers' education) into two block grants, with liberal waiver provisions. This has vastly increased the ability to shift resources from one budget priority to another. In addition, privatization of school functions is encouraged by the elimination of all statutory limits on outsourcing, contracting and downsizing. Previously bargained job rights of teachers and other employees have been eliminated from the school code, insuring that the mayor also has maximum flexibility in negotiating with unions. Just to underscore the point, the CTU was forbidden to strike for eighteen months after the third reform law was passed in 1995. Discretion in education decision making is further enhanced by the statutory requirement that Chicago's district leaders construct a series of "interventions" for schools in need of improvement, up to, and including, closing them.

In addition to eliminating the necessity for the system's top bureaucrat to be an educator, the law also codified a corporate management structure in which several second-level executives shared responsibility for the schools. A chief financial officer (CFO), chief purchasing officer, and chief operations officer were designated to control the business side of the schools, while a chief education officer — the only educator in the group — was authorized to make educational suggestions to the CEO. Not accountable to the public, the CEO and school board serve at the pleasure of the mayor (Illinois General Assembly 1995).

The formal structure of the principalship was also radically altered. No longer career-ladder employees in the district, principals are now hired and fired by Local School Councils (LSCs) on four-year renewable contracts. LSCs are mandated governing bodies at each of the system's 600 schools, statutorily composed of six parents, two community members, and two teachers (plus one student representative for high schools), elected every two years. Bolstering their authority over principals, LSCs also sign-off on the school budget, including as much as $1 million in discretionary funds per schoool.[4] In addition to being politically accountable to LSCs, principals of low-performing schools also answer to the CEO; others, though, are largely left alone (Hess 1991; Kyle and Kantowitz 1992; O'Connell 1991).

Having lost collective bargaining gains — but not their rights to bargain — teachers have little compensatory advantage in schools. They have only a minority vote on LSCs and an advisory role to the principal on those curriculum issues not settled by the CEO.

These formal changes have increased the mayor's flexibility in making school policy and his political accountability as the central school decision maker. Simultaneously, the LSC governing structure creates the potential for an alternative political accountability mechanism. Although only one mayor has governed the schools under the full benefits of this legal structure, as the section below describes, informal patterns of interaction have also developed in stages over the terms of three mayors: Jane Byrne (1979–1983), Harold Washington (1983–1987), and Richard M. Daley (1989–present).

Building Capacity for Regime Change

The legal sanction for these changes came from the state legislature and the governor. Yet the resources, priorities, agendas, and commitments were generated by coalitions of civic groups. These necessary conditions for reform did not simply flow from above, despite the enabling rhetoric of thoughtful politicians. Nor were all the substantive changes mandated. Instead, many of the broad expectations of the schools and all of the new social relationships came about because civic groups, and later city hall bureaucrats, improvised and experimented with new and unfamiliar responsibilities. Regime analysis alerts us to the process by which such structural changes are woven into a web of standard operating procedures, expectations, decision rules and informal evaluative criteria through countless negotiations between civic actors, politicians, and educators.

Changes in governing relationships, and the consequences for different sectors of Chicago, developed incrementally, as one coalition's hard won structural changes and patterns of interaction layered over another's. They are too many to detail in one chapter. However, the Chicago school board's evolving relationship to the mayor and other civic actors, and the subsequent alterations in its governing responsibilities, is one case study that illuminates the general pattern. Close examination of these alterations clarifies that the three school reform laws passed in 1980, 1988 and 1995 are road signs in an ongoing process of regime change. This governing history demonstrates how deeply regime change was contested, and how a fundamental institution of popular governance in American schooling has become a mechanism for managerial oversight.

1980: Business Initiates Reform

A fiscal crisis in the winter of 1979–80 lowered the school system's bond rating and spurred the city's top banking executives to search for a mechanism that would guarantee their financial return while controlling future educational costs (Shipps 1995). Newly elected Mayor Byrne, facing a recession that bankrupted other cities, declined to follow R. Daley Sr.'s practice of offering city assets as collateral for school refinancing (Green 1984; Rakove 1982). Instead, she watched from the sidelines as the city's bankers, all members of the elite Commercial Club, went to Governor James R. Thompson to hammer out a private bailout agreement. The executives agreed to loan the school system funds in exchange for oversight of its finances through a School Finance Authority (SFA) and control over a portion of the school tax receipts. Modeled after New York City's finance authority of the 1970s, the SFA was empowered to abrogate labor contracts, downsize the central office, and even close schools in order to force a balanced budget. It appointed an independent chief financial officer, stripping fiscal responsibility from the general superintendent for the first time in nearly thirty years. Legally mandated to fade away after three years of balanced budgets, the SFA held on, and even expanded its authority, until 1995. Only then was it disbanded (despite a projected deficit) in order to maximize Mayor Richard M. Daley's fiscal and managerial flexibility (Shipps 1997).

Not only did this "shotgun agreement" drastically curtail the school board's authority, it also required the sitting board to resign *en masse*, enabling Byrne to appoint an entirely new board. In search of allies in her losing battle to win the support of machine aldermen, Byrne decided to let the evidently interested and influential business executives provide her with a slate of candidates. She dismissed the president of the Advisory Commission on School Board Nominations and refused to reconvene the group, angering longstanding members in the process. Linked to the Commercial Club of Chicago and the city's banking elite by overlapping membership, Chicago United (CU) was chosen instead to serve as her nominating committee. CU, made up of equal numbers of Black civic leaders and white business executives, provided the city with its most racially balanced school board to date. That board, in turn, chose the city's first Black superintendent, Californian Ruth Love (Holli 1982; Shipps 1995).

Yet both the new board and Love's appointment divided, rather than united, Chicagoans. Jesse Jackson's Operation PUSH (People United to Save Humanity), the Chicago Urban League (CUL), The Woodlawn Organization (TWO), and other black community organizations believed that local Black career educators, poised by the late 1970s to take control of the system, rather than white "overseers," should be making district decisions. They had backed their own "inside" candidate for superintendent, Manfred Byrd, and mistrusted Love because she lacked local commitments and connections. Moreover, they resented the fact that the first Black superintendent would be sharing power with a CFO (Whitmore 1986). Then there was Byrne's effort to circumvent the law by appointing CU's Thomas Ayers, retired CEO of Commonwealth Edison, as board president. Ayers did not live in the city, (the technical reason he was not seated), and the majority of the board members were prepared to vote for a distinguished Black minister instead. Worse yet, Byrne changed her mind about two of CU's younger Black nominees after seating them, replacing them with two white women, one of whom was known to have vehemently resisted token desegregation in the 1970s (Kleppner 1985; Rivlin 1982).

These decisions and others like them — Byrne later replaced two Blacks on the city housing authority with two whites, triggering a boycott of the 1982 Chicago Fest — set in motion a campaign widely credited with bringing about the election of Harold Washington as the first Black mayor of Chicago (Gills 1991). Mayor Byrne failed to pull together a governing coalition while in office, and her abdication of leadership on the school board issue meant that the first reform of the era was led by a narrow coalition of bankers and other local business leaders. Subsequent reformers would of necessity respond to the processes and expectations they had set in motion. Ironically, Byrne's deference did not even win their electoral support. In the three-way race for the Democratic mayoral nomination in 1983, Chicago's business leaders backed another candidate, Richard M. Daley (Pinderhughes 1997; Shipps 1995).

1988: A Different Governing Strategy

Harold Washington beat both Byrne and Daley, largely due to his ability to mobilize the Black community. Four out of five eligible Black voters were registered as a result of aggressive efforts by Washington's campaign; an overwhelming seventy-three percent of Black voters cast their ballot for him. He promised to break up the white ethnic patronage and downtown development that kept Black (and Latino) neighborhoods at economic disadvantage (Clavel and Wiewel 1991). He narrowly won with an electoral coalition of blacks, Lakeshore liberals, and Latinos; and a vision of a city in which development meant neighborhood empowerment and grassroots groups had access to city hall. He brought a sense of hope to many accustomed to hearing their city disparaged as a patronage-bloated, decaying part of the Rust Belt, riven with racial and ethnic disputes. Perhaps to again make legitimate the mayor's authority in school matters, he campaigned against the politically unaccountable power of the SFA, and for the reinstitution of a voluntary school board advisory commission. When Superintendent Love's contract expired, he did not stand in the way of the board's decision to hire Manfred Byrd (Mirel 1993; Carl 2001).

Washington was also a pragmatic politician. He knew that, despite their lack of support for his candidacy, the city's well-organized business associations had resources he would need to govern effectively. He was deeply concerned about high unemployment among Black, particularly low-income Black, youth. As a graduate of the CPS himself, he believed public education could be part of the solution. After first reaching out for their financial advice with city hall, he approached business leaders to help him create a Learn/Earn Compact under which corporate executives would guarantee jobs for high school graduates in exchange for CPS setting higher graduation standards. However, the year-long summit of corporate and district leaders came to nothing. Superintendent Byrd resisted the executives' version of a graduation test, and the business leaders refused to promise more than 1000 jobs a year, agreeing to add more only if they saw performance rise to their satisfaction (Shipps, Kahne and Smylie 1999; Carl 2001).

Mayor Washington had hoped to avoid dictating decisions to the Black leaders of the union and the district. (In 1984, Jacqueline Vaughn was elected president of the CTU.) But strikes continued to plague the school system, ultimately forcing his hand. Payless paydays brought on

by the fiscal crisis had engendered a strike in January 1980, followed by
two more strikes in 1983 and 1984 to protest SFA cutbacks. A fourth,
begun as Washington entered his second term in 1987, proved to be the
longest in the history of the school system. The Black community was
divided: low-income Black (as well as white and Latino) neighborhood
groups held demonstrations, calling for an end to the strike. As its six-
teenth day passed, protestors gave up on the school board as a forum
for reaching compromise. Recalling Daley Sr.'s intercession during strike
negotiations, the Urban League, TWO, and PUSH joined the protests,
forcing Washington to intervene. They "put a demand" on city hall to
open schools by Monday morning or expect a call for the entire board's
resignation and thousands of parents to cross the picket lines according
to one activist (Personal Interview 1991). Seizing the opportunity to
harness this civic outpouring, Washington required Jacqueline Vaughn
and Manfred Byrd to sign an agreement to participate in a larger, rein-
vented summit as part of his brokered settlement (O'Connell 1991; Kyle
and Kantowitz 1992; Carl 2001).

Insisting on a wider representation of views than had been presented
in the deadlocked first summit, Washington added fifty community
members to the roster, dubbing them the Parent Community Council
(PPC). He made it clear that "the PPC [was] to lead his Summit and
develop a [reform] bill that the mayor would help shepherd through the
assembly" (Carl 2001, 339). Carl informs us that Washington sought
legislation that would protect collective bargaining, sustain mayoral appointments to the board, and avoid the privatization that some business
critics were then promoting. Although Washington died unexpectedly a
few weeks later, the summit continued and school reform engaged many
of the city's white and Latino activists in an historic debate with its
corporate leaders. The PPC, however, lost its leadership role.

Black community organizations were not pleased. Not only did they
lose a champion in city hall, but the summit also turned into a forum
for criticizing Superintendent Byrd and, to a lesser extent, Vaughn's leadership of the teacher's union (Smith 1990). The Urban League, PUSH,
TWO and other Black community groups recognized that, in addition
to their holding all the symbolically important leadership posts in the
system, Black teachers outnumbered white ones and held about thirty-
three percent of the principalships and forty-four percent of the central
office positions. Under the expectations of the system's career-ladder,
they were poised to become the dominant group. The range of opinions
Black community leaders expressed about the summit and school reform are detailed elsewhere (O'Connell 1995; Lewis and Nakagawa
1995; Shipps 1997; Shipps 1998; Carl 2001). But very few Blacks—
virtually none representing a group of any size—actively supported the

summit's deliberations after Washington's death. Nor did they contribute many proposals to the law that was passed less than a year later.

Despite the fact that the SFA had been unable to prevent debilitating strikes during its seven years of school oversight, corporate executives remained confident that they could make a difference and pressed their advantage. "If there is anything business executives can contribute . . . it is the ability to define the problems, establish priorities, sharpen the focus on a clear solution, build a lean organization, establish accountability for performance and then motivate and support . . . people until the job is done. That's what we're good at" (Bays 1988).

Latino community activists had different expectations. Latinos held very few professional jobs in the schools and had little reason to defend the system. One of the fourteen Latino principals at the time explained there was also internal competition for categorical funding. "Any government money that came through funded programs was for black children. Any other minority group that was trying to get money . . . was [perceived to be] getting their little hands on a pie that had not been won by their suffering" (Personal Interview 1984). Latinos strongly supported the idea that parents should elect principals through LSCs and successfully argued to extend the vote to non-citizen residents. When various summit participants broke away to draft legal language for what would be competing bills, United Neighborhood Organizations of Chicago (UNO), a Latino church-based group, joined CU and C.U.R.E., a multiracial coalition of neighborhood groups led by Donald Moore's parent advocacy organization, Designs for Change. Together they formed the Alliance for Better Chicago Schools (ABCs) coalition, and the law they drafted became the core of the legislation passed (Moore 1991; Kyle and Kantowitz 1992).

None of the competing bills attracted enough votes, but Illinois House Leader Michael Madigan agreed to push through compromise legislation on condition that no new funding would be requested. While corporate CEOs lobbied their favorite legislators, busloads of UNO parents descended upon the Democrats. The combination of grassroots and corporate support was irresistible to Democratic legislators, who passed a bill with no Republic votes. Business leaders had wanted a second oversight group to ensure the board would comply with the law's restructuring requirements. In the end, they prevailed: Governor Thompson held up the law until the SFA's oversight powers were extended over the entire operation of the central office.

Richard M. Daley was chosen to serve out Harold Washington's term in a 1989 special election. His electoral coalition included the city's ethnic whites, wealthier lakefront residents and Latinos, but conspicuously, not Blacks. Mayor Daley moved quickly to reconstruct his father's

(Richard J. Daley) governing coalition of corporate leaders and unions, expanding it to include opportunities for the city's fast-growing and politically active Latino population. He also reinvigorated his father's goal of attracting the middle class back to the city, while holding or attracting new corporate headquarters (Green 1991; Pinderhughes 1997; Shipps, Smylie, and Kahne 1999).

The timing of the special mayoral election was crucial for school reform because the 1988 law had given the mayor unfettered authority to appoint a seven-member Interim Board that would set the city's expectations during the initial eighteen months of the new reform's implementation. Selecting the Interim Board was also the mayor's best opportunity to assume leadership of a civic movement to which he had, so far, no ties. After the first eighteen months nearly all 600 LSCs would be elected and functional. At that point, LSCs would select a School Board Nominating Committee (SBNC) that would nominate all future central board candidates. This mandatory grassroots process of selecting the SBNC was intended to insure that Chicago's history of mayoral intervention through the school board could not resurface to trump the community will.

Daley picked an Interim Board that represented the broad coalition enacting the law. It was led by a trio of powerful business and political colleagues whom he trusted: the president of the Chicago Urban League, a former Democratic alderman, and the president of Leadership for Quality Education (LQE) — a business group formed by CU and the Commercial Club to help implement the law. This triumvirate fired Superintendent Byrd and hired another Black educator from California, Ted Kimbrough, to replace him. Enacting their deep distrust of district employees, the group also got the Interim Board to agree that LQE should hire (and pay for) a separate staff of advisors. Drawn from among the civic groups active in the summit, the advisors provided plans to balance the budget, increase cuts in the central office, and negotiate a consent decree concerning special education, further angering many Black board employees in the process. Unexpectedly, the Interim Board also signed a three-year teachers' contract that promised seven percent raises for each year, securing labor peace, but putting its own budget in jeopardy (Hess 1991; Personal Interviews 1991).

Quickly enough, however, the riveting first LSC elections (18,000 people ran for more than 5,000 seats) produced councils that in turn identified the nominating commission. Daley was obliged to replace his board with one made up of less-influential individuals, many of whom entirely unknown to him. As Daley's formal influence began to wane, it looked like the biannual election of LSCs could become a potentially threatening source of alternative political organizing. No less an established leader than the president of LQE argued for the creation of an organization of LSCs to counter the union's CTU power in the state capital (Personal Interview 1991). Such a group, if successful, might challenge the mayor's governing coalition by forcing his hand against the teachers union. Daley responded by denigrating the qualifications of the candidates sent to him by the LSC-picked SBNC, often sending back whole slates. He was also troubled that principals answered to LSCs rather than a superintendent. A nomination to the school board under these circumstances became a decidedly mixed blessing, and the board's potential as a meaningful forum for debate quickly deflated.

Although it was not a foregone conclusion, central office employees continued to be blamed for most implementation problems. Having been branded the "common enemy" in the summit, their motivations were suspect by some. Other critics began to realize that a central office designed to take the responsibility for all violations of federal, state and local regulations was not organized to operate as a service center, and would need a thorough redesign and, likely too, different kinds of employees (Wong 1996; Bennett and Carriedo 1995).

As district leaders and school board members redoubled their efforts or waited for the business leaders and activists to tire of running the schools, a remarkable outpouring of local foundation (and some corporate) financial support kept civic groups focused. Just as corporate leaders had been charged with implementing the 1980 law, so they, along with other civic groups, were charged with implementing the 1988 law. In both cases, this spurred activity that was not anticipated in the statutes. Local foundations dedicated substantial private resources to supplementing school discretionary dollars and to sustaining the community groups that made elections possible. Drawn by the discretionary dollars, local institutions of higher education and national reform organizations competed for school improvement contracts. By the early 1990s, more than one hundred nonprofit groups were working with one or more schools (McKersie 1996). A new cross-campus consortium of educational researchers dedicated itself to providing publicly available analyses of data on reform implementation and student performance (Consortium 1991). A monthly newsmagazine dedicated to disseminating information about the schools and reform was founded (*Catalyst* 1990). LQE initiated several projects intended to help the central office rebuild its technological and managerial capabilities (LQE 1994). One small group of activists committed to individual school experimentation and LSC-driven governance sought Annenberg Foundation support to keep their vision alive. Ironically, the $50 million in new resources and national recognition they garnered came just as a third governance law was being enacted (Shipps, Sconzert and Swyers 1999).[5]

Biennial LSC elections also gave community groups the most fruitful organizing opportunity they had seen in decades. The already well-organized Mexican-American community and cross-Latino collaborations like UNO ran slates of candidates for LSC elections. This helped boost the number of Latino principals from seventeen to forty-three after the first round, and continued to add to their numbers throughout the decade. At the grassroots level it felt like a participatory democracy equal to none anyone involved could remember (Katz et al. 1997; Bryk et al. 1998). It was also exhausting, frustrating, and mostly voluntary work. In five years, change had just begun, but private resources were drying up. Voter turnout and the number of volunteer candidates for LSC elections became much-discussed indicators of reform efficacy, but interest in both waned after the first year (Shipps 1997).

Despite their enhanced powers, SFA members also grew more disappointed. Its chairman grimly analyzed the situation: "across the board we had a central office that was failing, and we had fiscal crisis after fiscal crisis, and no sense of movement in schools that weren't working" (Personal Interview 1997). Another business leader clarified that board accountability was now their major concern. "This board is . . . accountable to no one because it's accountable to everyone . . . there's no person or . . . group of people that this board has to answer to, not the mayor, not the city council, because it is a bottom-up board" (Personal Interview 1991).

1995: Daley Gets Control

Primary impetus for the third change in governance law again came from Chicago's corporate community, joined this time by statewide, more conservative business association leaders. The Illinois Business Education Council (IBEC) was formed in the summer of 1994 to redesign education for the whole state. When the Illinois voters elected a Republican majority to their legislature that fall, its new leadership turned to IBEC for a plan. While declining to pursue the statewide implications, the legislature accepted nearly every IBEC proposal for a new Chicago school governance law in May 1995. Governor Edgar signed it immediately (Civic Committee 1995; IBEC 1995).

The 1988 law's reliance on civic volunteerism gave way to an ideology of privatization in the 1995 law. Most of the school board functions given to the SFA were transferred to a smaller Board of Trustees, while LSC powers were circumscribed. Mistrustful of the school board as a public forum, the business leaders had reconceptualized it in the familiar image of a corporate board. As CEOs themselves, they agreed that the relationship between a corporate board and organizational managers was better adapted to efficient operations than the relationship between a publicly accountable school board and district administrators. Customers — parents and community members — might be granted continuing influence over individual schools, but no longer over the central board. They wanted the board to function more like the SFA or the Interim Board, as "overseers of the school system," and thought selection of its members should be unconstrained by a nominating commission (Board of Education 2002). The system's CEO should be independently powerful as well, as they were in their own corporations. Thus, they suggested that the board president and the CEO might be the same person (IBEC 1995).

The key term was *accountability*, by which corporate leaders meant: "the mayor is accountable and he knows it . . . We want [his] ownership here. We want somebody to take responsibility" (Personal Interview 1997). Although Daley neither asked for control nor drafted the law — he had campaigned for reelection in 1995 on a platform that included dissolution of the SBNC, higher standards for principals, and report cards — their plan worked on parents. An aide to the mayor described why, from her point of view: "[Daley] was very willing, but had to play a little coy because of the Republican politics." A local public television journalist offered another explanation. "I think it is fair to say that the Republicans were much more inclined to give it to Daley than they would have been Harold Washington, because I firmly believe that Richard M. Daley is a great Republican mayor" (Personal Interviews 1997).

From the perspective of the Illinois legislature, the 1995 reform was a continuation of the 1988 decentralization. After having already given many school board responsibilities to the LSCs, they now gave state responsibilities to Chicago's mayor. Daley was charged with keeping the schools solvent, negotiating all labor contracts, and figuring out how to identify failing schools and fix them. While he received no new state funding, he was freed from SFA oversight, and from state laws that constrained contract negotiations and privatization. In addition he was given unprecedented budget flexibility.

With the pressure of this new accountability to the state and to the city's business leaders, Daley stepped to the plate cautiously. His first appointments were close associates, who knew their job was to make him look good. They proved trusted allies who would leave no doubt about who was making final decisions. He insured that his political appointments would bring symbolic benefits to his supporters. Latinos, mainstays of each of his electoral campaigns, had one of their own, Gery Chico, named school board president. Another Latino supporter was designated as a board member. Not part of Daley's electoral coalition, Blacks lost leadership positions. For the first time in fifteen years the chief administrator of the system was a white man. Only in 2001, when both Chico and CEO Paul Vallas resigned, did Daley appoint a Black business executive — Michael W. Scott — a former member of Harold Washington's staff, to be president of the school board. The CEO job, however, again went to a white man.

Responding to his strongest supporters was also a priority. Daley's electoral campaigns, like his father's, were routinely paid for by the city's developers, its real estate industry, and its CBD corporate leaders (Alexander 2000; Cohen and Taylor 2000). He knew that after decades of failed attempts by the SFA, the *sine qua non* for business remained a balanced school budget. Benefiting greatly from the accounting flexibility in the 1995 law, his fiscally oriented management team developed a balanced budget plan that declared a projected $105 million shortfall had been eliminated within a matter of months.

Once appointed, the board receded into the background, virtually never debating or turning down a CEO recommendation during its typically short meetings. Clarifying that it would function more like part of the mayor's management team than as an independent public forum, the board held meetings in the afternoon, often in one school or another, and gave citizens only a few minutes to make comments. Consequently, the board was rarely in the press. Instead, Daley and his CEO, represented the entire multiracial CPS and its reform to Chicagoans and the nation.

Those who wrote the 1995 law had no ties to school system's unions, but Mayor Daley did. He knew that, when indebted, unionized employees with both job security and regular raises could be more loyal than patronage workers. Before the law was voted upon, he asked the unions not to fight it, noting that passage was virtually assured anyway. For their restraint he promised to bargain back most of the offending restrictions after he was in control. He kept his promise. As one CTU leader put it: "Every right they took away, Daley gave them back in bargaining, every one of them" (Personal Interview 1997). Daley also offered a four-year contract with 3 percent yearly raises. One year before the contract was to end in 1999 (and several months before Mayor Daley came up for a third term), a second four-year contract was ratified, again with 2–3 percent yearly raises. Union President Thomas Reese claimed that the second contract was "the most positive experience I have ever had" in sixteen years of negotiating (Lawrence 1998).

Privatization may have been the most flexible policy instrument Daley was given. He has used it to wide and varied effect. The outsourcing of what had once been an internal process of mentoring the next generation of principals through career-ladders exemplifies a pattern of privatization throughout the system (Education Week 2001). In another example, when the CEO put schools on academic probation, they were partnered with a private group, often a university or a school reform group, rather than assigned to career specialists, as they would have been under the old regime. The total value of these contracts was about $7.3 million in 1998, and $25.5 million from 1996–1999 (*Catalyst* December 1998, 4). Other examples of private contracting include "renting" professionals from local universities to run central office departments, and hiring community organizers and news-reporters to work for the system in public relations. Corporate businesses have also gained large contracts for supplies (the school system's warehouse was closed), food services, construction, and the like (Wong et al. 1997).

Privatization proponents often tout it as a way to trim payrolls and save money; unions often fight it desperately for the very same reason. Although state law granted Daley authority to fire public employees whose jobs were made redundant, again his strategy was to keep unions at bay, which he did both by limiting privatization to the provision of new services and job displacement, when it did occur, to nonunion former patronage jobs and very small unions associated with the trades. Although admitting that all the contracting and outsourcing did not create fiscal savings — the budget has grown about by about $1.5 billion in the last five years — CEO Vallas extolled contracting as "more efficient" (Personal Interview, 1997). Whether or not every contract generated better service for the same cost, it was an efficient way to solidify strong political relationships between local businesses and civic groups and the mayor.

When he took control of the system, Mayor Daley made it clear that the schools were to become part of his plans for Chicago's economic development. He defined success as the ability of the school system to attract middle-class families from the suburbs and maintain the confidence of corporate executives who might otherwise relocate (Kass 1995). Neighborhood enrollment set-asides for special schools in gentrifying areas, and the International Baccalaureate Program and Advanced Placement courses in high schools were expected to lure a middle class whose eighth-graders left the system at the rate of forty-nine percent in 1996 (Weissman 1997). These goals were one justification for reporting only aggregated data on school and student performance. Data disaggregated by race or poverty status carried a dual risk: it might discourage the middle class from returning to the city by highlighting continuing disparities, and it might stir resentment among minority groups upset over those same outcomes. The ambitious $4 billion capital renovation plan for the schools also fits into Daley's overall governing strategy. The three most expensive of these schools (one will have cost $39,285 per student when at full enrollment) have opened or are targeted to open in gentrifying areas in the primarily white north side (*Catalyst* 2000). Not only do these new schools serve to attract middle-class students (Allensworth and Rosenkranz 2000), they also provide huge building contracts to local businesses and anchor neighborhood gentrification.

Consequences for Students

Daley inherited a mandate to improve failing schools from the 1988 law. Although little had been systematically attempted before 1995, he responded relatively quickly, but with more mixed results than are apparent from reading CPS press releases. In the summer of 1996 he endorsed ending "social promotions" and putting failing schools on academic probation. He has described both to the press as "the most important steps the Chicago Public Schools have taken" (Daley 1997). Until 2001 the policy of retaining students who did not receive a pre-specified score on two (math and reading) standardized tests affected about ten thousand elementary school students (14 percent) each year. Not all students actually spent a second or third year in the same grade, however. One-quarter to one-third of the students who failed the tests were "socially promoted" anyway. Failing Black students were four-and-one-half times more likely to be retained than failing whites. Failing Latino students were three times more likely to be retained. (Until 1999, Latino bilingual students were exempted from the retention policy.) The vast majority of retained students came from low-income elementary schools. And, retained youngsters did no better, and sometimes worse, than those with the same failing scores who were socially promoted (Moore 2000; Roderick, et al. 1999). A hidden elementary school dropout rate has also recently become apparent. Despite the fact that one-third of failing eighth graders never show up in high school, overall dropout rates have not declined, remaining steady at about 43 percent (Kelleher 1999; Duffrin and Dumke 2001). In 2000–01 a threatened lawsuit broadened the criteria for promotion to take into account student grades, teacher recommendations, and attendance, essentially the policy that existed before ending social promotion.

The same tests have been used to determine which schools are in need of probation, remediation, reconstitution, or other "interventions." Sanctions included firing principals and disbanding LSCs, forced pairings with external partners, mandatory scripted lessons, longer classes, summer school, and early school start, among other structural experiments. Schools were put on probation if 15 percent (upped to 20 percent in 1999) or fewer of their students read or did math at national averages on tests, and moved to progressively more severe sanctions if scores did not improve. Although at least twice as many might have been put on probation if the cutoff score were increased slightly, in the first year, probation netted about 20 percent of the schools. For each of the following six years, one or two dozen were eliminated from the probation list because they were judged to have either improved or moved to a more serious sanction, while others were added (CPS 2000a; CPS 2000b; *Catalyst* August 2000).[7] Yet the designation did not help failing schools. After three years under the severest of these sanctions, five high schools were judged to have worsened because teacher quality was depressed by defections and stigma—these were among the few schools singled out for teacher dismissals—and test scores in them subsequently fell to new lows (Rossi 2001; Newbart and Rossi 2001). Failures like this mean these sanctions, like the initial retention policy, would be retooled when district leadership changed in 2001 (*Catalyst* November 2001).

Nearly every independent study of the system has shown that Black children in "predominately" (over 85 percent) Black and/or "high-poverty" schools (more than 90 percent low-income students) fared the worst. By their own report, LSCs in these schools were the most likely to be troubled with corruption, or internal dissension, and unable to perform their duties (Ryan, et al. 1997). Children in Black or mixed minority schools, as well as high poverty schools receive by far the slowest instructional pacing, thus increasing the chances that these students will be retained because they were not given the opportunity to learn all the material on which they will be tested (Smith, Smith and Bryk 1998). Black children receive high levels of "didactic" and review instruction, which shows smaller learning gains when compared with the more "authentic" instruction used in racially mixed and "integrated" schools (Smith, Lee and Newmann 2001). Schools on probation fall disproportionately in the poorest (and therefore the most likely to be Black and Latino) neighborhoods (*Catalyst* November 1998). Magnet and college prep schools are least likely to be fully funded in predominately black neighborhoods (Weissman 1998). These differential effects raise troubling distributional questions about the new school regime.

Despite such mixed results, until mid-2001 the politics of this new regime looked extremely stable. The much-maligned professionals in the system had been either removed or, in the case of the teachers' union, had made peace with the mayor for the sake of relative job security. As the Republicans who handed Daley control understood quite well, organized teachers are among the constituencies a Democratic mayor must satisfy. Yet union leaders are no longer accepting the "anti-teacher" bias in the current regime (Reid 2001). The CTU recently voted overwhelmingly to oust the leadership of the union *en masse*, choosing instead a caucus that seeks to "challenge the . . . flawed contention that teachers are the reason Chicago's public schools students fail to achieve" (Walsh 2001). Deborah Lynch Walsh, the new white, reform-minded union president, is bargaining hard for a teacher role in reform that assumes teachers are decision-making professionals. She hopes to put teaching, rather than management, at the center of future changes (Walsh 2000; Personal Interview 1994). CTU pressure has also contributed to the abandonment of the severest sanctions on schools and students, and a new concern for teacher professional development (Temkin 2002).

The new union leadership appears to have sparked public concern over whether balanced budgets and labor peace are sufficient measures of school system success. Fully seventy-nine percent of those asked in a recent Chicago poll favored Daley's hiring a "career educator" when CEO Paul Vallas and the school board president resigned shortly after the CTU election (Guerrero 2001). Daley however, appointed another noneducator, prompting business pundits to remind him whom they intend to hold responsible. "It's Mr. Daley who remains" (*Crain's Chicago Business* 2001).

Regime Change in Chicago

In sum, a great deal has changed about the way the Chicago school board is constructed. Its membership, once limited by custom to well-organized civic sectors, now represents the city's corporate leadership and the mayor's political allies. Previous mayors had circumscribed formal authority and, as a matter of informal practice, left the school board to its own negotiations, taking a public stance of noninterference except when nominations or labor disruptions were imminent. In contrast, Richard M. Daley is the first mayor formally authorized to participate in all board decisions, although he need not, and does not, do so in open, public forums. Daley's new dominance (the integration of his informal power with the formal authority to make decisions) came only after Chicago passed through a fifteen-year period during which the SFA was more powerful. The SFA had an independent, open-ended legislative mandate, the ability to play one political party against the other by appealing equally to the Democratic mayor or the Republican governor, and ultimate control over all school spending. This transitional stage frustrated both Washington and Daley because each was forced to share some formal authority. It also gave the SFA independent political power that could trump mayoral decisions. The two mayors saw different causes, however, for the resulting gridlock. Washington blamed the SFA. Daley blamed the more democratic school board selection process in place when he took office, thus discrediting representational leadership and paving the way for a corporate-style board under his executive authority.

Board functions also changed over 15 years. Once responsible for buffering professional educators from public criticism, the new board is an overseer, expected to establish criteria for educators' performance and enforce them through rewards and sanctions. The board used to serve as a lively, often contentious, civic forum. Now a detached and distant executive council, it uses public meetings to report on and sanction decisions already made in private discussions among its members, the CEO and the mayor. Formerly criticized for micromanaging the schools, the board now virtually never contests CEO recommendations. Its many unanimous votes are dispatched in large, undifferentiated batches. Once expected to be a public decision-making body where political incorporation could lead to more than symbolic representation, it was criticized as incompetent and impotent during the late 1980s and 1990s, paving the way for the current board's largely symbolic political function.

At least some of these changes are likely the unintended consequences of a twenty-year process of building civic capacity for school reform. However intended, they reflect the priorities and agendas of those active in this civic movement, while similarly marginalizing the priorities of those less engaged. Mayors are one of the potent actors, and each of the three elected during the era has left his or her mark on reform, deciding whether and how to lead the groundswell, and which civic actors would be privileged in the process. But no mayor's leadership, or lack of it, spurred the groundswell. That came from Chicago's civic organizations.

Civic Capacity and Mayoral Leadership

Primary among the civic actors initiating school reform were Chicago's corporate business associations. These civic leaders imagined they were taking on a more limited and clearer goal when they began the reform process in 1979. But what began as short-term fiscal management quickly expanded, in part because Mayor Byrne washed her hands of the schools, but also because their activism spurred other organized civic actors to respond, disagree, and raise their own problems with the schools. Civic groups of all kinds—especially Latino neighborhood-based organizations and professional reformers' support groups — took the opportunity to press their favored educational solutions: "parent power," bilingual education, vouchers, and so on. The ferment did not yet constitute a cross-sector coalition, because no governmental actors participated. Neither school leaders nor city hall took an active role until a teachers strike in 1987 threatened political stability and unified the civic actors against a common enemy.

Harold Washington can be credited with forming the era's first cross-sector coalition for school reform; but his untimely death meant we will never know what his continued leadership might have produced. Washington was building a governing coalition that drew together Blacks, a handful of "Lakeshore liberals," corporate business, and a host of neighborhood groups, including Latinos. He had managed to create an inclusive multiracial electoral coalition, but the governing coalition he sought needed the active support of the powerful white corporate executives who had supported Daley Sr. And he had to find ways to satisfy a Black community splintering across class lines, while also fulfilling the yet unmet needs of Latinos.

Harold Washington belatedly made education the core of his efforts to forge that coalition. He deliberately constructed a process (the reform summit) that put both poorly resourced minority community groups and well-resourced business associations around the same table, insisting that they come up with a consensus reform plan to improve all the city's schools. This reflected his overall strategy for city governance: expand opportunities for the lower classes, but do so though political processes and neighborhood development, rather than direct redistribution programs. In the best of circumstances, it was a difficult governing strategy. His death left the coalition without a political leader committed to coordinating the unequal resources of such governing partners and sustaining that vision. By 1988, the school reform coalition was once again without political support.

Working against Washington all along had been the developing division between Latinos and Blacks. Latinos felt they had much to gain by engaging in "guerilla warfare" against the middle-class Blacks who ran the school system and who, they believed, withheld from Latinos the favors and resources of categorical programs and affirmative action. Blacks, who had been handed all the key leadership positions, chaffed against the implied racism in the anti-education professional bias of their (white) corporate "overseers" and the corporate management strategies for reform, to which Latinos had added grassroots legitimacy. Also surfacing then were differences and animosities between the middle-class Blacks and those (often white) activists who spoke up for low-income Blacks. These groups came together as an electoral coalition for Washington, but not over governance of the schools.

Even without strong and unified Black or educator participation, Daley inherited an uncommon civic capacity for school reform. Nearly all the city's foundations, most of its institutions of higher education, many community and neighborhood groups, professional and business associations were already engaged and contributing their ideas, resources, and time to school improvement when he was first elected. Many of the key compromises that sustained the civic coalition (e.g., parents given power over selection of principals in exchange for business leaders' power over the purse) also created structural changes in school governance that politically challenged the mayor. In order to lead, Daley, like Washington before him, had to harness the civic capacity he inherited and adjust the reform agenda. For Daley this meant walking a careful political line, criticizing the SBNC and the LSC's license, but praising reformers. His vision of an altered reform agenda was thus narrowly conceived during the 6 years that the 1988 coalition held together.

It is unclear how far this plan might have taken him if unexpected events had not occurred, providing Chicago's deeply engaged corporate executives with another opportunity to redesign the schools, this time without cross-sector compromises. The motives of executives were complex, but included frustration with their own failure to control school costs and produce the efficient, effective performance they clearly sought, and impatience with the slow implementation of their management advice. In addition, they were tired of public collaborative decision making. And they did not like being held publicly accountable for their mistakes (e.g., giving the CTU seven percent raises without the resources to pay them). Putting the mayor in charge gave them a more suitable role: holding an executive accountable for a performance judged in economic terms.

Having achieved formal authority over the schools through the auspices of his strongest supporters, Daley now fused the school reform agenda to an economic development rationale. Rather than ignoring the schools, as Mayor Byrne had done, or using them to further a neighborhood development and low-income advocacy agenda, as Washington had hoped to do, Daley integrated the public schools into his plans to make Chicago a global corporate hub and a tourist destination. The change has altered some of the civic capacity he inherited. It favors the views of his governing coalition supporters in the corporate community over those of Latino community activists, who reaped small benefits from their participation in his electoral coalition, but do not have the

same direct role in policy making. And it left white community activists
with the task of choosing whether to become personal advisors or external critics.

Importantly, it changed the way that Black nonparticipation was perceived. Blacks represented the largest segment of education professionals in the school system, but frequent downsizing and Latino succession had diffused their leadership in the middle ranks of the central
office, even as whites and Latinos replaced them in the top posts after
1988. After he gained control, and the SFA was eliminated, Daley was
required to give more attention to these Black professionals in order to
avoid the prospect of strikes, one of the most politically debilitating
problems of school governance. He chose to do so by turning the
union's quiescence and disengagement into a virtue to be rewarded.
Daley gave teachers steady raises and was perfectly willing to ignore the
more draconian limitations the 1995 legislation (and its business
drafters) had imposed on CTU bargaining. And, although the Mayor's
accountability sanctions have been stiff, the worst of them have by-
passed teachers, who were neither held accountable for student failure
on tests, nor, with near trivial exceptions, for school failure.

However, the coalition Daley forged by favoring corporate business,
mollifying the CTU, and handing small but significant benefits to Latino
supporters has recently been put at risk. Now that the CTU appears
unwilling to forgo a decision-making role in reform, further changes
could be inevitable. Some have already taken place. Recognizing the
political implications — the union would rival Daley's corporate partners
in the resources it could bring to the activist role that president Walsh
proposes, and could disrupt the implementation of his current agenda —
Daley has already signaled his own flexibility by replacing both the
board president and the CEO. Daley and his new (white, and relatively
inexperienced) CEO have also dropped, or promised to alter, many of
the more onerous sanctions that heretofore had accompanied his economic development reform agenda, especially those which disproportionately injured Black and Latino low-income children.[8] And the symbolically important appointment of school board president has been
given to a Black. If he had not made the change from Chico to Scott,
Daley would have risked the repercussions of sanctioning a complete
lack of Black representation among the decision makers on the management team. Instead, he has signaled that union leadership may not be
the only way for Blacks to benefit from reform.

But Daley's record has been less ambiguous than the current changes
suggest. Lacking strong commitment to low-income neighborhood development, he had, until recently, ignored or dismissed the disparities in
student performance that his alterations in the school reform agenda

helped produce. This is both a continuing moral problem, and a political vulnerability. No urban school reform can claim educational success if it is accompanied by Chicago's level of outcome disparities. After all, Black and Latino low-income students make up 80 percent of the children in the system. Nor can it claim political success if nearly 40 percent of the overall city population is disengaged, and the professional teaching force, also heavily Black, is effectively co-opted.

Consequences for Chicago's Black and Latino Communities

Race and class remained important to this regime change throughout the 20-year period of its development in Chicago. Although the 1980 reform explicitly addressed the costs of schooling, its cutbacks fell on overcrowded and underresourced schools no less than on schools in middle-class neighborhoods. The 1988 reform was enacted in a racially polarized environment. The third reform act in 1995 did nothing to mend the racial schism. Since then, low-income schools and neighborhoods have been the last to benefit from the new development agenda, and consequently, are the least likely to see long-term improvements now that the affluent years of the 1990s are receding. Examples drawn from this narrative clarify how the consequences differ, or are similar, for the two large "minorities" in Chicago.

Noted in this chapter was the fact that the number of Latino central office administrators and principals in the CPS dramatically increased, despite having only incrementally increased their representation among teachers. The racial politics of this regime change explains why. Under the old regime, the career-ladder from teacher-to-principal-to-central office meant a generation or two would have to pass for a fast-growing population subgroup to be represented in the decision-making positions of the school system. It took, for instance, three decades (1950–1980) before the first Blacks were hired for top decision-making posts. Black succession occurred only after a cadre of teachers and principals were in place from whom education leaders might reasonably have been selected. But the combination of a reform law that permitted principals to be hired without regard to their previous experience, and a mayor who rewarded his electoral supporters with symbolic leadership positions in the bureaucracy, changed the terms of ethnic succession for Latinos.

UNO's involvement in reform coalitions (e.g., ABCs) also gave Latinos a forum in which to press for favorable principal selection conditions. Absent this active participation, small opportunities could not have been seized, and fewer Latino principals would be working in the schools today. Nor, one might argue, would Danny Solis, an UNO organizer deeply involved with the 1988 reform, have been selected by Mayor Daley to fill a vacant city council seat, or had the opportunity to ascend to the council leadership position he holds today. In a similar way, the CPS's continuing commitment to bilingual education in the face of strong national criticism can be seen as a substantive benefit of the Latino community's active participation in reform coalitions and their electoral support for Daley. Overcrowding in Latino schools is a continuing problem — building middle-class schools in gentrifying areas still takes priority over rehabilitating schools in Latino neighborhoods — but the prospect of a political response by Daley remains viable. For Latinos then, both material benefits and symbolic success have accompanied political incorporation into the new school-governing regime.

Blacks have had a different experience of political incorporation into this regime. Because they already made up a large proportion of the school system's professional staff when educators were stigmatized as the enemies of reform, they found themselves fighting defensively as others sought change. Political incorporation began earlier than Latinos experienced, but was largely symbolic. Black leaders were appointed from outside the city, and local leaders did not feel represented by them. The backlash this engendered across both low-income and middle-class Black organizations brought Black authority and agency to city hall, as well as to the school system. In both instances, the authority would not come with ready-made power; that had to be wrested away from entrenched machine aldermen in city hall and from the corporate "overseers" of the school system. This battle was begun, but never finished.

Nor did Black professional educators and their middle-class supporters choose to participate in the only broad coalition that brought about reform after Harold Washington died. In part, this was because they were distracted by attempts to regain city hall. Yet apparent in the 1987 strike was another problem, a split between the Black middle class who worked in the schools and the low-income Black communities that sent their children to the worst of them. Such divisions rendered the presentation of a cohesive "Black" reform agenda an unreasonable expectation. Despite these hurdles and distractions, one might have hoped for an agenda backed by black professional educators and their middle-class supporters (if not by low-income Blacks), but no single reform proposal could produce their united support.

When Richard M. Daley won the 1989 primary, Black Chicagoans were still divided over whom to support as the next Black mayoral candidate and over their role in a school reform they had not sought, and which many of them had protested. Their lack of support for Daley and lack of participation in the reform coalitions that eventually handed him power left Blacks with fewer symbolic appointments than at the reform era's beginning, and far less power or authority over a school system that now has, ironically for them, greatly enhanced legitimacy. The realignments in the school reform coalition that have appeared in the last year (2001) do not substantially alter those facts; one or two high-profile appointments are small consolation.

Incrementalism Suggests a Future

Yet it may be that Chicagoans are awakening for a fourth time to a new school reform agenda. Given the economic downturn and the state and federal cutbacks that the system is already facing, education reform *cum* economic development may soon be nonviable. Moreover, unsolved educational problems loom larger now that dilapidated buildings have been repaired, budgets balanced, corporate commitments secured with contracts, and tough sanctions tried and rejected.

New coalition partners may be emerging. CTU members' resounding support for a new activist leadership portends an unprecedented desire to participate in reform. A new civic coalition between the CTU, the mayor, corporate leaders, and Latino community groups would necessarily involve a greater number of Black professionals as active reformers than has yet been seen. If it materializes, the new coalition will surely demand changes in the reform agenda affecting the large proportion of Chicago's public school children, so far primarily ignored or sanctioned. With a governing regime change having already taken place, the time may now be ripe for a change in educational regimen. This possibility raises new questions: Can Mayor Daley and his corporate supporters accept a broadening of the reform coalition to incorporate Black professional educators, not just symbolically, but as decision makers? Will Black educators follow a white leader into battle over the schooling of low-income Black and Latino children? Can the current corporate governing structure respond to the needs of the least powerful of Chicago's residents — its large majority of low-income students of color — or will another governance change be required? Open questions like these suffuse Chicago's regime change with promise. If the combination of answers is positive enough, and luck assists, there may still be reason for hope.

Notes

1. One exception in the early decades of the twentieth century was Mayor Edward Dunne (1905–1907) who ran a campaign to clean up the schools and

built a reform-minded and labor-oriented governing coalition to sustain this effort. However, his was a one-term mayoralty when school boards served a year longer than mayors.

2. Before 1947 the school governing structure had a "tripartite" leadership: a superintendent, a business manager, and a lawyer. In other respects this governing structure remained unchanged since 1917.

3. The informal nominating process began as an agreement between Mayor Kelly (1933–1947) and a blue ribbon advisory committee of university presidents called to squelch complaints about Kelly's appointment of known scalawags. Except Jane Byrne (1979–1983), every mayor until 1995 convened such a group.

4. As of 1995, 80 percent of state Chapter One (antipoverty) funds flowed directly to schools as a result of the 1988 law. In elementary schools this averaged $500,000 per year, while high schools averaged $800,000.

5. The activist leaders of the Chicago Annenberg Coalition were Anna Hallett, a local foundation executive turned national advocate for urban school restructuring; William Ayers, a former Students for a Democratic Society (SDS) anti–Vietnam War activist turned education professor at the University of Illinois at Chicago; and Warrant Chapman, a state school reformer and local foundation office. See Shipps et al. 1999, 5.

6. New federal requirements for schools seeking Title I aid require that all Chicago scores be disaggregated as of 2004–2005.

7. When the sanction policy was retooled, it eliminated probation and created new categories of sanctions, especially schools in crisis; accompanying the change in personnel and policy, the CPS ceased reflecting on its website all data referring to the earlier sanctions. Lists, however, have been preserved in hard copy and are in the possession of the author.

8. Arnold Duncan, 36 when appointed CEO in June 2001, was a former basketball player in Austria who formed in 1992 an initiative to adopt a 40-student sixth-grade class at one school in Chicago. In 1998 he was hired as director of magnet schools, then promoted to deputy chief of staff, overseeing service learning and after-school programs until he was selected for CEO. See *Catalyst* September 2001; Kelleher 2001.

References

Alexander, S. 2000. "Black and Latino Coalitions: Means to Greater Budget Resources for Their Communities?" In *The Collaborative City: Opportunities and Struggle for Blacks and Latinos in U.S. Cities*, ed. J. L. Betancur and D. Gills. New York: Garland.

Allensworth, E., and J. Q. Easton. 2001. *Calculating a Cohort Dropout for the Chicago Public Schools*. Chicago: Consortium on Chicago School Research.

Allensworth, E., and T. Rosenkranz. 2000. *Access to Magnet Schools in Chicago*. Chicago: Consortium on Chicago School Research.

Allswanger, J. M. 1987. "Richard J. Daley: America's Last Boss." In *The*

Mayors: The Chicago Political Tradition, ed. P. M. Green and M. G. Holli. Carbondale: Southern Illinois University Press.

Andrade, J. 2001. "Vallas Exit Gives Hope to Latinos." *Chicago Sun-Times*, 17 June.

Attinasi, J. J. 1991. "Hispanic Educational Research in View of Chicago Education Reform." In *Assessing School Reform in Chicago*. Chicago: Consortium on Chicago School Research.

Bays, K. D. 1988. "No More Business Coalitions!" *Crain's Chicago Business*, 20 August.

Beinart, P. 1997. "The Pride of the Cities: The New Breed of Progressive Mayors." *New Republic*, 30 June, 16–25.

Bennett, A. L., and R. Carriedo. 1995. *Restructuring the Research, Evaluation and Analysis Functions of the Chicago Public Schools*. Chicago: Consortium on Chicago School Research.

Betancur J. L., and D. Gills. 2000. *The Collaborative City: Opportunities and Struggle for Blacks and Latinos in U.S. Cities*. New York: Garland.

Bryk, A. S., J. Q. Easton, D. Kerbow, S. G. Rollow, and P. A. Sebring. 1993. *A View from the Elementary Schools*. Chicago: Consortium on Chicago School Research.

Bryk, A. S., P. B. Sebring, D. Kerbow, S. Rollow, and J. Q. Easton. 1998. *Charting Chicago School Reform*. Boulder, Colo.: Westview Press.

Carl, J. 2001. "Harold Washington and Chicago's Schools between Civil Rights and the Decline of the New Deal Consensus, 1955–87." *History of Education Quarterly* 41 (fall): 311–43.

Catalyst. 1990. "Chicago School Reform: A Beginning." 1 (February).

———. 1998. "Board Keeps Test Data under Wraps." 10 (November): 25–27.

———. 1998. "External Partners: By the Numbers." 10 (December): 4.

———. 1999. "Remediation and Probation Guidelines for Attendance Centers." August Web Extra <http:www.catalyst-chicago.org/04.99/LSCbill/May18bill.htm>.

———. 2000. "High School Accountability Strategies 1996–2000: A Scorecard." August Web Extra <http:www.catalyst-chicago.org/07-00/0700scorecard.htm>.

———. 2000. "Board Gives North Side Preps Lavish Facilities, Ample Planning Time." 11(4):4–9.

———. 2001. "'People's Choice' Candidates for CEO." 11(5):10–15.

———. 2001. "Duncan Charts a New Path for Chicago Public Schools." Interview. 13 (September): 24–29.

Chicago Public Schools. 2000a. "Intervention Status" (02-P36-C). <http:www.CPS.k12.il.us>.

———. 2000b. "Lists of Schools on Academic Probation (FY1999–2000)." <http:www.CPS.k12.il.us>.

———. 2002a. "Iowa Tests of Basic Skills: Citywide Results over Time, 1997–2002." <http:www.CPS.k-12.il.us/itbs−over−read−a.pdf>.

———. 2002b. "FY 2003 Capital Projects Funds." <http:www.CPS.k12.il.us/aboutCPS/financial−Information/FY2003/X.Capital-Projects-Funds.pdf>.

Chicago Tribune. 1997. "Schools Go from Worse to . . . Better." 31 October.

Civic Committee of the Commercial Club of Chicago. 1995. "Business Leaders: Education Is Our Top Priority." Press Release. 20 March.

Clavel, P., and W. Wiewel, eds. 1991. *Harold Washington and the Neighborhoods: Progressive City Government in Chicago 1983–1987*. New Brunswick, N.J.: Rutgers University Press.

Cohen, A., and E. Taylor. 2000. *American Pharaoh: Mayor Richard M. Daley*. Boston: Little, Brown and Co.

Consortium on Chicago School Research. 1991. *Assessing School Reform in Chicago*. Chicago: Consortium on Chicago School Research.

Crain's Chicago Business. 2001. "Keeping School Reform on the Move Is Daley's Job." 4 June.

Cuban, L. 1976. *Urban School Chiefs under Fire*. Chicago: University of Chicago Press.

Daley, R. M. 1997. "Speech to the National Press Club." Video recording. Washington D.C.: CSPAN-2, 5 June.

Duffrin, E., and M. Dumke. 2001. "Thousands of Kids 'Disappear': Researchers, CPS Tussle over Stats." *Catalyst* 12(9):12.

Easton, J.Q., T. Rosenkranz, and A. S. Bryk. 2001. *Annual CPS Test Trend Review, 2000*. Chicago: Consortium on Chicago School Research.

Education Commission of the States. 1999. *The Changing Landscape of Educational Governance*. Denver: Education Commission of the States.

Education Week. 2001. "Group to Train Chicago Leaders: News in Brief." 4 April.

Forte, L. 1995. "New Law Lets Board Shift Money to Balance Budget." *Catalyst* 12:7–10.

Gills, D. 1991. "Chicago Politics and Community Development: A Social Movement Perspective." In *Harold Washington and the Neighborhoods: Progressive City Government in Chicago, 1983–1987*, ed. P. Clavel and W. Wiewel. New Brunswick N.J.: Rutgers University Press.

Green, P. M. 1984. "The Primary: Some New Players, Same Old Rules." In *Making of the Mayor: Chicago 1983*, ed. M. G. Holli and P. M. Green. Grand Rapids, Mich.: Eerdman's.

———. 1991. "Chicago's 1991 Mayoral Elections: Richard M. Daley Wins Second Term." *Illinois Issues*, June, 17–20.

Grimshaw, W. J. 1979. *Union Rule in the Schools: Big City Politics in Transformation*. Toronto: Lexington Books.

Guerrero, L. 2001. "Public Favors Picking an Educator." *Chicago Sun-Times*, 27 June.

Hess, G. A., Jr. 1988. "Who Benefits from Desegregation Now?" *Journal of Negro Education* 57(4):536–51.

———. 1991. *School Restructuring: Chicago Style*. Newbury Park, Calif.: Corwin Press.

Hinz, G. 1998. "Teachers, CPS Hit the Books on Long-Term Pact." *Crain's Chicago Business*, 9 March.

———. 2001. "New Student Dropout Report Shakes Up Biz." *Crain's Chicago Business*, 19 March.

Holli, M. G. 1987. "Jane Byrne: To Think the Unthinkable and Do the Undoable." In *The Mayors: The Chicago Political Tradition*, ed. P. M. Green and M. G. Holli. Carbondale: Southern Illinois University Press.

Illinois Business Education Council (IBEC). 1995. *Proposal to the Illinois General Assembly*. 9 February.

Illinois General Assembly. 1995. "Eighty-ninth General Assembly Conference Committee Report on House Bill 206." State of Illinois.

Kass, J. 1995. "Daley Names School Team; Now Comes the Difficult Part: Turning Everything Around." *Chicago Tribune*, 30 June.

Katz, M., M. Fine, and E. Simon. 1997. "Poking Around: Outsiders View Chicago School Reform." *Teachers College Record* 99 (Fall): 117–57.

Kelleher, M. 1999. "Dropout Rate Climbs as Schools Dump Truants." *Catalyst* 10(9):1.

———. 2001. "Team Player Duncan Named CEO." *Catalyst* Web Site Extra (June). <http:www.catalyst—chicago.org/06-01/061duncan.htm.

Kleppner, P. 1985. *Chicago Divided: The Making of a Black Mayor*. DeKalb: Northern Illinois University Press.

Kyle, C. L., and E. R. Kantowitz. 1992. *Kids First — Primero Los Niños: Chicago School Reform in the 1980's*. Springfield: Illinois Issues.

Latino Institute. 1994. *A Profile of Nine Latino Groups in Chicago*. Chicago: Latino Institute.

Lawrence, C. 1998. "Delegates Approve Teachers Contract." *Chicago Sun-Times*, 31 October.

Leadership for Quality Education. 1994. *T.I.M.E.: To Improve the Management of Education, Phase I*. Chicago: LQE.

Lenz, L. 1988. "School Summit Wants Outsiders Kept Out." *Chicago Sun-Times*, 29 April.

Lewis, D., and K. Nakagawa. 1995. *Race and Education Reform in the American Metropolis*. Albany: SUNY Press.

McKersie, W. S. 1996. "Reforming Chicago's Public Schools: Philanthropic Persistence, 1987–1993." In *Advances in Educational Policy*, ed. K. Wong, vol. 2. Greenwich, Conn.: JAI Press.

Meyer, J., and B. Rowen. 1978. "The Structure of Educational Organizations." In *Environments and Organizations*, ed. M. Meyer. San Francisco: Jossey-Bass.

Mirel, J. 1993. "School Reform, Chicago Style: Educational Innovation in a Changing Urban Context, 1976–1991." *Urban Education* 28(2):116–49.

Moore, D. 1990. "Voice and Choice in Chicago." In *Choice and Control in American Education*, ed. W. H. Clune and J. Witte, vol. 2. Bristol, Pa.: Falmer Press.

———. 2000. *Chicago's Grade Retention Program Fails to Help Retained Students*. Chicago: Designs for Change.

Newbart, D., and R. Rossi. 2001. "Scores Drop at Schools under Tightest Rein." *Chicago Sun-Times*, 6 June.

O'Connell, M. 1991. *School Reform, Chicago Style: How Citizens Organized to Change Public Policy*. Chicago: Center for Neighborhood Technology.

Peterson, P. E. 1981. *School Politics, Chicago Style*. Chicago: University of Chicago Press.

Pinderhughes, D. M. 1997. "An Examination of Chicago Politics for Evidence of Political Incorporation and Representation." In *Racial Politics in American Cities*, ed. R. P. Browning, D. R. Marshall, and D. H. Tabb. New York: Longman.

Pois, J. 1964. *The School Board Crisis: A Chicago Case Study*. Chicago: Educational Methods.

President Reagan. 1981. "The State of the Union Speech." Washington, D.C.: The White House, 27 January.

Rakove, M. L. 1982. "Jane Byrne and the New Chicago Politics." In *After Daley: Chicago Politics in Transition*, ed. S. K. Gove and L. H. Masotti. Chicago: University of Illinois Press.

Reid, K. S. 2001. "Challenger Topples Teacher's Union President." *Education Week*, 6 June, 11.

Rivlin, G. 1982. *Fire on the Prairie: Chicago's Harold Washington and the Politics of Race*. New York: Henry Holt and Co.

Roderick, M., A. S. Bryk, B.A. Jacob, J. Q. Easton, and E. Allensworth. 1999. *Ending Social Promotion*. Chicago: Consortium on Chicago School Research.

Rossi, R. 2001. "Study Faults Low Scoring High Schools." *Chicago Sun-Times*, 11 March.

Ryan, S., A. S. Bryk, K. P. Williams, K. Hall, and S. Luppescu. 1997. *Charting Reform: LSCs-Local Leadership at Work*. Chicago: Consortium on Chicago School Research.

Scott, M. 2002. Open letter to "Chicagoans." *Chicago Public Schools*, 26 June <http:www.CPS.k12.il.us/aboutCPS/Financial-Information/FY2003/I.MessagefromPresident.pdf>.

Shipps, D. 1995. "Big Business and School Reform: The Case of Chicago, 1988." Ph.D. diss., Stanford University.

———. 1997. "The Invisible Hand: Big Business and Chicago School Reform." *Teachers College Record* 99 (fall): 73–116.

———. 1998. "Corporate Involvement in School Reform." In *Changing Urban Education*, ed. C. N. Stone. Lawrence: University Press of Kansas.

Shipps, D., J. Kahne, and M. Smylie. 1999. "The Politics of Urban School Reform: Legitimacy, City Growth and School Improvement in Chicago." *Education Policy* 13(4):518–45.

Shipps, D., K. Sconzert, and H. Swyers. 1999. *The Chicago Annenberg Challenge: The First Three Years*. Chicago: Consortium on Chicago School Research.

Simpson, D., O., with J. Adeoye, R. Feliciano, and E. Howard. 2002. "Chicago since September 11, 2001: An Uncertain Future." Paper delivered at "Resurgence of America's Great Cities," a Lanier Public Policy Conference, 26 April.

Smith, J. B., V. E. Lee, and F. M. Newmann. 2001. *Instruction and Achievement in Chicago Elementary Schools*. Chicago: Consortium on Chicago School Research.

Smith, J. B., B. Smith, and A. S. Bryk. 1998. *Setting the Pace: Opportunities to*

Learn in Chicago's Elementary Schools. Chicago: Consortium on Chicago School Research.

Smith, K. B. 1990. "Give School System Time, Helping Hand, a Break." *Catalyst* 1 (February): 18–19.

Stone, C. N. 1989. *Regime Politics: Governing Atlanta, 1946–1988.* Lawrence: University Press of Kansas.

———. 1993. "Urban Regimes and the Capacity to Govern: A Political Economy Approach." *Journal of Urban Affairs* 15(1):1–28

Stone, C. N., J. R. Henig, B. D. Jones, and C. Pierannunzi. 2001. *Building Civic Capacity: The Politics of Reforming Urban Schools.* Lawrence: University Press of Kansas.

Temkin, J. 2002. "Politics Strain School Board, Teachers Union Relations." *Catalyst* 13 (May): 8–10.

Travis, D. J. 1987. *An Autobiography of Black Politics.* Chicago: Urban Research Press.

Vallas, P. G. 1998. *Saving Public Schools.* New York: Center for Educational Innovation, Manhattan Institute.

Walsh, D. L. 2000. *Labor of Love: One Teacher's Experience.* New York: Writers Club Press.

———. 2001. "Involving Teachers Would Improve School Reform." *Chicago Sun-Times,* 25 June.

Weissman, D. 1997. "Can Middle Class Kids Be Lured Back?" *Catalyst* 9 (November): 1–6.

———. 1998. "Everyone Wins, Some Win More." *Catalyst* 10 (November): 1–9.

Whitmore, J. 1986. "Behind Chicago School System's Shakeup." *Crain's Chicago Business,* 2 June.

Wong, K. K. 1996. *Advances in Educational Policy: Rethinking School Reform in Chicago.* Vol. 2. Greenwich Conn.: JAI Press.

Wong, K. K., R. Dreeben, L. E. Lynn, and G. I. Sunderman. 1997. *Integrated Governance as a Reform Strategy in Chicago Public Schools.* Philadelphia: National Center on Education in the Inner Cities.

Zimmerman, S. 2001. "Crowding Woes Continue." *Chicago Sun-Times,* 10 June.

Chapter Four

Boston: Agenda Setting and School Reform in a Mayor-centric System

JOHN PORTZ

"I want to be judged as your mayor by what happens now in the Boston public schools. . . . If I fail to bring about these specific reforms by the year 2001, then judge me harshly."
—*Mayor Thomas M. Menino, State-of-the-City Address (1996)*

MAYOR MENINO'S PLEDGE to improve public education in Boston high-lighted a major shift in governance of the city's school system. When a mayoral-appointed school committee replaced the elected committee in January 1992, the mayor's office moved to center stage in school poli-tics.[1] This shift in governance launched Boston down a path followed by Chicago, Detroit, and other cities where mayors assumed control of urban school systems (Kirst and Bulkley 2000). Boston's transition to mayor-centric governance, however, preceded most of these other cities. In fact, mayoral control of public education in Boston emerged from a local history of tensions and discord around school governance that focused on the ineffectiveness of the school committee and concluded with a local referendum and state legislation creating a mayoral-appointed board.

What has this change to a mayor-centric school governance system meant in the city of Boston? How has it impacted school politics and educational leadership? And how has this change affected communities of color? To answer these questions, this chapter begins with an intro-duction to the Boston Public Schools and a brief overview of the gov-ernance battles that led to mayoral control. The impact of this govern-ance change can be seen in a number of areas, including the agenda status of education, the nature of public discourse, school spending, and school reform initiatives. We also review changes in academic achievement as the most visible challenge facing the school system. The general public has supported these changes, although the minority community is more guarded in its assessment. We conclude with some final comments on school politics and policy-making under a mayor-centric system.

Boston Public Schools

The Boston Public Schools (BPS) is the smallest school district represented in this volume. However, like the student populations of other urban school systems presented here, Boston's student population of sixty-three thousand is predominately non-white: forty-eight percent African American; twenty-eight percent Hispanic; fifteen percent white; and nine percent Asian. The learning needs of this student population are diverse. Approximately 12,600 students—twenty percent of the total—receive special education services, while 9,400 students—sixteen percent of the total—participate in bilingual programs (Boston School Department 2002).

The school district employs approximately 8,500 individuals; fifty-six percent being teachers and thirteen percent, aides and monitors. The teachers in the district are typically experienced, with advanced degrees. Although the student population of the school district is predominately non-white, its cadre of professional educators is predominately white. Sixty-one percent of the teachers are white; twenty-six percent African American.[1] Among administrators, the racial breakdown is similar.

The school department's general fund budget, which includes most state aid, was $639 million in fiscal year 2002. An additional $113 million was received through other competitive and formula grants, and other external sources. The largest single area of expenditure was regular education, accounting for 35 percent of the budget. Special education accounted for 21 percent of the budget. The per-pupil cost based on the general fund budget in fiscal year 2001 was $9,545.

The boundaries of the school district are coterminous with the city of Boston. With the 2000 Census, Boston became a "majority minority" city. Of its 589,000 residents, 49.5 percent are white; 23.8 percent, African American; 14.4 percent, Hispanic; and 7.5 percent, Asian.[2] As in many other American cities, the public school population has a much higher non-white composition than does the overall city population: 85 percent minority in the schools, as compared to 50.5 percent in the city. In general, white residents of the city are less involved with the city's public schools. They are more likely to be childless. Among those who do have children, they typically have fewer children and are more likely to pursue private school options.

School Governance

The debate over school governance—elected versus appointed school committee and the role of the mayor—dominated school politics in the late 1980s and early 1990s (Portz, Stein and Jones 1999). The thirteen-member elected school committee was at the center of the debate. It was widely criticized for political opportunism, policy fragmentation, and fiscal irresponsibility (Mayor's Advisory Committee 1989). Battles over school closures were commonplace, and racial divisions were prominent. Claims of fiscal mismanagement were rooted in an institutional arrangement that clouded accountability. In particular, the school committee controlled the allocation of resources within the school budget, while the mayor and city council set the total appropriation for the school department. In this fiscally dependent arrangement, the school committee often decried city hall for providing inadequate financial resources to operate the school system, while city hall complained of having no control over the allocation of school monies. The school committee typically refused to make expenditure adjustments equal to those requested by city hall and would end the year in a deficit, requiring a last-minute appropriation from the mayor and city council.

Criticism was widespread of school governance generally, and the school committee in particular. The Boston Municipal Research Bureau, a business-supported government watchdog organization, had long-advocated greater clarity in governance roles, with the school committee focusing on policymaking and the superintendent managing the school system (Boston Municipal Research Bureau, 1989). During the late 1970s and mid-1980s several legislative changes were made to clarify the relationship among the superintendent, school committee, and city hall, but problems persisted. Amidst the growing debate, the school committee received the sharpest criticism. A *Boston Globe* editorial described the school committee as "a disaster." The editorial continued, "Infighting, grandstanding, aspirations for higher political office, and incompetence have become mainstays of the 13-member committee. The system is floundering" (*Boston Globe* 1992).

The Boston Municipal Research Bureau and several blue-ribbon commissions recommended major changes. In 1989, for example, a commission appointed by the mayor declared that "frustration with school performance had reached an historic high," and that changes in governance were critical to the future of the system (Mayor's Advisory Committee 1989, 1). After reviewing the governance system for the schools, the study concluded: "Boston is unique. The buck does not appear to stop anywhere" (27).

The mayor's role was limited in this system. Boston's strong mayor-council form of government granted the mayor extensive authority over the city side of local government, but a limited role in school policy. Administrative control of the schools resided with the superintendent and school committee and, as noted earlier, the allocation of funds within the school budget was outside the formal power of the mayor. Boston's mayors typically maintained an arm's length distance from the public schools. Mayor Kevin White (1967–1983) was a coalition builder who played a cautious role in desegregation debates and other discussions of school policy. Mayor Flynn (1984–1993) also was hesitant during the early years of his tenure to become involved in school politics. As Flynn noted in remarks prepared for the business community, "public education is an area that can swallow up the most promising career and politicians are counseled at every step to 'stay away from the schools'" (Flynn 1993, 19).

Calls for a change in governance became increasingly widespread in the media and among many in the city, particularly in the business community (Boston Municipal Research Bureau 1989; Portz 1996). Mayor Flynn also became more vocal in his criticisms and began to propose changes in governance. Among the governance proposals floated for consideration were elimination of the school committee along with direct appointment of the superintendent by the mayor and, as a less drastic alternative, a school committee composed of a mix of mayoral appointees and elected members. The mayor and other policymakers were cautious in pushing one proposal over another, but city hall was increasingly aware of the growing importance placed on education by city residents and the role of education as a key quality-of-life issue that defined the city.

The most popular governance proposal was to replace the elected committee with one appointed by the mayor. This would lodge overall fiscal and political accountability with the mayor. In November 1989, a city-wide advisory referendum on the issue yielded mixed results: 37 percent favored an appointed committee; 36 percent opposed it; and 26 percent left the referendum question blank. The movement to an appointed committee was temporarily shelved, but in late 1990 the effort resumed. Advocates for an appointed committee, like the Boston Municipal Research Bureau, continued to lobby for change. In January 1991, the *Boston Globe* called for an appointed committee; in April, the city council approved — by a 9–4 vote — a home rule petition to the state to create a seven-member committee appointed by the mayor. The two Black members of the city council voted against the change, criticizing the loss of voting power for Boston's residents (Rezendes 1991). Debate continued, but the new committee structure received state approval, and Mayor Flynn appointed seven individuals from a list provided by a nominating committee to begin terms in January 1992.

The shift to mayoral control marked a sharp break in school governance. Yet to be resolved, however, was how leadership within the school system would mesh with the new political control exercised by the mayor. More specifically, Superintendent Harrison-Jones, Boston's second Black superintendent, who was hired in mid-1991 by the elected committee, now found herself working for the newly appointed committee and, indirectly, for the mayor. The honeymoon was brief. Disagreements between the mayor and superintendent became increasingly public. The controversy subsided, at least temporarily, when Mayor Flynn resigned in mid-1993 to join the Clinton administration as ambassador to the Vatican. City council president Thomas Menino became acting-mayor, then won the special election in November 1993.

With a new mayor in city hall, the relationships among the superintendent, school committee, and mayor were less volatile. But tensions continued. From the superintendent's perspective, the problem was the intervention of Boston politics into public education, and the persistent criticism of her role as superintendent. As Harrison-Jones emphasized in a *Globe* interview, there was a key difference between Boston and other cities: "Boston will not respect the agenda or the plan or the vision put forth by the superintendent. It has happened here for the past two decades" (Hart 1995, 1). On the other side, however, Mayor Menino, the *Boston Globe*, and some business leaders were increasingly critical of the superintendent. The *Globe* editorial staff produced a "report card" on the superintendent that included such comments as "limited vision," "poor management skills," "strained relationship with outside parties," and "meager overall progress in academic achievement." The *Globe's* conclusion: it was time for new leadership in the schools (*Boston Globe* 1994).

The final step came in early 1995 when Superintendent Harrison-Jones was informed that her contract, due to expire in July, would not be renewed. The school committee initiated a broad public search process. Mayor Menino made it clear that he would take a central role in the process, albeit behind the scenes. In July and August 1995, three finalists were interviewed, and an offer was extended to Thomas Payzant, assistant secretary in the United States Department of Education and former superintendent in San Diego, California, and Oklahoma City, Oklahoma. Payzant accepted, becoming superintendent in September 1995.

Since 1995, key actors in school governance and leadership have remained in place. Quite unlike the city's previous history—or the history of most urban school systems—Boston is in the midst of one of the longest periods on record of stable and cooperative leadership for public education. Thomas Payzant continues as superintendent, and now has a contract through 2005. Thomas Menino was reelected in 1997, without opposition, and again in 2001, giving him a term of office through 2005, as well. Membership on the seven-member appointed school committee has slowly changed, but continuity is quite strong. And on the teacher side, Edward Doherty continues through 2003 as president of the Boston Teachers Union, a position he has held since 1983.

What has this new mayor-centric governance system meant for school politics and public education? In several areas, the change has been quite significant. As described below, Mayor Menino has raised the agenda status of education, while the general nature of public discourse about education has shifted. Continuity in leadership has facilitated numerous reform efforts, and the mayor has supported an increase in financial resources for the schools. While many applaud these changes, improvements in academic achievement have been slow, and support within the minority community remains tentative. Mayoral control has yielded some positive achievements, but the overall "report card" remains mixed, as the school system strives to improve student academic achievement.

Agenda Status

Setting the policy agenda is one of the most important sources of mayoral power. Particularly in strong-mayor cities, mayors have numerous opportunities to direct the course of public policy for the city. Inaugural addresses, "state-of-the-city" speeches, budget messages, executive appointments, and public forums provide mayors with numerous opportunities to fundamentally shape the policy process.

As mayors have assumed more authority over public education, a critical question becomes whether they have used their agenda-setting powers to elevate education as a policy concern in the city. In Boston, the mayor's new authority over school affairs has been accompanied by a significant elevation of public education on the policy agenda. Mayor Flynn appointed the first committee and devoted considerable time and resources to education, although his parting comments upon joining the Clinton administration included doubts over the efficacy of the new appointed committee. Under Mayor Menino, however, there is little hesitancy: public education is a top priority for the city. Mayor Menino, a self-proclaimed "urban mechanic," accepts his responsibility for public education as an integral part of building the human and physical infra-

TABLE 4.1

State-of-the-City Address (percent of each speech devoted to public education)

Elected Committee		Appointed Committee	
Year	Percent on Education	Year	Percent on Education
1985	0	1992	25
1986	1	1993	14
1987	8	1994	12
1988	8	1995	23
1989	NA	1996	68
1990	3	1997	23
1991	12	1998	34
Average	3.7	1999	48
		2000	28
		2001	48
		Average	32.3

Source: Author's review of State-of-the-City Addresses.

Note: Percentages in this table were calculated by dividing the number of lines in the speech devoted to education by the total number of lines in the speech, as published in the City Record. The 1989 State-of-the-City Address was not published.

structure of the city. Education stands alongside public safety, housing, and economic development as central goals for city government. Indeed, at times Mayor Menino has characterized public education as the most critical issue facing the city.

Exemplifying this shift in attention are two excerpts from state-of-the-city messages. In early 1991, when the school committee was elected, Mayor Flynn emphasized traditional goals for Boston: The priorities in Boston are clear. Government has a job to do. We're going to keep providing the basic city services that you need and deserve, like maintaining the parks, picking up the trash, and having dedicated fire fighters and EMTs there when you need them . . . Our number one priority is safe neighborhoods (City Record 1991, 29).

Five years later, in a speech delivered at the Jeremiah Burke High School, which had just lost accreditation, Mayor Menino offered a different list of priorities: Economic security. Good jobs. Safe streets. Quality of life. Public health. Those are the spokes of the wheel — but do you know what the [HUB] of that wheel is? Public education! . . . [GOOD PUBLIC SCHOOLS ARE AT THE CENTER OF IT ALL]!" (City Record 1996, 70).

The elevation of education on the policy agenda is apparent in both quantitative and qualitative terms. Based upon a review of sixteen annual state-of-the-city messages, Table 1 shows the shift in attention to education from the elected committee period (1985–1991) to that of the appointed committee (1992–2001). This shift is quite dramatic, from an average of only 3.7 percent of the speech devoted to education during the earlier period to 32.3 percent during the later one.

This quantitative shift has been accompanied by a qualitative change in the aspects of education that received attention. Prior to mayoral appointment of the school committee, education was invariably linked to another mayoral goal, typically job skills or employment opportunities. Education was a means to an end and as such, received limited attention. With the assumption of mayoral control, the aspects of education under consideration expanded well beyond employment issues. Access to college for Boston high school graduates received prominent attention in 1994 and 1995. In subsequent years the mayor raised a broad range of education issues including more extended-day programs, more computers in the classroom, more and better school buildings, expanded literacy programs, better teacher recruitment, and improvement in test scores. The state-of-the-city message became an important forum for the mayor to identify key education policy goals.

This prominent placement of education on the policy agenda was not done in racial terms. Race, in fact, was never mentioned in any state-of-the-city discussions of education. Given the very public nature of these speeches, this was not surprising, but it was indicative of the way in which race was downplayed as a consideration in policy discussions of education. Although most policymakers recognize that race is an important current in city and school politics, in this case the agenda focus was on the quality and utilitarian nature of education, rather than the racial dimensions that lay beneath the surface.

Public Discourse

Related to the heightened agenda status of education is a change in the nature of public discourse around school issues. In a mayor-centric system, the mayor's political style shapes the debate and discussion about school matters. This governing system has raised the agenda status of education, but it has limited public debate and discussion of alternative paths to education reform. Public discourse in this environment tends to be dominated by the mayor, school committee, and superintendent. And it is less contentious than it was under the elected committee.

This change in discourse is evident in how the school committee operates and relates to the public. Under the elected school committee, discussions concerning public education were often contentious and lengthy. Committee meetings were noted for their duration, averaging three hours in 1989 and 1990, and a divided committee was typical. In

1989 and 1990, 88 percent of committee votes included at least one dissenting member (Avenoso and Wen 1996). On occasion, a member would leave the meeting in disgust. Racial divisions were sometimes prominent in these debates. In 1989, for example, the committee approved a controlled-choice busing plan, with all four Black members in opposition. In the following year (1990), the four Black members walked out in protest before the committee voted 7-1 to fire Laval Wilson, the district's first Black superintendent.

In the elected committee environment, interaction with the public was frequent and service-oriented. In 1989 and 1990, the committee held ten public hearings on a range of topics. Outside of hearings, committee members frequently responded to complaints from parents. Each member received a $52,000 office allotment, typically used to hire a staff person to receive telephone calls from parents and other residents with complaints about school services. This constituent orientation provided a readily accessible avenue for citizen concerns, and also prompted committee involvement in school operations.

Public interaction and discourse have changed significantly under an appointed committee. A more consensual, elite dialogue has replaced contentious debate, racial divisions, and constituent services. In contrast to long meetings and divided votes, the typical meeting of the appointed committee is both shorter and less contentious. In 1994 and 1995, for example, committee meetings averaged 1 hour and 35 minutes, half as long as those of the elected committee, and the board voted unanimously 98 percent of the time during those two years (Id). A common criticism is that few issues are truly debated by the appointed committee; many decisions are made prior to a public meeting. One community activist described the committee as a "rubber stamp," while a long-time educator questioned the committee for not "challenging" more of the proposals from the superintendent and mayor (Vaishnav 2001). Increasingly, community activists and others are turning to the city council and its education committee as a venue to raise concerns and grievances.

In this consensual and elite decision-making environment, public participation is less constituent-based. Appointed committee members lack the electoral incentive to seek parental input. For outreach, the appointed committee occasionally holds meetings in school buildings around the city and sponsors periodic public forums, but citizen participation has generally declined. In 1994 and 1995, for example, the committee held five public hearings, compared to twice that number in 1989 and 1990.

The style of the appointed school committee reflects the generally professional background of the members. Of the seventeen members who have served on the appointed committee, most have professional or administrative experience, including higher education, business, and

community organizations. Although the elected committees also included individuals with such backgrounds, they were generally more
diverse groups, with members attuned to the campaign trail of community meetings and voter forums.

Surprisingly, perhaps, the appointed committees are more representative, in racial and ethnic terms, than were the elected committees. In
1989 and 1990, of the fifteen members who served on the elected committee, only four were Black (27 percent); there were no Asians or Hispanics. In contrast, the first committee appointed by Mayor Flynn in
1992 included two whites, two Blacks, two Hispanics, and one Asian.
Although the appointed committee is more representative of the city's
population, in demographic terms, all members, must face scrutiny by
the mayor on their educational philosophies. Individual members may
occasionally stray from the mayor's stated positions, but this is relatively rare. The only appointed member to be denied reappointment
was an individual who had frequently disagreed with positions taken by
the other committee members, the superintendent, and the mayor.

This decision-making pattern has both detractors and proponents. A
common criticism, particularly from the minority community, is the
lack of meaningful opportunities for discussion and debate of key policy
decisions. As one long-time observer of the schools note in an interview,
there is very limited "space for discussion" of positions that conflict
with those of the mayor. A consensual, elite dialogue is viewed as not
receptive to criticism and challenges. Historically, communities of color
have relied upon protest and criticism as important avenues for the expression of grievances. To have this avenue closed off, particularly in a
city with a predominately white power structure, is a major concern to
many in the minority community (see Taylor 2001).

Proponents, however, highlight the greater efficiency and effectiveness
of an appointed committee aligned with the mayor and operating in a
consensual manner. Although admittedly less independent, it is seen as a
more effective forum for discussions of educational policy. Even among
many in the minority community, there is recognition that the appointed
school committee has been relatively successful in focusing on educational matters. The committee, for example, approved successive district-wide improvement plans, citywide learning standards, and other
reform initiatives, as noted below.

Public Support

The clearest test of public approval for the new governance system
came in 1996, when a ballot question was put to the voters. Required

by the state legislation that authorized the appointed committee, this ballot gave voters the choice of returning to a thirteen-member elected committee (a "yes" vote) or keeping the seven-member appointed committee (a "no" vote).

Mayor Menino, joined by business leaders, the *Boston Globe*, and many community leaders — including some from the minority community — defended the appointed committee and urged voters to keep the current governance system. Arguing for stability and continuity as well as accountability through the mayor, the defenders of the appointed committee launched an extensive campaign to sway voters. Proponents of an elected committee, including former superintendent Harrison-Jones, many members of past elected committees, and some minority leaders, emphasized the importance of minority involvement and representation through an elected body. Advocates for keeping the appointed committee raised about $600,000 in their bid to retain the existing governance structure, while supporters of an elected committee raised only $5,000 in a less-organized effort to convince voters to change the system (Chaçon 1996a).

In the November election, the appointed committee won the day, receiving 53 percent of the votes, compared to 23 percent for returning to an elected committee and 23 percent blank votes. Said Menino, "The message was clear throughout Boston that we should continue the progress we've made in the schools" (Ibid, 1996b). Although the appointed committee won by a 2-1 margin among votes cast, it received less support within the minority community. In two of Boston's twenty-two voting wards, the appointed committee was defeated. These two wards are in the heart of Boston's minority population in the neighborhoods of Roxbury and Dorchester.

A closer look at Boston's 254 voting precincts also reveals this racial split. By precinct, the range of the vote tally in favor of returning to an elected committee was quite large, from 15 to 93 percent. To explore the racial dimensions of this vote, our analysis compares the vote in favor of the referendum with precinct-level census data involving the percent of individuals over the age of eighteen in different racial/ethnic groups. Such a comparison must be done with caution. In statistical terms, it is an "ecological fallacy" to draw conclusions when the units of analysis being compared are not appropriately related (Neuman 2000). In our voting case, for example, we do not know which individuals identified in the census actually participated in the election. However, as the percent of a particular racial group increases within a precinct, our inference linking the actual vote to this racial group becomes stronger.

An initial look at the data indicates that the racial split was most likely between African Americans and whites, while Hispanics seemed

TABLE 4.2

Pearson Correlation Coefficient between Racial Percentages in the Population and Percentage Voting 'Yes,' by Precinct

Racial/Ethnic Group	Percent of Overall 1990 Population	All Precincts Pearson Correlation	Precincts with 70% or More of Racial Group Pearson Correlation
African American	21	.713*	.829*
White	55	−.576*	−.819*
Hispanic	12	.006	**
Asian	8	−.254*	**

*Significant at the .01 level.

**There are no precincts that include 70 percent or more Hispanic or Asian.

Sources: (1) Census 2000 Redistricting Data, Boston, PL4: Hispanic or Latino and Not Hispanic or Latino by Race for the Population 18 Years and Over; (2) City of Boston, Elections Commission, Question 2 Vote on November 5, 1996, by Ward and Precinct.

to be more divided on the vote. The Pearson correlations are listed in Table 4.2 for each racial group. The strongest correlations between racial percentages of the population and percentage voting "yes" on the referendum involve whites and African Americans.

Given the statistical challenges noted above, a focus on predominately white or predominately African American precincts provides a clearer picture. Of the 254 precincts, 33 had a population that was 70 percent or more African American, and 94 had a population that was 70 percent or more white. As listed in Table 2, the Pearson correlation coefficients are even larger for these precincts, indicating a stronger association between race and referendum vote. A second measure that captures this difference is the average vote in the predominately Black and predominately white precincts. In the predominately Black precincts, the average vote in favor of returning to an elected committee was 55 percent; in the predominately white precincts the comparable average was 28 percent. As both measures indicate, the African American community was considerably more inclined to support a return to an elected committee.

The preference for an elected committee among African Americans reveals the strong interest in electoral representation (Taylor 2001). The demise of the elected committee in 1992 resulted in the loss of four Black elected officials in city politics. Even though the thirteen-member elected committee often voted in opposition to issues important in the African American community, including the dismissal of the first African American superintendent, having elected representatives was important, particularly when minority representation on the city council became even more difficult to achieve. Furthermore, the elected committee did hire two African Americans as superintendents for the school system. Although, the appointed committee included broader minority representation, the mayor, not the voters, chose the committee members. For many in the African American community, this loss of electoral representation was an important diminution of their role in city and school politics.

As one other measure of public support for this new governance system, Mayor Menino has maintained strong favorability ratings throughout most of his mayoral career. In 1997, one year after the appointed committee versus elected committee referendum, the voters reelected Menino to a new four-year term. Menino ran unopposed, the first time in recent decades that a Boston mayor had not faced an opponent. In 2001, Menino again stood for reelection, this time winning by a very strong 72–28 percent spread over City Councilor Peggy Davis-Mullin. Menino beat Davis-Mullin in each of the city's twenty-two wards (Mooney 2001). Davis-Mullin's campaign strategy included a focus on public education, but the voters were content to stay with Menino.

Leadership and Reform Initiatives

The move to a mayor-centric system in public education has facilitated greater continuity in leadership and extensive reform activity. Stability in leadership began with the hiring of Payzant as superintendent in 1995. As one school principal commented in an interview, successful school reform requires that the mayor, superintendent, school committee, and school administrators be in accord, or as he put it, "all the planets have to be lined-up." With Payzant's move into the superintendent's office and mayoral appointment of the school committee, this alignment was in place. As one business leader Harold Hestnes commented, "For the first time we have a mayor, a superintendent and a school committee singing from the same sheet of music"(*Boston Globe* 1996).

This alignment continues today. Payzant and Menino still hold their respective offices of superintendent and mayor, and membership on the school committee has evolved, but with no dramatic shifts. Since 1996, only two individuals have served as chair of the school committee, and three of the seven committee members have served throughout this period.

This leadership structure is, in turn, closely aligned with the business community. The Private Industry Council and the Boston Plan for Excellence, for example, work closely with the mayor and superintendent in shaping school reform. Both organizations, rooted in the business sector, predate the appointed committee, but under the mayor-centric system they have increased their involvement and influence. The Private Industry Council provides staff support for the Boston Compact, an agreement among city government, the public schools, business, labor, higher education, and community groups to support the Boston Public Schools. The Boston Plan for Excellence, a business-sponsored group that provides financial support to the schools, has been a primary supporter of the whole-school change model adopted by the BPS. Mayoral accountability and an appointed school committee composed of concerned and knowledgeable citizens appeal to the business community as rational ways to exercise leadership in the otherwise fragmented world of public education.

The prominence of the business community in the mayoral-led coalition has diminished the role of other actors, including the teachers union and the minority community. Even under an elected committee it was difficult to exercise influence, but the current leadership structure and elite model of discourse groups such as the teachers union, education activists, and minority leaders find it even more difficult to have an impact on education policy. The forums for their input are limited and the current emphasis on testing and accountability leaves even less space for discussions about race, alternative paths to increase student achievement, and other education concerns.

With the support of this leadership structure, Superintendent Payzant has launched a number of major reforms within the school system. In 1996, for example, he reorganized the school department. In the same year he proposed — and the school committee adopted — *Focus on Children*, a five-year reform plan for the schools (Boston School Department 1996). Whole-school change is the guiding educational philosophy of this reform plan. Since 1996 individual schools have adopted whole-school change models that focus on improving literacy. Support for this reform effort has come from the business community and a grant from the Annenberg Foundation. In 2001, the school committee adopted *Focus on Children II* as the next five-year plan to continue whole-school improvement within the system.

A number of other reform initiatives have been put in place in recent years, some of which were prompted by the state through the Education Reform Act of 1993. The school department, for example, adopted citywide learning standards aligned with state standards. Along with adopting these standards and extending the whole-school change another major focus is improving literacy and mathematical skills. A rigorous promotion policy is in place that includes additional academic support

for students who fail to meet promotion standards, including mandatory summer school for many students. At the high school level, a number of schools are being restructured into smaller learning communities
to support closer teacher-student interaction and better learning opportunities.

School reforms are present in a number of other areas as well. Since
1998, for example, all five-year-olds are guaranteed full-day kinder-
garten. The school committee negotiated a class size reduction plan
with the teachers union, and undertook a technology initiative to dramatically increase the number of computers in the classroom. To expand school options, the school committee and teachers union agreed to
the establishment of "pilot" schools within the district that operate with
greater flexibility from school department regulations and union work
rules. And to increase accountability, the school department put in place
an extensive review system that includes an in-depth analysis with site
visits at all schools.

Financial Support for the Schools

These reform initiatives are indicative of the increase in financial support for the school department. From the state and the city, the Boston
Public Schools has received a growing piece of the city's fiscal pie, particularly in the mid– and late 1990s. The agenda status accorded to the
schools has translated into financial support. Although the recent economic and fiscal downturn has hit the schools as well as most other
departments, the overall level of financial support remains significant.

Financial support for the schools is evident by a number of measures.
As a percentage of general fund expenditures from the city, the school
department's portion has increased steadily for the last fifteen years (see
Table 4.3). This increase is most prominent during the period of mayoral control. During the last eight years of an elected committee, from
fiscal years 1985 through, and including, 1992, the school department
averaged 31.3 percent of the city's general fund expenditures. During
the first eight years of an appointed committee, the average was 35.9
percent, reaching a peak of 37.2 percent in fiscal year 2000.

The increase in school spending reveals a similar trend, although the
school department was not alone in receiving generous support. Table
4.4 shows that under an elected committee the increase in school department spending exceeded the increase in total spending, but the police and fire departments received even larger increases. Under mayoral
control and an appointed committee, the school department has received quite favorable treatment as spending by the department in-

TABLE 4.3
City General Fund Expenditures (excluding health and hospitals) Percent by
School Department

Elected Committee		Appointed Committee	
Year	Percent by School Dept.	Year	Percent by School Dept.
1985	29.3	1993	33.4
1986	29.7	1994	34.8
1987	29.6	1995	35.5
1988	30.4	1996	36.6
1989	32.3	1997	36.1
1990	32.7	1998	36.9
1991	33.2	1999	36.5
1992	33.5	2000	37.2
Average	31.3	Average	35.9

Source: Boston Municipal Research Bureau and City of Boston, Audited Financial
Statements.

creased twice as much as total spending. The police and fire departments also received quite favorable treatment, at a level slightly below
that of the school department.

As another financial indicator of city support, the mayor and city
council have held the school department harmless from loss of revenues
due to Boston students attending charter schools. Under the state's charter school law, school districts are assessed by the state for every student
from the district who attends a charter school. This assessment, based
on the average cost of educating a student in the district, is sent to the
charter school. To cushion this financial loss, however, the state reim-
burses the district for part of the assessment. For Boston, the estimated
net loss due to city youth attending the ten charter schools in the city
was $14 million in fiscal year 2002. Under Mayor Menino the city has
absorbed this loss, rather than passing it along to the school district.

These indicators of support are important, but two other points
should temper them. First, credit for this financial support must be
shared with state government. In 1993, Massachusetts adopted a comprehensive education reform law that included a major revision of the
state's school aid formula. Under this new formula urban centers, such
as Boston, have received substantial increases in state aid for schools. In
Boston, these funds are placed in the city's general fund and are included in the data already cited.

When school spending is broken down by its component revenue
parts, it becomes apparent that the increase in school spending already

TABLE 4.4
Changes in General Fund Spending (percentage increase during each
time period)

	Elected Committee 1985–92	Appointed Committee 1993–2000
Total general fund spending	38%	24%
General fund spending by the school department	49%	55%
General fund spending by police and fire departments	57%	52%

Source: Boston Municipal Research Bureau and City of Boston, Audited Financial Statements.

noted is due in large part to the increase in state aid. In fact, 70 percent of the increase in school department general fund spending from 1994 to 2000 can be attributed to that increase. During these years state aid increased a dramatic 180 percent, from $66.6 million to $186.2 million. This increase also served as the foundation for the school department's spending increase from $408 million to $579 million. The mayor was a strong advocate for this increase in state aid; without it he would have faced a much more difficult challenge in meeting the financial needs of the school department.

The more recent economic and fiscal downturn offers a second cautionary note. Due to less-than-projected state aid and local revenues, the city's general fund budget increased by only 2.9 percent between fiscal years 2002 and 2003, significantly less than the increases for previous years. In the belt-tightening required to accommodate this budget, the school department shared the burden by cutting positions in the central office and making a number of other cost savings. Nevertheless, the increase in the school department's operating budget exceeded the average 2.9 percent increase, but most of the increase was for employee benefits. Exclusive of employee benefits, the school department's budget increased by only one percent (Boston Municipal Research Bureau, 2002).

Academic Achievement

The key test in assessing school improvement is student academic achievement. To be certain, changes in governance discussed in this chapter do not directly link to student test scores. There are many intervening variables involving teachers, curriculum, and other key elements in the education setting that will fundamentally influence student achievement.

TABLE 4.5
Percent of Students Failing MCAS Exams by Year of Test and Grade

Grade	English Language Arts		Math	
	1998	2001	1998	2001
4	*	29%	56%	42%
8	32%	21%	70%	54%
10	57%	39%	74%	47%

*Different performance standards were used in 1998 so these scores are not comparable.
Source: "MCAS Report for Spring 2001 Testing," Boston School Department.

Governance, however, is important. Governance arrangements are best viewed as enabling. They provide a context within which resources are more — or less — effectively brought to bear in support of student learning.

For the mayor and his appointed school board, student test scores have shown some improvement in recent years, but the challenge is still quite formidable. The task ahead is evident in the results on the state-mandated Massachusetts Comprehensive Assessment System (MCAS). MCAS is a criterion-referenced test based on the curriculum developed under the Massachusetts Education Reform Act of 1993. The test was first administered in 1998 in grades 4, 8, and 10 in the subjects of math and English language arts, and is slowly expanding into other grades and subjects. Most importantly, beginning with the graduating class of 2003, all students must pass the tenth grade English language arts and mathematics tests to receive a high school diploma. Students who fail the test in the spring have four additional opportunities to pass. This high-stakes requirement is the subject of intense debate among educators and legislators, but at the present time it remains part of the assessment system.

MCAS scores have improved since 1998, but a significant challenge remains (Boston School Department 2001). In 2001, for example, 47 percent of tenth-grade students failed the math exam and 39 percent failed the English language arts exam (see Table 4.5). These students must pass the exam to receive a diploma. On the first retest in December 2001, about half of each group failed each exam again, while almost a third did not take the retest (they either left the system or otherwise were absent on the test day).

The achievement gap by racial group adds an additional challenge for the school district (Boston School Department 2001). In grade 10, for example, the MCAS math exam reveals a particularly wide achievement

TABLE 4.6
Achievement Gap by Race (percent of students passing 2001 MCAS exams by
grade and race)

	English Language Arts				Math			
Grade	Asian	White	Hispanic	Black	Asian	White	Hispanic	Black
4	85%	84%	61%	68%	87%	80%	53%	51%
8	93%	90%	75%	73%	84%	72%	39%	32%
10	78%	81%	49%	50%	91%	80%	42%	40%

Source: "MCAS Report for Spring 2001 Testing," Boston School Department.

gap. Whereas ninety-one percent of Asian students and eighty percent
of white students passed the 2001 MCAS math test, only forty percent
of Black students and forty-two percent of Hispanic students passed the
test (see Table 4.6). In general, the gap is less prominent at the lower
grade levels, but it remains a significant concern.

Conclusion

Important changes in political institutions are rarely neutral. They typically reshape political and policy processes, often shifting advantages
and disadvantages among different groups and interests. So also, Boston's move to a mayor-centric governance structure for public education
has altered the city's political and policy world. Boston is ten years into
this experiment and the general public appears to accept the system,
although there is a current of dissent as well. A mayor-centric system is
praised for the attention and resources it has brought to public education, but it also has raised concerns over the changing nature of school
politics, policy debate and citizen participation.

    Placing the mayor at the center of school politics has raised the visi-
bility of public education, and it has linked city hall and the school
department in a cooperative manner not seen under the elected committee structure. Mayor Menino's frequent references to education in his
state-of-the-city speeches are indicative of this trend. The substantial
financial resources provided to the schools also highlight significant city
support. Along with this support and visibility has come a more elite
and consensual style of decision making in which the mayor plays a key
role. As the mayor stated in a speech before the Education Writers Association, "In a nutshell, when it comes to school change—the mayor
must be like the hub in a wheel—you have got to be in the center to
keep things rolling" (Menino 1999).

Importantly, the mayor is part of a stable leadership structure that is rare among big city school systems. Mayor Menino and Superintendent Payzant have been working together since 1995, and likely will continue that partnership to at least 2005. Leadership of the teachers union also has not changed, and the appointed school committee has maintained relatively stable leadership. This ten-year period will match what Richard Wallace, a highly-acclaimed superintendent in Pittsburgh in the 1980s, noted as the necessary period to bring about significant change in an urban school system (Wallace 1996).

With mayor-centric governance, however, there are concerns about the changing nature of school politics. In this system the mayor's goals, aspirations and style can dominate educational policymaking. "It all depends on who the mayor is," commented one community leader in an interview with the author. Mayor Menino has been supportive of public education, but a future mayor may be less inclined. For a mayor counting votes in a close race, public education may not be a top priority. By one estimate, only twenty percent of households in Boston have children in the public schools (Clay 1991). Also, a mayor could turn the schools into a political "commodity" for patronage and other political purposes (Hunter 1997). While Mayor Menino has not pursued this path, it could happen under a different mayor.

In a mayor-centric system, school policy is subject to the governing and political style of the mayor. As elected officials, mayors typically are sensitive to criticism and wary of potential competitors. Mayors expect to be the focus of attention. When this governing style is applied to school policy, dissent and dialogue around alternative school programs and strategies can be easily muffled. Thus, in Boston, the mayor is sensitive to criticisms of school policies. Debate over school initiatives is much less public than it was in the past and less contentious. Along with this change has come a shift in power to the electoral and governing coalitions of the mayor. In Boston, this has diminished the role of many school activists and leaders, including some in the minority community. The mayor's supporting coalition, with its emphasis on accountability, has a closer affiliation with the business community.

For communities of color, particularly the African American community, mayor-centric governance has not fostered a larger role in school affairs. Although Boston's population is now just over 50 percent minority, and school enrollment over 80 percent minority, the power structure in the city remains predominately white, in both the political and economic worlds. In the school system as well, whites hold many of the leadership positions and are the largest employee group. Unlike some of the other cities in this volume, the schools are not a major source of employment for the minority community. The minority community has supported Mayor Menino at the polls, but as the 1996 referendum vote indicated, support for a mayoral-appointed school committee is weaker. The preference among many Blacks is for greater electoral representation as an avenue for participation in school and city politics.

The pace of school reform is also subject to the style of the mayor, as well as that of the superintendent. Mayor Menino's political style is generally deliberate and cautious, a style compatible with Superintendent Payzant's approach to school reform. To some community leaders, particularly in the minority community, this caution has stymied the pace of school reform. To these individuals, the low scores in student achievement require major — not incremental — changes. A community-based watchdog group, for example, called for an "immediate shift from rhetoric to radical action" when it concluded that reform initiatives were not producing the fundamental changes needed in the system (Critical Friends 1997). More recently, the *Boston Herald,* the daily newspaper with the largest circulation within the city, gave Menino a "failing grade" for stagnant test scores and inadequate physical facilities (Crummy 2001).

In general, a mayor-centric system of school governance creates a form of accountability that is both more direct and complex. One of the major appeals of the mayoral-appointed school committee is the alignment of accountability directly with the mayor. The mayor now has general authority over school policy, via the appointed school committee, as well as fiscal policy, via the budget process. Mayor Menino often highlights this direct accountability. On the other hand, accountability through the mayor is more complex. As chief executives, mayors are responsible for most city services, including public safety, physical infrastructure, and community development. When education is added to the list, it loses separate identity and becomes part of a larger calculus by voters in judging the merits of a particular candidate for mayor. A mayor can perform well in other areas and still maintain overall political support, despite weak support for the schools. To education advocates, this loss of status for education as a separate area of policy accountability is a cause for concern.

On balance, as a policy approach, mayor-centric school reform has been supported in Boston. Mayor Menino has benefited from a supportive political and economic environment. Importantly, the governance turmoil of the late 1980s and early 1990s created considerable policy and political space for changing the structure of school leadership. In contrast to most other cities, Boston's venture in mayor-centric control of education was built upon a local history of governance battles and widespread disillusionment with an elected school committee. The call for a change in governance by the business community, *Boston Globe* editors, and others created a receptive environment for mayoral control. Mayors Flynn and Menino stepped into that space with all the status and resources they possessed in a strong-mayor system. Accountability through the mayor's office continues to garner broad support in the community.

In addition, a strong overall economy, state support, and relatively successful public safety programs have helped create a supportive environment. Through much of the period of mayor-centric governance, the Boston economy has remained quite strong. City revenues increased and job opportunities remained plentiful. Increases in state funding for public education provided critical support for the city and helped the mayor to take a leadership role in education.

The economic times are changing, however, and patience with mayor-centric reform is not unlimited. The next few years will truly be a test for mayor-centric governance. Raising test scores in a time of fiscal belt-tightening will challenge the mayor and other educational leaders. Mayors cannot change these scores themselves, but they can play an important role in providing resources for schools and rallying general community support for public education. In this new institutional world schools are now part of the larger political and policy dialogue in the city. In contrast to the Progressive Era legacy of removing schools from politics, mayor-centric governance has placed the schools squarely in the larger political arena of the city. There are trade-offs with such a strategy, but in an era of tight fiscal constraints, as exists in most large cities, winning a share of resources requires competing in the political process. In this regard, casting one's lot with the mayor may be the most viable governance strategy for improving urban education.

Notes

1. Nine percent are Hispanic; 4 percent Asian.
2. The balance (4.8 percent) are "other."
3. In Massachusetts, the term school committee is used rather than school board.

References

Avenso, Karen, and Patricia Wen. 1996. "Elected, Appointed Panels Show Differences in Style." *Boston Globe*, 28 October.
Boston Globe. 1991. Editorials. 16 January and 10 April.
———. 1992. Editorial. 30 August.
———. 1994. Editorial. 21 December.
———. 1996. "Massachusetts Business Roundtable: Six Views from the Top." 1 December.

Boston Municipal Research Bureau. 1989. *Special Report. Bureau Supports Appointed School Committee.* Boston: Boston Municipal Research Bureau.
———. 2002. *Special Report. Boston's BY03 Budget: Tighter but Still Full Service.* Boston: Boston Municipal Research Bureau.
Boston School Department. 1996. *Focus on Children: A Comprehensive Reform Plan for the Boston Public Schools.* Boston: Boston Public Schools.
———. 2002. "About the BPS: Facts and Figures." <http:www.boston.k12.ma.us>.
Chaçon, Richard. 1996a. "School Committee Vote Reflects Menino's Influence." *Boston Globe,* 6 November.
———. 1996b. "Menino: School Panel to Be 'More Accessible.'" *Boston Globe,* 7 November.
City Record. 1991. "State of the City, January 9, 1991." 83(3):1, 30–32.
———. 1996. "Mayor Thomas M. Menino, State of the City Address," 29 January 88(5):1, 70–71.
Clay, Philip. 1991. "Boston: The Incomplete Transformation." In *Big City Politics in Transition,* ed. H. Savitch and J. Thomas. Newbury Park, Calif.: Sage Publications.
Critical Friends of the Boston Public Schools. 1997. *Status Report on Boston's Public Schools after Two Years of Reform.* Boston: Critical Friends of the Boston Public Schools.
Crummy, Karen. 2001. "Failing Grade: Menino Not Living Up to Promises on Education." *Boston Herald,* 2 May.
Flynn, Raymond. 1993. "A Vision for Public Education Reform." Prepared for Presentation to the Boston Business Community, 29 January. Boston: Mayor's Office.
Hart, Jordana. 1995. "Harrison-Jones Sees a Lack of Respect for Role." *Boston Globe,* 19 January.
Hunter, Richard. 1997. "The Mayor versus the School Superintendent: Political Incursions into Metropolitan School Politics." *Education and Urban Society* 29:217–32.
Kirst, Michael, and Katrina Bulkley. 2000. "'New, Improved' Mayors Take Over City Schools." *Phi Delta Kappan* 81 (March): 538–46.
Mayor's Advisory Committee. 1989. *The Rebirth of America's Oldest Public School System: Redefining Responsibility.* Boston: Office of the Mayor.
Menino, Thomas. 1999. "Mayors' Roles in School Change." Remarks by Mayor Menino to Education Writers Association, 16 April.
Mooney, Brian. 2001. "Mayor Promises 'Best Term Ever.'" *Boston Globe,* 7 November.
Newman, W. Lawrence. 2000. *Social Research Methods: Qualitative and Quantitative Approaches.* 4th ed. Boston: Allyn and Bacon.
Portz, John. 1996. "Problem Definitions and Policy Agendas: Shaping the Education Agenda in Boston." *Policy Studies Journal* 24:371–86.
Portz, John, Lana Stein, and Robin Jones. 1999. *City Schools and City Politics: Institutions and Leadership in Pittsburgh, Boston, and St. Louis.* Lawrence: University Press of Kansas.

Rezendes, Michael. 1991. "Council Votes to Back Appointed School Panel, Abolish Current Board." *Boston Globe*, 11 April.

Taylor, Steven. 2001. "Appointing or Electing the Boston School Committee: The Preferences of the African American Community." *Urban Education* 36 (January): 4–26.

Vaishnav, Anand. 2001. "Are They Acting as Advocates or Appointed Rubber Stamps?" *Boston Globe*, 28 January.

Wallace, Richard. 1996. *From Vision to Practice: The Art of Educational Leadership*. Thousand Oaks, Calif.: Corwin Press.

Chapter Five ⸻

Detroit: "There Is Still a Long Road to Travel, and Success Is Far from Assured"

JEFFREY MIREL

THE REPUTATION of the Detroit Public Schools closely tracks the modern trajectory of American urban education — a rise to national prominence in the first half of the twentieth century, and a slow, but dramatic, decline in the last half. Detroit participated in — and in some cases led — virtually every important reform effort involving urban schools in the twentieth century. This chapter examines the most recent of these reform initiatives in Detroit — a takeover of the public school system by the mayor that centralized power in the hands of an appointed school board and a strong education executive.[1] My analysis of this initiative concentrates on several broad areas that have given shape and substance to education politics and school reform in Detroit, and Michigan overall, for several decades.

The first area is the growing power of the state over education policies in Detroit, as well as over every other local school district in Michigan. Since the 1930s, state power over local schools has increased dramatically, often in direct relation to increases in state funding. In the mid-1990s, the state government took responsibility for supplying nearly 80 percent of local school district funding, including funding for the Detroit Public Schools, a development that gave it unprecedented power over education. That change also exacerbated racial tensions between the overwhelmingly black city and the rest of the state.

The second area is the role of teachers unions. From the early 1970s to the early 1990s, teachers unions in Detroit, and Michigan generally, were the most powerful education interest groups in the state. By the mid-1990s, however, the unions had been beaten nearly into submission by a Republican governor and Republican-controlled state legislature. This development has changed the political landscape almost beyond recognition.

The third area that the chapter explores is how reformers, both inside and outside city, have struggled within a dramatically shifting political environment to improve Detroit's failing school system. The mayoral

takeover of the public schools is the most recent of these efforts. Together, the changes in the late 1990s in these three areas appear to have
created the possibility for some positive changes in the Detroit system.

Detroit's Changing Social and Education Contexts, 1982–1992

During the last part of the twentieth century, Detroit came to symbolize
the transformation of America's great industrial cities into centers of
unemployment, poverty, and crime. In some ways, however, Detroit was
unfairly stigmatized by that symbolic status. In 1989, for example, just
over half of all Detroit households had middle incomes and almost 10
percent had high incomes. While these figures were somewhat lower
than the nation as a whole, they show the need to at least qualify the
stereotype of Detroit as a post-industrial wasteland.[2] Yet, Detroit's negative symbolic status is not entirely undeserved either. During the 1980s
and early 1990s, the city continued to suffer greatly from the consequences of serious economic decline. Poverty was widespread; in 1989,
almost forty percent of Detroit households — nearly twice the national
average — had low incomes. Moreover, between 1969 and 1989 trends
in all in the income data for the city moved in the wrong direction.
Low-income households doubled; high-income households fell by almost
half, and middle-income households dropped by almost 9 percent. Moreover, during the second half of the twentieth century, the city lost population at an alarming rate. The 2000 United States Census found Detroit had fewer than a million inhabitants, less than half the number of
people it had in 1950. Equally important, Detroit continues to be the
most racially segregated large city in the nation. African Americans account for 80 percent of Detroit's residents.[3]

All of these factors battered the Detroit schools as they struggled to
educate the city's children. Beginning in 1978, the school system began
running annual budget deficits that ranged from $10 million in the
mid-1980s to $150 million in 1989. In this period elementary students
made some modest educational gains, but Detroit's senior high schools
(with the exceptions of Cass Technical and Renaissance High School)
were education disaster areas. During the 1980s, the high school dropout rate was well over 40 percent. As late as 1996, researchers estimated that almost two-thirds of Detroit's entering freshman did not
graduate, and, among those who did, less than 10 percent could read at
grade level.[4]

In the 1980s and early 1990s, a series of developments within Detroit
and Michigan bedeviled attempts to end the financial woes of the school
system or improve the educational achievements of the city's students.

The power of the Detroit Federation of Teachers (DFT) complicated every effort by the board to gain some control over worsening budget problems. Teachers, who saw the DFT as an island of stability and source of protection in a highly turbulent educational environment, gave union leaders strong unified support throughout this period. This support helped make the DFT, perhaps, the strongest education interest group in the city. Although the union did not win all its battles, it was clear in the 1980s and early 1990s that nothing would be accomplished, either financially or educationally, without the agreement of the union.[5]

If union strength increased during this period, the power of race to shape local educational issues declined relative to its power in the 1960s and 1970s, when it was the defining factor in all aspects of educational and municipal politics. Beginning in 1981, when John Elliott became the first African American president of the Detroit Federation of Teachers, virtually every major local figure involved in educational issues — the school board president, the superintendent of schools, the union president, and the mayor — were African American. However, the fact that local politics were dominated by African-Americans did not mean that race had disappeared as a factor in educational politics. Whites still controlled such powerful local institutions as the Greater Detroit Chamber of Commerce, the two daily newspapers, the *Free Press* and the *News*, and, indeed, almost every other major media outlet in the city. Above all, whites played a dominant role in the state government, which in the 1980s provided between 50 to 60 percent of Detroit's school revenue. Because of the racial tension between a majority Black city and a majority white state, and because Detroit depended so heavily on state funding for operating its schools, race often reemerged as a powerful force in debates about school governance, policy, and practice in the Motor City, especially during periods of financial crisis.[6]

The Changing Educational Landscape, 1993–99

In their insightful book, *Tinkering Toward Utopia*, David Tyack and Larry Cuban argue that school reform has "often resembled shooting stars that spurted across the pedagogical heavens, leaving a meteoric trail in the media but burning up and disappearing in the everyday atmosphere of the schools."[7] Typical of such shooting star reforms was the short-lived HOPE campaign to transform the Detroit schools in the late 1980s and early 1990s. Its failure helped set the stage for the mayoral takeover of the system. In 1988, when the four HOPE candidates won resounding elections to the Detroit Board of Education the promise of school reform indeed seemed to light up the educational sky above the Motor City. One local education reporter called their election "the biggest shake up in Detroit school leadership in at least two decades."[8] Representing a diverse coalition of Blacks, whites, labor unions, business groups, grass-roots activists, and major political leaders, the HOPE team came to office committed to transforming a school system noted mainly for poor educational performance, chronic mismanagement, and growing budget deficit estimated in 1989–90 at as high as $150 million (equal to almost 20 percent of the system's operating budget). Over the next two years, that promise appeared to burn even brighter as the HOPE team got control of the budget, reduced the deficit, and developed what appeared to be a strong working relationship with the DFT.

Yet, by late 1992, the HOPE reform effort was all but consumed in its plunge through the dense political atmosphere surrounding the system. A growing array of critics opposed its two main educational initiatives — specialized magnet schools (known as "schools of choice") and empowered schools (characterized by principals and teachers having considerable control over such areas as school finances, curriculum, and testing). Grassroots organizations denounced the schools of choice as "boutique schools," claiming they drained funds away from neighborhood schools. Simultaneously, the DFT and the administrators' union attacked the empowered schools as unwieldy and potentially destructive of union contracts. This opposition, particularly that of the DFT, contributed to the defeat of three of the four HOPE candidates in their 1992 reelection bid. Within a year, the reconstituted board hired David Snead, a long-time Detroit education insider, as superintendent, and, for all intents and purposes, restored the old order. Except for having produced a stable school budget, certainly an impressive achievement but not a revolutionary one and creating a number of new Afrocentric schools of choice, the public schools of Detroit were much the same in 1993 as they had been in 1988. The promise and early brilliance of the HOPE reforms faded quickly.[9]

Yet as apt as the shooting star metaphor often is in describing many school reforms, it leaves little hope that other efforts might actually achieve dramatic change. If most attempts at changing schools begin — and end — as dazzling but ultimately ineffective efforts, then reform campaigns are little more than exercises in futility. In systems as deeply troubled as Detroit, that vision can only lead to despair. Equally important, not all reform efforts are as evanescent as shooting stars on warm summer nights. In fact, in the 1990s, several developments in Michigan and Detroit demonstrated that some school reforms could be enormously effective, although whether their ultimate consequences are positive or negative still remains unclear. To push the Tyack and Cuban metaphor a bit farther, sometimes the shooting stars of education reform can be so large that they survive their fiery journey earthward, and hit the ground with such force that they utterly transform the political and education landscape.

Between 1993 and 1999, four reform efforts had exactly that effect in Michigan. The first was the radical restructuring of school finance in the state, a change that simultaneously increased state power and weakened teachers unions. The second was a direct attack on the state's teachers unions by legislation that, for all practical purposes, eliminated their right to strike. The third was the passage of a $1.5 billion bond issue to improve the educational infrastructure in Detroit and the subsequent failure of the school board to spend the funds in an expeditious manner. The fourth change, spurred by this failure and coupled with chronic complaints about poor administration of the system, was mayoral take-over of the school system.

The transformation of how schools are financed in Michigan was rooted in long-running problems in many of the state's districts related to raising money and the growing financial disparities between poor and wealthy districts. As in most states, school finance problems in Michigan were due to the state's reliance on local property taxes for most of its educational revenues. Michigan, however, was different from other states in two ways. It levied some of the highest property taxes in the country (in 1993, the statewide average was 35 mills), and it received an enormous amount of national notoriety when, in March 1993, the Kalkaska School District declared bankruptcy, closing its doors after voters turned down three consecutive attempts to increase school taxes.[10]

Pressures to solve the school finance problem were intense. In June 1993, the state's political leaders placed a constitutional amendment on the ballot calling for a major cut in property taxes offset by an increase in sales taxes. The amendment also called for greater equity in funding among districts. Despite support from virtually every major political and educational interest group in the state, ranging from the Michigan Chamber of Commerce to the state's largest teachers union, the Michigan Education Association (MEA), the amendment lost by a 54–46 percent margin.[11]

The defeat of the amendment stunned Michigan's political establishment. But less than two months later the politicians returned the favor. In an astonishingly audacious political act, the legislature deliberately created a financial and political crisis by banning the use of property taxes to fund education beginning with the 1994–95 school year. This bipartisan action — initiated by Debbie Stabenow, a liberal Democratic state senator, and strongly endorsed by Governor John Engler, a conservative Republican — compelled the state's political leaders to fashion a new approach to school funding or face the closure of every public school in the state.[12]

Over the next few months, state leaders struggled to draft a funding package that would restore the $6.3 billion lost by the ban on property taxes. Two possible approaches quickly emerged: increasing sales taxes from 4 to 6 percent, or increasing income taxes. In addition to these options, the legislators sought to achieve somewhat greater equity in funding by proposing that base per-pupil revenues for poorly funded districts be only $2000 lower than those of wealthier districts (approximately $4,500 and $6,500, respectively). Initially, the governor also called for an open enrollment plan for the entire state, a flexible charter school law, and a proposal to protect teachers who did not want to join a union.[13]

The bill that the legislature finally drafted did not contain any of those controversial measures. Instead it offered the Michigan electorate a simple choice to vote for either the 2 percent increase on sales tax or the increase in the state's income tax. Each option included identical increases in cigarette taxes and real estate transfer taxes, and allowed districts to levy up to six mills of property taxes. Each also promised a $4,200 per-pupil base for poorly funded districts that would rise to $5,000 over the next five years. On March 15, 1994, Michigan voters overwhelmingly opted to increase sales tax rather than the income tax. The margin of victory was more than two-to-one, 69–31 percent.[14]

There were several major consequences of this referendum. The most obvious and immediate was the enormous increase in state involvement in local education. As Lonnie Harp, a reporter for *Education Week*, wrote, "The tax shift has vastly changed the role of the state government in supporting public schools. Last year [1993], aid checks from the state capital accounted for, on average, 30 percent of a district's funding. This year, the state foots 80 percent of the bill. And while the overall size of the pot stayed almost constant, it is the state's new grip on the purse strings of school districts that is stoking the concerns of local educators." Compounding the problem were the limits on "the growth of assessed valuation of property, virtually locking in the portion of school funding that can be raised locally."[15]

The consequences of the tax change were also profoundly important for teachers unions. Governor Engler was a staunch opponent of teachers unions, not merely because they tended to be strongly Democratic in their political orientation but also because he believed their salary demands were a major factor leading to high educational costs. He frequently clashed with the MEA, reputed to be the most politically powerful union in the state and one of the most powerful, if not the most powerful, teachers unions in the country. In the early 1990s, Engler began to win virtually all of these confrontations. The MEA, for example, was the only major education organization to support an income, rather than sales, tax increase. Many analysts saw the lopsided victory of the sales tax proposal as a rebuke to the union.

Within the new school funding package was a far more significant setback for teachers unions than the electoral defeat, a setback that affected not only the MEA but also the smaller Michigan Federation of Teachers (MFT), of which the DFT was the largest local. Because the law shifted the main source of school funding from the districts to the state, local school boards had little room for maneuvering when faced with union demands for higher salaries. The districts could no longer go to the voters to ask for property tax increases to pay for salary increases. School finance reform essentially ended what had become a routine pattern in DFT and Detroit school board relations: teachers demanding — and then striking — for raises, followed by new millage elections to pay for the increases. Moreover, both the MEA and MFT joined forces to pressure the state into increasing funding for education, funds that often mainly went to increase teachers' salaries. Engler had no doubt about the importance of the new law in curbing the power of the unions in the area of school finance. At the signing ceremony for the school finance law, he stated simply, "[T]he power and control the teachers unions have had over educational policies in Michigan ended this morning."[16]

Worse was to follow for the unions. In April 1994, the Republican-controlled legislature passed a law that superseded the 1948 Hutchinson Act, which had outlawed strikes by public employees. Since the late 1960s, teachers unions had routinely ignored the earlier law, in essence daring school districts to enforce it. But the 1994 law put teeth into efforts to end, or at least shorten, teacher strikes. The new law, strongly endorsed by Governor Engler, penalized unions $5,000 a day for each day they were on strike and fined individual teachers the equivalent of their daily salary for each instructional day they were off the job. Reimbursement of the fines was outlawed. In addition, the new law limited the scope of collective bargaining. It forbade discussions of such issues as health insurance providers, "the starting time for the school day and school year, the makeup of site-based-decision making councils, and the use of volunteers. The structure of open-enrollment policies, pilot programs, and technology uses also would be off limits in contract talks." The only ray of hope for the unions was that the bill provided local districts with the option of not implementing these measures, if they chose. But that was small consolation to the unions. Outraged teachers from both the MEA and MFT responded by solidly supporting Engler's opponent, who promised to repeal the bargaining law, in the 1994 election. Despite their efforts Engler easily won reelection.[17]

On the same day John Engler was returned to the governor's mansion, Detroit voters rocked the political status quo in the city with another electoral decision, one with major long-range consequences. They approved an enormous bond levy to fund the rebuilding of Detroit's crumbling educational infrastructure. When Superintendent Snead took office in 1993, he made improving the educational infrastructure his highest priority. To tackle the problem, Snead proposed a $1.5 billion bond issue to refurbish old buildings and construct fourteen new schools. This was the largest amount of money any local school district had ever attempted to raise, but Snead realized that Detroit could afford such a massive bond proposal because the city's local property tax levy had plunged due to the state's shift to the sales tax to fund education.[18]

There was little doubt among "Detroiters" that the board needed such an enormous amount of money to renovate the system's decaying schools. Since the late 1940s, Detroit had failed to provide enough schools to accommodate enrollment increases; most schools in the system suffered from decades of neglected or inadequate maintenance. The average age of Detroit's schools was sixty years, but in some cases, as board members pointed out, children were attending schools built during the McKinley administration. Despite this obvious need, local leaders and key civic organizations including Mayor Dennis Archer (who had replaced Coleman Young as mayor in 1994), the Detroit Chamber of Commerce, and the DFT were wary of the measure. These individuals and organizations were particularly concerned about the board's lack of a detailed construction plan. As DFT president John Elliott put it, "This is an instance where we don't think the administration and board are giving us and the public full information as to what they intend to do and how they plan to do it." Yet even without the endorsement of such important members of the city's political and education establishment, the measure passed with over 60 percent of the vote. In addition, five of the six incumbent board members who endorsed the proposal were re-elected, a development that Snead proclaimed was a "clear vote of confidence" that these board members would be wise stewards of this new-found wealth.[19]

Over the next three years, however, it became apparent that this confidence was badly misplaced. Indeed, the concerns voiced by leaders such as Archer and Elliott about the lack of a construction plan appeared to be right on target. As of June 1997, over two and one-half years after the voters approved the bond issue, "not a lick of paint or trowel of mortar ha[d] been applied with the money." The reasons behind the board's failure to begin any of the renovation or new construction projects were numerous, and telling. After getting approval from the state treasurer to sell the initial $89 million in bonds, the board refused to sign-off on the first set of construction plans and ordered the planning process to begin again. The board then tossed out the revised set of plans, stating that the engineering surveys that guided them were based on "dated, incomplete, and erroneous data." The board also rejected the person nominated by Snead to oversee the program. Instead it gave control of the operation to two local businesses "with records of campaign contributions to school board members." Compounding the problem, starting in 1996, four key administrators, including the chief of accounting "who cited with her department's work as a reason for quitting," had quit. Finally, a Ford Motor Company executive who had been hired as the supervisor of the district's physical plant left the job after less than a year, having found the support and expertise in the department inadequate.[20] Compounding these problems was the simple fact that, for each year that the money went unspent, the value of the bonds was decreasing due to inflation. Given the huge amount of money at stake, even assuming a very low rate of inflation, the purchasing power of the bonds was falling by over $30 million per year. Not spending the funds was costing money.

As Snead and the board tried to ward off criticism about the unspent funds, other problems emerged. In March 1997, the board asked a group of business leaders from New Detroit, Inc.—a nonprofit organization active in school and municipal politics since the late 1960s—to audit the system's books. The impetus for the audit was a looming $25 million deficit in the district's operating budget. Five months later, New Detroit issued a report strongly criticizing attempts by board members "to run the day-to-day operations of the school system" and usurping powers "properly delegated to the Superintendent's office." It criticized how the board handled the district's finances; how it was swayed by unwarranted influence from outside groups in making "hiring, purchasing, and other decisions" and how it failed to delegate authority, particularly to building principals. The audit also noted that "the district lacked financial checks and balances as well as a comprehensive maintenance program." Over the next few months, neither the board nor the superintendent took any significant steps to implement the changes recommended by New Detroit.[21]

By the fall of 1997, the continuing failure of the board to get the construction projects underway and Snead's uncertain commitment to carrying out New Detroit's recommendations for reorganization had become highly politicized. Rumors flew that Mayor Archer, in collusion with "corporate interests" (i.e., New Detroit, Inc.), was maneuvering to oust Snead and take over the board. These rumors were fueled, in part, by Governor Engler's announcement earlier in the year that he would seek legislation permitting state takeovers of "failing districts." He pointedly declared that Detroit was one of the districts he had in mind and that he had approached Archer about gaining mayoral control of the school system, much as Richard M. Daley had done in Chicago. At the time, Archer refused the offer. But Engler had planted a seed that would eventually take root.[22]

In late October 1997, after two board members privately urged Snead to step down, he handed in his resignation. The board accepted the resignation in a divided vote, and recriminations flew. Snead's critics condemned his failure to get the construction program off the ground and his foot dragging on the New Detroit recommendations. They also accused him of not having the administrative skills necessary to lead the system. His defenders pointed to his success in bringing the budget into balance and improving district-wide test scores.[23]

Removing Snead and replacing him with Eddie Green, another long-time Detroit administrator, did not end the board's problems. For example, as late as April 1998, virtually none of the renovation or construction projects from the $1.5 billion bond issue were underway. Compounding the growing perception that the board and its top administrators had lost control of the situation, the state treasurer, who was authorized to approve the sale of new bonds, balked at the board's request for another $200 million. Noting that the board had barely used the money from the $89 million approved in 1996, the treasurer declared, "Is it appropriate for me to allow [the district] to borrow $200 million more when there's more than $89 million sitting in the bank?" More ominously, he wondered whether the board's failure to spend the money might have compromised the tax-exempt status the bonds had with the Internal Revenue Service.[24]

While Detroiters were arguing and anguishing about the failure of local school leaders to make improvements in the system, political leaders in Lansing were preparing to act. In September 1998, in the midst of his campaign for reelection, Governor Engler floated a new idea for taking over the Detroit schools. His victory in November, coupled with Republican majorities in both the Michigan House and Senate, guaranteed that his campaign promise to change school governance in Detroit would be realized in 1999. In December 1998, recognizing the marked shift in Michigan's political ground, Mayor Archer addressed the Detroit school board and directly stated, "Either improve our public schools, and do so in a serious, significant, and timely manner, or get out of the way." By the beginning of 1999, it was clear that the center would not hold.[25]

The Mayoral Takeover, 1999–2001

In 1999, all the pressures that had been building throughout the decade coalesced into a seemingly unstoppable force aimed directly at transforming the governance structure of the Detroit Public Schools. The collapse of the HOPE initiative in 1992 sent the message that local political forces could thwart even an initially popular and promising movement for reform in Detroit. The subsequent restoration of the "old guard" on the Detroit school board and its failure to expeditiously use the enormous funds it received from the voters, convinced many Detroiters that the continuation of the status quo would lead only to further stagnation. The dramatic increase in the power of the state following the successful reform of the school tax structure meant that local districts generally would have to bow to demands from the state, even when those demands threatened important aspects of local control. The anti-teachers union measures passed by Governor Engler and the Republican-dominated legislature drastically reduced the power of these once-formidable interest groups and made possible certain types of reforms that hitherto had been unthinkable. Finally, the positive educational news out of Chicago, where a Republican governor and a Democratic mayor worked in tandem to take over a troubled school system, provided a powerful impetus for political leaders in Michigan to follow a similar course.[26]

The "Chicago experiment" in mayoral control had begun four years earlier in 1995. When a state law engineered by then-Governor James Edgar eliminated the school board and gave the mayor (Richard M. Daley) authority to appoint a five-member board of trustees whose policies would be carried out by a powerful chief educational officer (CEO). The board of trustees appointed Paul Vallas, who had been active in Illinois politics for many years, but was new to education, to be the first CEO of the system. Vallas, whose political background was in the area of finance, quickly got the budget into balance, negotiated a four-year contract with the Chicago Teachers Union, and streamlined the central administration. He then set about eliminating questionable educational practices such as social promotion, and introducing new programs such as mandatory summer school for students who failed to master the knowledge and skills necessary for promotion. Once derided as the "worst in the nation," the Chicago school system entered a period of almost unprecedented political calm and financial stability. Most important, students demonstrated better achievement in the elementary grades. News of the seeming success of mayoral control in Chicago spread quickly.[27]

In his State of the State address in late January 1999, Governor Engler had the Chicago model in mind when he called on the legislature to give mayors the power to "disband their local school boards and name new leadership in ailing school systems." Recognizing that the governor was specifically targeting Detroit's system, the city's elected school leaders held a protest rally several days before the speech. They pointed to the strong financial situation of the school system and to improving student achievement. They specifically denounced any attempt by the governor to remove them from office. With the battle lines between the governor and the school board clearly drawn, the key question was where Mayor Archer would stand.[28]

In February, Archer used his State of the City address to criticize both the governor's proposed action and the Detroit school board's inaction. Yet Archer was also cognizant of the new political realities in Lansing. He declared, "I have never coveted authority over the school system. My position has simply been 'Let's do the right thing for our children.'" In terms of serving the children, Archer argued, the city had reached "a critical period of decision regarding Detroit Public Schools." He continued:

> Two years ago, in this very chamber, after the governor floated a plan for state control, I plainly stated that such a plan was extreme and that Lansing should not try to dictate the terms of school reform to Detroit. Subsequently, I offered to participate in a local reform plan that would engage a broad spectrum of our community. My proposal was tabled by the Detroit school board. Last year, in two major addresses, I emphasized the need for immediate, aggressive reforms by the board.
>
> Now, the Republican-controlled State Legislature is working on a reform plan for Detroit Public Schools that appears to be on a fast track. I wish to caution that the plan's provision for removing a duly elected school board and replacing them with an appointed board should not be embraced without a lot of careful and sensitive thought, legal consideration and respect for the voters.
>
> But we have to face facts. Michigan has a Republican governor and Republican majorities in the House, Senate and the Michigan Supreme Court. The Republican legislators appear to be united on this issue. Clearly, they have the votes. Most Detroit legislators are in opposition and some religious and community leaders and Detroit parents oppose any change. However, it is abundantly clear that many, many Detroit parents, community and civic groups, religious leaders and business organizations support some form of legislative educational reform. Several education union leaders share the same view.
>
> So, we must face the probability that some form of legislation will be deemed legal, make it through the required committees, be passed by both houses — and signed into law.

Archer then listed the things that would be required to insure his cooperation in this effort. These included "direct participation" in drafting the legislation, additional funding to help dramatically reduce class size, expanded summer and after-school programs, and incentives for attracting large numbers of new teachers. He concluded by calling on all Detroiters to unite and create a community "that is committed to academic excellence for our children . . ."[29]

One week later, in a speech to the Economic Club of Detroit, Archer was considerably more forthright about supporting a mayoral takeover of the schools. He stated directly, "I want to remove any doubt about my willingness to take this bull by the horns if Lansing decides to send it charging in my direction."[30]

At the time, survey data revealed that Detroiters were divided about the issue. A *Detroit News* poll taken in late February 1999 found that almost 80 percent of Detroiters were dissatisfied with the administration of the Detroit Public Schools and over 70 percent were dissatisfied with the schools their children attended. Nevertheless, only 49 percent of the respondents favored the takeover, while 44 percent opposed it. With a 5 percentage point margin of error, the results were essentially even. The *News* reported that whites were stronger supporters of the takeover than Blacks, with about 75 percent of whites favoring the move, compared to slightly more than half of Blacks opposing it.[31]

As the takeover bill moved through the legislature, it provoked vigorous protests that aggravated many of the traditional political antagonisms between the city and the state. In this case, most of the Detroit protesters saw the takeover as a blatant attempt by a white Republican governor and a largely white Republican legislature to impose their will on a Black Democratic city. Many Detroiters, including the local chapter of the National Association for the Advancement of Colored People, saw the takeover as the latest racist outrage by politicians whose past indifference to Detroit's problems was only surpassed by their habit of race-baiting the city. Some critics viewed the takeover as an attempt to disenfranchise Black voters by ending their ability to choose their school leaders. Others saw Engler's targeting of Detroit as a form of educational "racial profiling." They pointedly emphasized that some predominantly white school districts had problems as serious as those of the Motor City, but none were slated for takeovers. A state representative from Detroit bluntly declared, "Engler wants to be master of the plantation — not the governor." A Detroit minister proclaimed, "The governor may wear a suit by day, but at night he puts on a white sheet."[32]

Not all of opponents of the takeover were inspired by fears about racism. Some predominantly white suburban districts from the Detroit area also vigorously resisted the measure. Leaders in these districts saw the takeover bill as a dangerous precedent that could eventually undermine local control in every district in the state.[33]

Supporters of the takeover responded to these criticisms by reminding Detroiters of the miserable record of the current board and by pointing out that control of the schools was not going to rest in Lansing, but in the office of a Black mayor accountable to the city's electorate. These arguments, however, spurred new charges. Opponents countered that Dennis Archer was a pawn of white politicians, an accusation that may have stemmed from Archer's being less confrontational than his predecessor, Coleman Young. In addition, some critics charged that white politicians planned to use the takeover to steer contracts for the $1.5 billion construction program away from minority businesses and towards white ones. As one school board member put it, "Archer is pressured by whites in private business and expected to conform to the wishes of European Americans."[34]

Despite these allegations, support grew for the mayoral takeover. Given the chronically poor performance of the school system on almost every measure of educational achievement or organizational effectiveness, it was nearly impossible to defend the status quo other than with the racially charged rhetoric the opponents used. No amount of angry speeches could overcome the findings noted in the earlier *News* survey that the vast majority of Detroiters believed the school administration was inept and their children's schools were not doing their job. Supporters of takeover promised that the reform would change that situation. Ultimately, a broad biracial coalition, including many business and church leaders, the Detroit Urban League, the high-profile community organization 100 Black Men, all the major unions in the city including the DFT, New Detroit, Inc., the (*Detroit*) *Free Press*, the (*Detroit*) *News*, and the *Michigan Chronicle*, the leading Black newspaper in the state, endorsed the takeover.[35] And, as the legislature debated the bill, public attitudes in Detroit about it shifted strongly in favor of the change. In mid-March 1999, a *Free Press* survey found 63 percent of Detroiters supported the takeover, and only 31 percent opposed it.[36]

These later indications of changing public attitudes may have influenced the vote on the bill in the legislature. Given the unity of the Republican majorities in the House and Senate on this issue, the result was a foregone conclusion. Nevertheless, when the legislators actually cast their votes, the big surprise was the degree of Democratic support that the bill received. The senate version, for example, received unanimous backing from Republicans, eight of the fifteen Democrats, including two Black senators from Detroit, voted for it, as well. When Governor Engler signed the bill into law on March 26, 1999, it looked less like a hostile state takeover and more like a bipartisan, and, to a lesser extent, biracial initiative.[37]

In several important ways, Michigan Public Act 10 of 1999 was similar to the Chicago school reform bill of 1995. Both bills abolished existing school boards (although the Detroit board members were allowed to serve in an advisory capacity until their terms expired). The powers and duties of both original boards were transferred to the mayors. Both laws created reform school boards that were appointed by the mayor (five members in Chicago, seven in Detroit although one of the seven would be appointed by the governor). Once constituted by the mayors, the Chicago and Detroit boards gained the power and authority to set policy for the school system. In both cases, the law eliminated the position of school superintendent and in its stead created a new, more powerful position of chief executive officer (CEO) to manage day-to-day operations. Both provided modest amounts of additional funding to the beleaguered school systems and options for ending or re-evaluating the takeover after a set number of years. Detroit voters will vote on whether to continue the new governance structure in 2005. One major difference in the two laws was that in Chicago the mayor appointed the CEO; in Detroit that authority rested with the reform board (although the Detroit mayor could dismiss the CEO without cause). The other major difference was that the Illinois law gave the reform board and CEO broader powers than the Michigan law in terms of dismissing incompetent principals and teachers, reconstituting failing schools, and getting waivers on union contracts.[38]

Early steps in the takeover process in Detroit were difficult and, at times, hostile. As *Detroit News* columnist Pete Waldmeir described it, within hours of Engler signing the bill into law, "Archer had letters hand-delivered to the board member's homes ordering them out of their offices by [March 31] . . . [and demanding they] turn in their keys, ID cards, cell phones, credit cards, pagers and any other district-owned property they may have accumulated." For their part, in their last official meeting, members of the old board "approved two-year contract extensions for fourteen top school administrators whose salaries ranged from $90,000 to $110,000 a year. They also approved generous two-year deals with twenty-eight lower-level administrators as well [one of whom was the wife of a board member]." Less than two weeks later, supporters of the old board filed suit to stop the takeover.[39]

Yet in a number of important ways the transition also went relatively smoothly. One week after Engler signed the new law, Archer appointed his six board members and the governor appointed the seventh.[40] In May 1999, the new board picked David Adamany as the interim CEO and offered him a one-year contract during which he would lay the groundwork for the appointment of a permanent CEO. A distinguished scholar, Adamany had served as president of Wayne State University for seventeen years, and was known as a strong, skillful educational and political leader. His accomplishments at Wayne State were considerable. He expanded research funding, staunchly supported affirmative action (consequently making the school one of the top three producers of Black physicians in the country), and eliminated a substantial budget deficit. On the downside, some critics voiced concerns about having a white academic who had never worked in public schools guide the initial steps of the reform board. More troubling was his stormy history with the university's unions. In any event, he had good relations with politicians on both sides of the partisan divide in Michigan; indeed, both Archer and Engler had urged him to take the job.[41]

Adamany faced a formidable set of challenges as CEO, not the least of which was to bring order and focus to the still chaotic $1.5 billion construction program. One of the first actions that the new board took was to reassure the community that it would not steer most of the construction contracts to white, suburban firms. In late June, Adamany's team announced that almost half the renovation money slated to get schools ready for the 1999–2000 school year would go to Black contractors.[42]

Another large challenge was negotiating the contract with the DFT. On the surface, Adamany and the city's teachers agreed about basic problems and solutions. Teachers routinely complained about truancy, which was serious at every level of instruction, but rampant in the city's high schools. The district had no minimum number of days students had to be in school to receive credit for the year. Teachers also denounced the long-standing policy of social promotion that seriously short-changed students who were promoted without having the necessary skills, and penalized teachers who devoted disproportionate amounts of time giving remedial instruction to these students while neglecting those who were working at grade level. Teachers placed responsibility for these problems squarely on the shoulders of school administrators. They claimed that administrators failed to enforce attendance and discipline policies and that they either overruled or threatened poor evaluations to teachers who failed "too many" students. Above and beyond these demands, Detroit teachers were dismayed by the size of their classes, a problem that had festered for years. Teachers complained bitterly about elementary classes containing thirty-five to forty students. In all these cases, Adamany supported the teachers.[43]

Adamany and the DFT parted company, however, over a series of proposals that he believed were crucial to improving educational quality in the district. These included: increasing the length of the school day and year without additional compensation; introducing a merit pay plan to reward high-performing schools; penalizing teachers for excessive absences, particularly their using sick days as personal leave; and giving the CEO the authority to "reconstitute" failing schools, which meant removing all the administrators and teachers from those schools without the promise of rehiring them. Not surprisingly, union leaders rejected all these proposals. They assumed that Adamany would use the anti-teacher strike bill passed in 1994 to force them into accepting the proposals, a tactic they denounced as a form of union-busting. As one DFT leader put it, "None of us wants to go on strike, but if Dr. Adamany falsely believes he can use that law to destroy our union and our union protections, we will strike."[44]

Throughout the late summer, union and board negotiators struggled to find common ground. An indication of the difficulty the negotiators faced was that discussions of salaries were among the least contentious items in the talks. In late August 1999, hoping to gain some breathing space for resolving the most troublesome issues, negotiators on both sides agreed to a ten-day extension of the existing contract, an agreement that would allow the schools to open on time. However, union members rejected the contract extension and voted to strike. The vote was a sharp rebuke to DFT president Elliott and revealed deep divisions between the older union leaders and a small, militant group of teachers who felt the leadership was too accommodating to the reform board.[45]

The strike was the first by the DFT since 1992, and because the DFT was the largest and strongest local in the state, the walkout was the first serious test of the 1994 anti-strike law. The law gave local school leaders the option of invoking penalties against the union and striking teachers, an option that Adamany and the board decided *not* to take during the first week of the strike. That decision infuriated Republican legislative leaders, who then threatened to convene a special session of the legislature to enact a bill removing the local option and making the penalties mandatory the moment teachers walked out.[46]

Though none of the negotiators admitted it, the threat of additional state action seemed to focus everyone's mind on settling the strike quickly, which they did. On September 8, 1999, union members voted overwhelmingly to accept the three-year contract their leaders had negotiated. The vote was an important victory for Elliott and signaled that he had regained control over the union (a development that became even clearer less than a year later when he resigned and handed control to one of his allies).[47]

The contract contained clear compromises by both sides. Adamany and the board dropped their demands for a longer school day and year, even though under the 1994 law they could have compelled the teachers to accept those changes. The administration also pulled back on efforts to introduce a merit pay system, although Adamany insisted he could impose such a plan without union approval. The board agreed to a 6 percent raise for all teachers over the three years and a 10.5 percent raise for teachers at the top of the salary schedule during that same period. The board also agreed to lower class sizes in forty-four elementary schools, an important, but still mostly symbolic, step in the direction of that crucial union demand. For its part, the union agreed to a process in which the CEO could reconstitute schools, but with some safeguards for transferred teachers. In addition, it accepted revisions of the sick-day policy by allowing administrators to penalize teachers for unauthorized absences and agreed to changes in the tenure policy by reducing to one year the period during which teachers could be evaluated before being terminated. Both sides claimed victory and the schools opened.[48]

As the teachers headed back to work, Adamany instituted a number of reforms that he believed were vital to improving the schools. He introduced a series of practice tests based on the Michigan Educational Assessment Program (MEAP) exams that, on the one hand, would give students greater experience and confidence in taking the MEAP exams and, on the other, would serve as a source for evaluating schools, principals, and teachers. He stiffened school policies regarding social promotion for students in second, third, fifth and eighth grades. In order to be promoted students would need an attendance rate of 90 percent or better *and* a "C" average or better in such core classes as English, math, and reading. For students who failed to meet promotion standards, the district began setting up special summer academies. The district also started working with the Wayne County prosecutor and Family Court in dealing with chronic truancy. Groundwork was laid to give principals greater control over their buildings, including the hiring of faculty.[49]

By far the most controversial step that Adamany took was asking Michigan legislators to approve a bill abolishing unions for school principals and administrators in Detroit. The bill immediately evoked cries of union-busting, and—given the ham-fisted way the legislature carried out the measure—even louder cries of racism. Adamany saw the bill as an essential tool for improving the school system. Like the HOPE reformers, Adamany believed that site-based management was essential for school improvement. Consequently he wanted principals to be the "chief executives of their schools," exerting substantial control over "academic, fiscal, [and] financial" aspects of their buildings,. But he also felt that without a means for weeding out incompetent administrators that crucial effort would fail. He noted that under the current system, "We have central staff who evaluate principals, and principals who evaluate assistant principals, and they're all in the same union." As they did with the HOPE initiative, union leaders denounced this effort claiming that the CEO already had more than enough power to remove incompetent administrators.[50]

Republican legislators, however, seemed to see the bill primarily as another opportunity to bludgeon education unions, especially in majority Black school districts. One of the later versions of the bill included two additional districts, both of which, like Detroit, primarily served black students. "My, my, my," one dissenting Detroit representative declared during the debate on the bill, "who is the population of those three cities? If it's such good public policy, why don't you decertify [the unions] in your district? Why don't you throw out the principals in your district?" He concluded bluntly, "This is a racist bill." In the end, the bill that Engler signed into law covered only Detroit, but the bitterness remained. Following its passage, one Detroit school principal declared: "If you are going to do something like this to the principals, then do it across the board. Do it statewide . . . It's hard to believe that this is not based on racism."[51]

This action by the legislature re-ignited the racial and political passions that had cooled somewhat after the initial takeover. Simultaneously, a veto cast by the governor's representative on the reform board during its search for a permanent CEO set off yet another firestorm of controversy. By mid-December 1999, the board had narrowed their search for a replacement for Adamany to two African American school administrators from the Sunbelt. The board was slated to choose one of the two candidates at its January meeting. However, at that meeting the governor's representative voted against the majority's candidate citing poor test scores in the candidate's current school district. According to the law, five of the seven board members including the governor's representative had to agree on a new CEO, or a new candidate had to be found. The vote was 5-1, with one abstention. Following the vote, community members who attended the meeting "erupted in anger." In a statement greeted by loud applause, a Wayne county commissioner declared that the governor's representative "doesn't understand a community that fought for its rights. I feel like a slave. I feel like my master just told me what to do." Deputy mayor and chair of the reform board Freman Hendrix commented, "There has been a gulf between Lansing and Detroit and tonight I'm afraid that gulf broadened."[52]

Despite the setback, over the next four months the board united and in early May voted unanimously to hire Kenneth Burnley, superintendent of the Colorado Springs, Colorado school system, to replace David Adamany. Burnley was a strong candidate. He had run the Colorado

Springs schools for fourteen years and in 1993 had been voted Superintendent of the Year by the American Association of School Administrators. As an African American who had grown up in Detroit and had attended the Detroit Public Schools, he was well-positioned to help heal some of the emotional scars the takeover had inflicted.[53]

Burnley took over as CEO on July 1, 2000. Four months later, John Elliott announced that he was stepping down as president of the DFT, ending some nineteen years as the head of the union. At almost the same time, federal court Judge Nancy Edmunds ruled against the suit that supporters of the old board had brought against the state takeover. Resting her decision on long-established legal precedent, Edmunds rejected the argument that the legislature had violated the constitutional rights of Detroit voters, affirming that the state was well within its rights to mandate the takeover. "School districts are state agencies," she declared, "Contrary to the plaintiff's assertion, there is no fundamental right to vote for members of a school board." The U.S. sixth Circuit Court of Appeals upheld that ruling in June 2002. With the legality of the reform board assured and important changes in the leadership of the district and the union underway, a new era for the Detroit Public Schools appeared to be at hand.[54]

Yet even as these developments promised some smooth sailing for the reform effort, two new clouds appeared on the horizon. The first, and the most immediately consequential, was the announcement by Dennis Archer that he would not seek re-election in November 2001. The second was that John Engler was barred by Michigan's term limit law from seeking another term in 2002. Thus, by January 2003, the two men who helped launch the Detroit reform effort would not be in office to help direct its course.[55]

The future of the reform effort did indeed become less clear when Kwame Kilpatrick won the mayoral election in Detroit. Kilpatrick, who had been the minority leader in the Michigan House of Representatives when the battle over the reform bill took place, had opposed the takeover. During his campaign for mayor, however, he declared, "We cannot go back to what we had." Nevertheless, he argued that ". . . [W]e also have to have some elected representation from the community on the school board."[56] Where that contradictory stance will lead remains uncertain. However, in the past year, Kilpatrick has essentially stayed aloof from educational issues.

The burden of running the schools appropriately has fallen on the shoulders of Kenneth Burnley. He has had a challenging first two years, which was to be expected, given the enormous problems facing the system. These problems include: restructuring the school bureaucracy so that the system provides efficient and effective service to school administrators, teachers and students; spending the $1.5 billion infrastructure funds quickly and carefully; negotiating contracts with the DFT and other unions without acrimony or threats of strikes; finding enough funds during a statewide economic downturn to pay for salary increases, hire teachers, and introduce effective new programs; and, finally, focusing clearly and consistently on improving teaching and learning within every classroom in every school in the city.

Burnley has made some progress in each of these areas. In his first year as CEO, he strongly supported the completion of a system-wide audit that had been commissioned by Interim Superintendent Green. Its initial findings on about a fourth of the schools in the district uncovered $1.5 million in misappropriated funds, a sizable portion of which were used illegally. This finding led to four criminal indictments (including a high school principal). Burnley also reorganized the notoriously inefficient payroll office that had consistently failed to pay teachers and other employees on time. He outsourced such operations as food service, grounds maintenance, and information technology. Moreover, he saved the system over $7 million annually by purchasing buses to replace the taxi service that the previous regime had used to transport special education students to school.[57]

Burnley's progress in making school operations more effective was matched by his success in finally getting the massive $1.5 billion infrastructure project underway. By April 2002, principals in each school in the district knew what kinds of renovations their building would get and how much would be spent. In addition, Burnley announced that the fourteen promised new buildings would indeed be constructed, including a new home for the system's premier high school, Cass Tech.[58]

In addition, despite union anger over the issue of outsourcing, Burnley was able to negotiate a new three-year contract with the DFT well before the start of the school year, an almost unprecedented achievement. Insuring a 3 percent annual raise for teachers and a 4.1 percent raise for those at the top of the salary schedule, the contract also committed the board to reducing class sizes in grades K–3, providing a planning period for all elementary teachers, and eliminating lunch room duty and hall monitoring for high school teachers. DFT president Janna Garrison, called the contract "a win–win situation. It is a win for our students, it is a win for teachers, and it is a win for the district."[59]

Burnley's accomplishments in these areas provide some evidence of the wisdom behind the reform effort and of his strong skills as an administrator. In a number of ways, he has followed in the footsteps of Paul Vallas who used his first years as Chicago's CEO to bring order, stability, and efficiency to that deeply troubled school system. Yet in one crucial way, the challenges that Burnley faces are quite different from those that confronted Vallas. When he assumed power over the Chicago schools in the mid-1990s, Vallas worked within the context a strong and sustained national economic expansion. Burnley took over in Detroit just as the economic bubble burst.

As the Michigan economy slowed in 2001, state tax revenues, including revenues to support the now enormous burden of providing about 80 percent of the funds for public schools began to fall. Since the Michigan government is legally bound to have a balanced budget, the governor and legislators had to cut promised increases for local schools to keep within the law. By January 2002, Detroit school leaders predicted they would have a $70 million deficit for the 2001–02 school year and estimated it would grow to $135 million in 2002–03. Complicating matters was the new contract with the DFT, which added an estimated $27 million annually to district expenses, money that could not be raised by increasing local taxes.[60]

Detroit's financial situation was worse than many other Michigan school districts because it had been losing students and, as a result, per-pupil state aid since 1997. In Burnley's first year as CEO, for example, Detroit lost over 4,700 pupils, which cost the district some $31.5 million in state funding. In the face of declining revenues and rising expenses, Burnley's only option was to cut jobs. Early in 2002, he "pink-slipped" about seven hundred employees, including social workers, custodians, and clerks, an action that provoked angry protests at several board meetings. Joining these protestors were people who used the cuts as a pretext for denouncing the mayoral takeover itself once again. These people saw Burnley's actions as further evidence of the perfidious nature of the reform. At the February 2002 board meeting, the anti-takeover protestors were so loud and disruptive that representatives of the laid-off workers could not make their case, a situation that forced the board to limit access to future meetings.[61]

The budget crisis ultimately may have more serious consequences than just reawakening political opposition to the takeover. A long-running shortage of funds has the potential for undermining efforts to improve student achievement even before they are implemented. After some false starts, in April 2002, Burnley unveiled an "aggressive" school improvement plan. In issuing the plan, Burnley committed his reform administration to improving test scores. To date, a major criticism of the reform effort has been that since 1999 the scores of Detroit students on the Michigan Educational Assessment Placement (MEAP) tests have been stagnant or have fallen. Given that Detroit's MEAP scores were among the worst in the state prior to 1999, the need for improvement was urgent.[62]

The school improvement plan marked a shift in the emphasis of the

reform effort from construction and contracts to children and curriculum. As the president of the Cass Tech parent and community organization put it, "Everything has been focused on bricks and mortar. . . . I
am happy that Dr. Burnley is now going to focus on the curriculum part
of it."[63] While some of the measures that Burnley called for may not
involve substantial amounts of new money (e.g., a zero tolerance policy
on school violence, greater emphasis on reading, an individualized academic achievement plan for every student and school in the system,
tougher annual student promotion standards, and the creation of a
common curriculum throughout the district), others were predicated on
resolving the system's budget problems. For example, two key goals of
the school improvement plan are reducing class size and hiring certified
teachers (at the time almost 20 percent of Detroit teachers were working with temporary certificates). Unfortunately, given the looming budget problems, school officials estimated that it would cost the district an
additional $100 million just to hire enough K–3 teachers to meet the
goal of reducing classes in these grade alone. How the district will be
able to address this problem in a period of financial restraints is one of
the great challenges Burnley and the reform administration will face in
the next few years.[64]

Despite these continuing controversies about the takeover, the budget,
and the poor performance by students on the MEAP tests, Detroiters
generally and the reform board members specifically have given the
takeover good marks to date. An April 2002 survey of Detroiters found
that 69 percent "strongly" or "somewhat" favored the reform process;
only 19 percent opposed it. While the survey revealed some residual
anger about the loss of the elected school board, most of these polled
seemed willing to give the reforms more time to prove their mettle.
Similarly, the reform board strongly praised Burnley in its second annual evaluation of his leadership. Though some board members expressed concern about the poor MEAP scores, all agreed Burnley could
have done little in that area during the only three semesters that he had
been on the job. In all, as Burnley entered his third year in office, Detroiters seemed content to wait and hope for progress in their schools.[65]

Conclusion

During the 1990s, the changes that have taken place in education politics, power relations in Michigan, and school governance and organization in Detroit are as significant as any in history. Indeed, one must go
back to the Progressive Era to find reforms of equal magnitude in Detroit. Progressive Era education innovations helped propel the Detroit

Public Schools to excellence and national prominence. It is unlikely that these latest changes, important as they are, will have so profound an effect. The more realistic measure of success will be whether these changes bring order and efficiency to the school system and improve educational outcomes for students.

This chapter concludes by speculating about five broad questions, the answers to which will influence the degree of success Detroit might have in realizing these goals: (1) How well will school leaders in Detroit be able to negotiate the unequal and highly racialized power relationship with the state? (2) How effective will the "Chicago-style" reform be in making the Detroit schools more financially stable and efficient? (3) How will teachers unions and teachers respond to their dramatic loss of power? (4) What pedagogical reforms must complement the governance and organizational changes in Detroit? (5) To what extent can these pedagogical reforms be carried out during a period of severe budgetary constraints?

In regard to the first question, no aspect of educational politics changed so markedly in the 1990s as the relationship between Detroit schools and state government. Following the 1993 school funding reform and the 1994 anti-teacher union legislation, state power over education in Detroit reached an unprecedented level. Adjusting to this shift in power relationship would have been difficult under any circumstances but two factors, race and political partisanship, have compounded the problem for Detroit. Since the 1970s when Blacks became the majority of the city's population, and especially after 1973, when Coleman Young became its first Black mayor, clashes between the city and the rest of the state have had strong racial overtones. These conflicts were mitigated to some extent when Democrats controlled either the governor's mansion or the legislature. But in the 1990s, as Republicans came to dominate every branch of the Michigan government, it became increasingly difficult to separate race and politics especially as sides regularly played the "race card." Some white Republicans, for example, consistently used "*Detroit*" as a code word for Blacks, and some prominent Black Democrats denounced virtually every criticism of the city or its schools as *racist*. In this context, it is not surprising that the rhetorical battles about the takeover were fought in racial terms.

Yet viewing the controversy about the mayoral takeover of the Detroit schools solely, or even mainly, as being about race ignores some important points. While it is true that white Detroiters supported the takeover more strongly than Blacks, on the eve of the legislature's vote over 60 percent of Black Detroiters supported the measure, as well. Moreover, many of the city's most prominent Black organizations, institutions, and leaders supported the change. On the other side of the issue, political and education leaders from a number of predominantly white suburbs opposed the Detroit takeover due to fears about growing state power over local school systems.

In the political debate, a number of Democrats joined Republicans in supporting the takeover. Moreover, Governor Engler appeared to realize that despite his party's majority in the legislature, he could not force his will on Detroit. Without the cooperation of leading politicians and organizations in the city, changing the governance structure of the Detroit schools would have been impossible. Mayor Archer, for his part, recognized that the education status quo was untenable, and that working with Engler offered the best possibility for improving the system. The relatively smooth takeover process was, at least, a partial vindication of the pragmatic approach taken by the two political leaders.

In short, rather than viewing the takeover as a stark racial or partisan conflict, it might be more useful to see it as a multifaceted struggle marked by fluid alliances that defied traditional categories. Neither Blacks nor whites, neither Democrats nor Republicans, spoke with a unified voice. Most importantly, within Detroit's Black community at least two major factions emerged. One continued the Detroit-centered, race-based politics that had been perfected in the 1970s and early 1980s by leaders such as Coleman Young. This faction allied itself with the elected board and viewed mayoral control of the schools as a hostile takeover that would cut jobs and steer contracts away from the Black community. The other faction had a more metropolitan focus and was less racially oriented. It was akin to the HOPE coalition and to Mayor Archer's less confrontational approach to state politics. This group saw the takeover as a way to shake up and improve a dysfunctional school system. It is unclear at this time whether the new mayor, Kwame Kilpatrick, will align with either faction or strike out on his own to forge a "third way" in Detroit politics. The results of the upcoming gubernatorial race — offering the best hope for returning a Democrat to the state house in more than a decade — could also play a significant role in shaping the future of the reform effort.

But even assuming the best possible political scenario for mayor-centered school reform in Detroit, the second question about the overall effectiveness of such efforts remains, especially given the long history of mismanagement and malfeasance in the administration of the system. While the mayoral takeover in Detroit appears to have had an early positive effect in terms of bringing some order and efficiency to the Detroit schools (similar to what occurred in Chicago), the reasons behind this positive change are problematic. Clearly, mayoral control of the schools is only as good as the people in charge and the people they promote and hire. The seeming success of Chicago's experiment may have had as much, if not more, to do with the political skills and educational wisdom of Mayor Richard M. Daley and CEO Paul Vallas as it did with the structural changes introduced in 1995. In fact, historically, mayoral control of school boards has not been a panacea, as even a brief look at the Chicago public schools demonstrates. Since the Progressive Era, all Chicago school boards have been appointed by the mayor, and for much of the last century, the school board and the system it ran were awash in political manipulation, corruption, bureaucratic stagnation, financial crises and, in the 1970s and 1980s, massive educational failure. There are clearly differences between the current system of mayoral appointments in Chicago and what preceded it, but it is important to note that there is nothing about mayoral control *per se* that leads inevitability to better schools.[66]

From that perspective, questions about who the mayor and governor will be, what their relationship to each other is, whom they will pick to serve on the reform board, whom the board will choose as CEO, and who will be chosen for lower-level administration posts are essential. The possibilities are ever present that mayors could use these appointments to pay off political cronies or strengthen their overall political position, rather than seek people committed to improving the schools. The importance of these questions and the recognition of the potential political problems of mayoral control can be seen readily in Detroit. As early as 1977, Mayor Coleman Young urged the state to give him control of the Detroit schools, a call he repeated in 1988 following the HOPE election. Yet neither Democratic nor Republican governors, nor the legislature, regardless of which party had a majority, responded positively to these calls.[67]

To date, Detroit's reform board appears to have been untouched by overt political manipulation. Despite some missteps, the general quality of the board members has been good, and the board's choices for CEO in both cases have been strong. Whether the same is true of people promoted and hired at lower levels of the administration remains an open question. Will the reformers be able to find lower-level administrators capable of bringing efficient, honest, and effective leadership to the Detroit schools? Moreover, as in other aspects of the reform effort, the future effectiveness of the administration is uncertain due to the change in municipal leadership in Detroit. Will Mayor Kilpatrick choose the same type of board members that Dennis Archer appointed? Will he reach out to different, less conciliatory constituencies? Will he support the return of an elected school board for Detroit?[68]

The third large question, the answer to which will shape the future of the Detroit Public Schools, concerns the survival of teachers unions as effective organizations in the city and in the state. As recently as 1992,

the DFT and the MEA were the strongest education interest groups in
Detroit and Michigan, respectively. Three years later, both had been
beaten down by Engler and the Republican-dominated legislature to a
point at which their most potent weapon, the strike, had been almost
eliminated, and their political power seriously weakened. In examining
the teachers unions' rapid fall, commentators from all sides of the political spectrum argued that at least to a considerable extent, the unions
had it coming. The assumption was that their arrogance and high-
handed methods proved to be their undoing. Clearly, John Engler and
the Republican Party tapped into this sentiment when they "demonized
the MEA as one of the principal obstacles to educational reform . . ." a
position that appeared to appeal to large numbers of Michigan voters.[69]

Throughout the 1990s, Engler's willingness to work with political opponents such as Archer on the takeover did not extend to building
bridges with teachers unions. Indeed, he was relentless in his campaign
against teachers unions and showed them no quarter. From a political
perspective Engler probably took some pride in humbling them, and he
may believe that their defeats signal better days for Michigan schools.
But as the United States enters a period in which teachers will be in
desperately short supply, one wonders about the consequences of state
actions that deprive teachers in Michigan of their most effective way to
demand better salaries, working conditions, and educational changes.
As Boyd, Plank and Sykes argue, "Politicians cannot do without the
energetic collaboration of teachers if the long-term goal of improving
public schools is to be achieved; but their short-term interest in restrain-
ing public expenditures, strengthening the institutions of public control,
and winning elections may preclude the kinds of concessions that would
win the trust and cooperation of organized teachers." Without that
trust and cooperation significant educational improvements on the classroom level are unlikely. For that reason, the "take-no-prisoners" approach to this aspect of education politics in Michigan might not only
damage the prospects for improving schools in Detroit, but it might also
weaken the quality of education in the entire state.[70]

As with the other large questions under consideration here, the possible political changes on the state level in November 2002 make the
future of teachers unions in Michigan unclear. A Democratic governor
would certainly moderate the political tone of the debate about teachers
unions. However, even if the Democratic gubernatorial candidate wins,
it is unlikely that the Republican Party will lose control of the legislature. Thus, the constraints under which teachers unions now operate in
Michigan will likely continue indefinitely.

Related to these large political, governance, and organizational
changes is the fourth question, concerning pedagogy. Ultimately, even if

the answers to the preceding three questions are as positive as anyone could hope for—namely that the major political issues between the city and state are resolved, that mayor-centered reforms produce an efficient and service-oriented school system, and that an era of unprecedented labor peace is at hand—there still would be no guarantees that the children of Detroit would demonstrate improved educational outcomes. While all these factors are *necessary* for improving the Detroit schools, they are not *sufficient* for improving achievement. If nothing else is changed, it is unlikely that student achievement will improve. As Derek Meinecke and former Detroit CEO David Adamany cogently observed, "Despite an array of efforts in cities across the country, there is at best only modest evidence that restructuring of school governance produces significant improvements in student performance. . . . There is yet little proof—except for some improvements in the Chicago public schools— that these measures have a significant effect on student achievement."[71]

Yet in his short term as CEO, Kenneth Burnley *has* taken some important steps that could lead to better student achievement. Building on the foundation laid by Adamany, Burnley's school improvement plan proposes policies and practices, which, if wisely implemented, could bolster student performance. Such efforts as reducing class size in the lower elementary grades, emphasizing reading, toughening promotion standards, and increasing the use of summer school are all positive steps. Among the best of these policy directives is his call for creating a district-wide curriculum.[72] This policy dovetails nicely with one of the fundamental ideas animating the mayor-centered, strong-CEO approach to school reform, namely, that highly centralized control of urban schools can bring about swift and dramatic changes to the entire system. Mandating a common, coherent curriculum for every school in the district is such a change especially if the content standards for that curriculum are well-defined, specific, and oriented to state standards and assessment.[73]

Such a well-designed common curriculum has the potential to address several crucial problems in urban systems, notably, student mobility, teachers' knowledge of subject matter, creation of effective new methods and materials, and student assessment. For example, Burnley's immediate concern in touting a common curriculum is the high mobility rate of Detroit students. Like families in all large urban school systems, families in Detroit, particularly those that are poor, move frequently. When all, or even many, of the schools in a district follow different curricula, students moving within the district find themselves confronting uncertainties and academic challenges for which they were unprepared at their previous school. In all likelihood, with each move they will fall further behind and slide into a cycle of frustration and failure. A common curriculum would provide these children with a considerable amount of educational stability, despite their frequent moves. It would make at least one aspect of going to school a fixed haven in their often too fluid lives. A common curriculum would also enable teachers to quickly assess children's skill and knowledge levels, and allow them to make appropriate accommodations for their new students.

In addition, a district-wide curriculum would make it easier to create effective professional development programs for teachers. Detroit, like other large urban school systems, has large numbers of teachers who are not trained in the subject areas they teach.[74] A clearly defined common curriculum would at least provide an essential body of information from which teachers could begin to prepare their lessons. Strong professional development programs, perhaps linked to major universities in the area, could improve teachers' knowledge of subject matter, help them prepare new materials for their classrooms, and train them in new methods. Finally, a common curriculum would provide the content and skill knowledge that evaluators could assess to gauge the progress of individual students, schools, and the district.

As with every approach to education reform there are pitfalls to relying on curriculum as a key element for change. The curriculum standards produced in most subject areas in most states, for example, are so poorly conceived that, in the final analysis, they are useless for helping teachers create units, lessons, or classroom activities. If the curriculum produced in Detroit follows this pattern, if the content standards are so vague that they cannot effectively guide instruction, the effort will be a waste of time and money, and the waste of a golden opportunity for improving achievement.

Yet even if the district introduced a finely crafted district-wide curriculum, the overall Detroit reform effort could still founder because of the looming financial problems. The fifth and final question about this reform effort, then, is to what extent can pedagogical reforms be carried out effectively during a period of severe budgetary constraints? Finding enough funds to hire substantial numbers of well-educated teachers, reduce the size of early elementary classes, introduce effective reading programs, provide summer schools for poor performing students and implement the district-wide curriculum are vital for improving achievement. Whether during the current period of financial distress Burnley can mobilize the various groups supporting reform to fight for better funding will be, perhaps, the major test of his leadership. Given that Dennis Archer and John Engler, the two prime architects of the reform, have left the field, that task is particularly daunting. As it has in the past, money and politics may yet trump pedagogy in shaping education in the Motor City.

The effort to improve the quality of the Detroit schools through mayoral control has brought about some positive developments in the system. Whether these developments will continue apace and student achievement rise accordingly remains to be seen. As David Adamany observed in his final report to the board in 2001, while there are some reasons to be hopeful, "there is still a long road to travel, and success is far from assured."[75]

Notes

I would like to thank Robert Bain, Paul Bielawski, Jenny DeMonte, Anne-Lise Halvorsen, Deborah Michaels and Maris Vinoskis for their thoughtful and helpful comments on various drafts of this chapter. They are not responsible for any errors or inaccuracies.

1. On the history of the Detroit schools in the twentieth century, see Jeffrey Mirel, *The Rise and Fall of an Urban School System: Detroit, 1907–81* (Ann Arbor: University of Michigan Press, 1999). On recent developments in Detroit, see Wilbur C. Rich, *Black Mayors and School Politics: The Failure of Reform in Detroit, Gary, and Newark* (New York: Garland Press, 1996), and Jeffrey R. Henig, Richard C. Hula, Marion Orr, and Desiree S. Pedescleaux, *The Color of School Reform: Race, Politics, and the Challenge of Urban Education* (Princeton, N.J.: Princeton University Press, 1999).

2. Department of Housing and Urban Development Office of Policy Development and Research, "Percent of Household in National Income Brackets," *SOCDS Census Data: Output for Detroit, MI*, <http://www.socds.huduser.org/scripts/odbic.exe/census/incpov.htm>.

3. Ibid.; James G. Hill, "Detroit Census Drop Attributed to White Flight," *Detroit Free Press*, 29 March 2001; Genaro C. Armas, "Report: Races Still Live Apart," *Detroit Free Press*, 4 April 2001; "Census 2000: Race in the Cities," *Detroit Free Press*, 13 August 2001. According to a recent *Detroit News* series, in 2000 there were fewer racially balanced neighborhoods in Detroit and its surrounding metropolitan area than in 1980. Not surprisingly, therefore, more than seventy percent of Detroit school children attend schools that are either ninety percent Black or ninety percent white. Gordon Trowbridge, "Racial Divide Widest in U.S.," *Detroit News*, 14 January 2002; Jodi Upton, "Segregated Schools Hurt Students' Bid for Success," *Detroit News*, 21 January 2002. On the overall decline of the city into the 1980s, see Joe T. Darden, Richard Child Hill, June Thomas, and Richard Thomas, *Detroit: Race and Uneven Development* (Philadelphia: Temple University Press, 1987). For a more recent assessment see, Jodi Wilgoren, "Detroit Urban Renewal without the Renewal," *New York Times*, 7 July 2002, <http://www.nytimes.com/2002/07/07/national/07DETR.htm>.

4. Henig et al., *The Color of School Reform*; Mirel, *The Rise and Fall of an Urban School System*, 411–20; Rich, *Black Mayors and School Politics*. See also Laura D. Varon, "Red Ink," *Detroit News*, 21 June 1988. Bryan Wittman and

Robert Wittman, "Extraordinary Measures: An Historical and Comparative Analysis of the Mayoral Takeover for the Detroit School District as Contained in Public Act 10 of 1999" (Lansing, Mich.: TEACH Michigan Education Fund, 1999), 5. On Renaissance High School, see Deborah Viadero, "Higher Standards," *U.S. News and World Report*, 18 January 1999, <http://www.usnews.com/usnews/issue/990118/18detr.htm>. See also Derek W. Meinecke and David W. Adamany, "School Reform in Detroit and Public Act 10: A Decisive Legislative Effort with an Uncertain Outcome," *The Wayne Law Review* 47 (spring 2001): 28.

5. On the power of the DFT in the 1980s and early 1990s, see Mirel, *The Rise and Fall of an Urban School System*, 416–18; Rich, *Black Mayors and School Politics*, 34–39.

6. On the confrontational atmosphere between Detroit and the rest of state during the administration of Mayor Coleman Young, see Tamar Jacoby, *Someone Else's House* (New York: The Free Press, 1998), 295–353. With regard to school finance, in 1984–85, Detroit received 55.2% of its revenue from the state, 34.3% from local taxes, and 10.5% from the federal government. By 1991–92, the schools were getting 60.1% of their funds from the state, 28.6% locally, and 11.2% from the federal government. National Center for Education Statistics, *Digest of Education Statistics 1988* (Washington, D.C.: U.S. Government Printing Office, 1988), 88–89; idem, *Digest of Education Statistics 1993* (Washington, D.C.: U.S. Government Printing Office, 1993), 100.

7. David Tyack and Larry Cuban, *Tinkering towards Utopia: A Century of Public School Reform* (Cambridge: Harvard University Press, 1995), 111, 110–13.

8. Ron Russell, "New School Board Hopes to Fix Financial Mess without State Help," *Detroit News*, 1 January 1989. The HOPE campaign took its name from the last names of a group of candidates for the school board who ran in the 1988 school board election as a team committed to major reforms of the Detroit schools: Frank Hayden, David Olmstead, and Lawrence Patrick for Education.

9. The most comprehensive account of the HOPE electoral campaign is Richard W. Jelier, Jr., "Challenging Bureaucratic Insularity: A Regime Analysis of Education Reform in Detroit, 1988–1994" (Ph.D. diss., Michigan State University, 1995). For additional information on HOPE, see Henig et al., *The Color of School Reform*, 99–104; Richard C. Hula, Richard W. Jelier, and Mark Schauer, et al., "Making Educational Reform; Hard Times in Detroit, 1988–1995," *Urban Education* 32:4 (1992): 202–31; Mirel, *The Rise and Fall of an Urban School System*, 418–20; Rich, *Black Mayors and School Politics*, 39–46, 52–53.

10. An excellent article on the developments covered in this section, particularly on the dramatic loss of power and influence of teachers unions in Michigan is William Lowe Boyd, David N. Plank, and Gary Sykes, "Teachers Unions in Hard Times," in *Conflicting Missions? Teachers Unions and Educational Reform*, ed. Tom Loveless (Washington, D.C.: Brookings Institution Press, 2000), 174–210. Peter Schmidt, "Lack of Funds Forces Mich. District to Close Early," *Education Week*, 13 March 1993; Peter Schmidt, "Mich. Voters to Decide Fate of Finance Amendment," *Education Week*, 7 April 1993; Peter Schmidt, "Broad

Coalition in Michigan Backing Tax Reform and Finance Amendment," *Education Week*, 26 May 1993; Lonnie Harp, "Mich. Law Bans Property Tax Use to Fund Schools," *Education Week*, 4 August 1993.

11. Boyd et al., "Teachers Unions in Hard Times," 178; Schmidt, "Broad Coalition in Michigan Backing Tax Reform and Finance Amendment"; Lonnie Harp, "Mich. Voters Reject Amendment to Retool Tax System," *Education Week*, 6 June 1993.

12. Boyd et al., "Teachers Unions in Hard Times," 178–79; Lonnie Harp, "Mich. Law Bans Property Tax Use to Fund Schools," *Education Week*, 4 August 1993; Lonnie Harp, "Mich. Officials Scramble in Wake of Property-Tax Decision," *Education Week*, 8 September 1993.

13. Lonnie Harp, "Curtain Goes Up on Proposal to Overhaul Michigan Schools," *Education Week*, 13 October 1993; Lonnie Harp, "Some Uneasy with Quick Timetable for Mich. Reform," *Education Week*, 20 October 1993; Lonnie Harp, "After New Programs Pass, Mich. Panel Weighs Taxes," *Education Week*, 10 November 1993.

14. Lonnie Harp, "Mich. House Seeks Accord on Finance Measure," *Education Week*, 15 December 1993; Lonnie Harp, "Funding Plans Again Debated in Mich.," *Education Week*, 16 February 1994; Lonnie Harp, "With Mich. Vote Comes the Inevitability of Change," *Education Week*, 9 March 1994; Lonnie Harp, "Mich. Voters Back 2 Cent Sales-Tax Hike to Pay for Schools," *Education Week*, 23 March 1994. See also Boyd et al., "Teachers Unions in Hard Times," 179.

15. Lonnie Harp, "Mich. Law Does Little to Change the Bottom Line," *Education Week*, 7 December 1994; Boyd et al., "Teachers Unions in Hard Times," 179. For another discussion of the changes in Michigan school finance, see Barbara Miner, "Michigan Reforms School Funding," *Rethinking Schools* 9:4 (summer 1995). In 1995–96, Detroit received 78.6% of its revenue from the state. See U.S. Department of Education, National Center for Education Statistics, *Digest of Education Statistics, 1999* (Washington, D.C.: GPO, 2000), 112.

16. Engler is quoted in Boyd et al., "Teachers Unions in Hard Times," 179; Harp, "Mich. Law Does Little to Change the Bottom Line."

17. On the Hutchinson Act see Mirel, *The Rise and Fall of an Urban School System*, 184–85, 271. Lonnie Harp, "Mich. Bill Penalizes Teachers for Job Actions" *Education Week*, 27 April 1994. See also Joanna Richardson, "The Declining Fortunes of Michigan's Teachers' Unions," *Education Week*, 17 May 1995; Joanna Richardson, "Teachers' Unions Fighting Some Losing Battles in State Races," *Education Week*, 2 November 1994; Boyd et al., "Teachers Unions in Hard Times," 180–81.

18. Taylor and Wittman, "Extraordinary Measures," 9; Peter Schmidt, "Detroit District Stumps for $1.5 Billion Bond Issue," *Education Week*, 26 October 1994; Peter Schmidt, "Detroit Voters Back Unprecedented $1.5 Billion Bond Issue," *Education Week*, 16 November 1994.

19. Elliott is quoted in Peter Schmidt, "Detroit District Stumps for $1.5 Billion Bond Issue"; Snead is quoted in Schmidt, "Detroit Voters Back Unprecedented $1.5 Billion Bond Issue."

20. By comparison, in April 1997 Los Angeles passed a $2.4 billion bond

issue for school renovation and construction (which was then the largest bond issue ever passed by a local school district), and began work on the project two months later. Bess Keller, "Building Plan in Detroit Still Only a Dream," *Education Week*, 11 June 1997. See also Taylor and Wittman, "Extraordinary Measures," 9–10.

21. This summary of the New Detroit report draws from Meinecke and Adamany, "School Reform in Detroit and Public Act 10," 11–12; "Detroit Seeks Audit Help," *Education Week*, 5 March 1997; "Detroit Officials Accept Audit Help," *Education Week*, 6 August 1997; "Principals Gain Power," *Education Week*, 17 September 1997.

22. Caroline Hendrie, "Plan to Allow Mich. School Takeovers Assailed," *Education Week*, 12 February 1997; "Mayors, Superintendents Pledge Greater Cooperation," *Education Week*, 22 October 1997; Bess Keller, "With Board Opposition Mounting, Snead Resigns as Detroit Superintendent," *Education Week*, 5 November 1997.

23. Bess Keller, "With Board Opposition Mounting, Snead Resigns as Detroit Superintendent," *Education Week*, 5 November 1997.

24. Bess Keller, "Detroiters Await Repairs from '94 Bond Vote," *Education Week*, 8 April 1998; Meinecke and Adamany, "School Reform in Detroit and Public Act 10," 29. One of the absurdities of the situation was uncovered later by two *Detroit News* reporters who found a September 1998 memo written by the head of the system's physical plant department to Acting Superintendent Green. At the time, nearly four years after the bond proposal had been passed, precious little work was being done on the schools. In light of that stagnation, the administrator urged Green to stop referring to the project as the 1994 Bond Program because it gave people the impression they were behind schedule! Green agreed to start calling call it the Proposal S Bond program instead. DFT president, John Elliott, summed up the feelings of many Detroiters commenting, "The whole business has become a kind of Keystone Kops project when we should be calling it a tragedy." Melvin Claxton and Charles Hurt, "Bad Management Cronyism Waste School Repair Money," *Detroit News*, 10 October 1999. Elliott is quoted in Bess Keller, "Detroiters Await Repairs from '94 Bond Vote," *Education Week*, 8 April 1998.

25. Mary Ann Zehr, "Engler Pitches New Plan for Detroit School Takeovers," *Education Week*, 16 September 1998. Archer is quoted in Robert C. Johnston, "Accountability on Deck in Mich," *Education Week*, 20 January 1999. See also Meinecke and Adamany, "School Reform in Detroit and Public Act 10," 32.

26. In a recent study, Barry Franklin offers another interpretation of the mayoral takeover in Detroit. His well-researched and thoughtful study argues that the battle over the takeover was shaped primarily by racial politics. Barry Franklin, "Race, Restructuring, and Educational Reform: The Mayoral Takeover of the Detroit Public Schools," in Louis R. Miron and Edward P. St. John, eds., *Reinterpreting Urban School Reform: Have Urban Schools Failed or Has the Reform Movement Failed Urban Schools?* (Albany: State University of New York Press, forthcoming). Another alternative interpretation of the mayoral

takeover in Detroit can be found in an online essay by Rich Gibson who was program coordinator for social studies at Wayne State University. Gibson argues that vouchers, standardized curricula, high-stakes tests, and mayoral takeovers such as the one in Detroit "seek to deepen segregation, regulate knowledge, and intensify the alienation of citizens from the institution which holds their highest aspirations: education." Rich Gibson, "Suit in Detroit Strikes Back at Assaults on Democracy in Education," 24 April 2000 <http://www.pipeline.com/~rgibson/Dpsuit.htm>.

27. Since 1988 when the first wave of school reform began in Chicago, there has been a constant flow of reports and studies. A good overview of the two waves of reform is Anthony Bryk, "Policy Lessons from Chicago's Experience with Decentralization," in Diane Ravich, ed., *Brookings Papers in Education Policy 1999* (Washington, D.C.: Brookings Institution Press, 1999), 67–126. A typical example of the journalism about educational developments in Chicago is Cameron McWhirter and Sheryl Kennedy, "Windy City Shines as School Reform Success," *Detroit News*, 21 March 1999. On the use of Chicago as a model for Detroit, see Meinecke and Adamany, "School Reform in Detroit and Public Act 10," 13.

28. Robert C. Johnston, "Engler Proposes Takeover Plan for State's Urban Districts," *Education Week*, 2 February 1999, 16, 18.

29. Dennis Archer, "State of the City Address, Parts 1 and 2," *Detroit News*, 16 February 1999.

30. Mario G. Ortiz, "Ready to Run Schools, Archer Says," *Detroit Free Press*, 23 February 1999.

31. Cameron McWhirter, "Most Blacks Oppose Engler Plan, Poll Finds," *Detroit News*, 21 February 1999.

32. Cameron McWhirter and Brian Harmon, "Parents Say Archer Let Down Students," *Detroit News*, 16 February 1999; Brian Harmon and Kenneth Cole, "Despite Some Outcries of Racism, Most Emphasis Is on Who Can Do the Best Job," *Detroit News*, 21 February 1999; McWhirter, "Most Blacks Oppose Engler Plan, Poll Finds"; Lekan Oguntoyinbo, "NAACP Opposed to School Takeover," *Detroit Free Press*, 17 February 1999; Kerry A. White, "Power Shift for Michigan Moves Ahead," *Education Week*, 3 March 1999. Keith Bradsher, "Mayor Is Step Closer to Control of Detroit School," *New York Times*, 5 March 1999; Meinecke and Adamany, "School Reform in Detroit and Public Act 10," 33–37.

33. Tamara Audi, "Opposition Mounts over Takeover Plan," *Detroit Free Press*, 11 March 1999.

34. Harmon and Cole, "Despite Some Outcries of Racism, Most Emphasis Is on Who Can Do the Best Job."

35. "Businesses Plead for Overhaul," *Detroit News*, 21 February 1999; Bradsher, "Mayor Is Step Closer to Control of Detroit Schools." T. Van Moorlehem & D. Bell, "Takeover Gains Favor of 2 More City Groups," *Detroit Free Press*, 18 February 1999; T. Van Moorlehem, "School Takeover Bid Gets Endorsement," *Detroit Free Press*, 27 February 1999; Michael Goodin, "Lansing Circus Reminds Me of the Worst Antics of the School Board," *Michigan Chron-*

icle, 9 March 1999; *Michigan Chronicle*, 10–16 March 1999; Mario G. Ortiz, "School Plan Gets Support, Ideas," *Detroit Free Press*, 9 March 1999.

36. Cameron McWhirter, "Most Blacks Oppose Engler Plan, Poll Finds," *Detroit Free Press*, 17 March 1999. A February *Free Press* poll had reported fifty-four percent in favor and thirty-two percent opposed the takeover. See White, "Power Shift for Detroit Moves Ahead."

37. Gary Heinlein, Brian Harmon, and Ron French, "Takeover Heads to House," *Detroit News*, 3 March 1999; Greta Guest, "House Adopts Detroit School Bill," *Detroit Free Press*, 17 March 1999. "Michigan Legislature OKs Chicago-style Ouster of Detroit's School Board," *Chicago Tribune*, 26 March 1999; Bess Keller, "Mich. Lawmakers Approve Takeover Bill for Detroit," *Education Week*, 31 March 1999; Meinecke and Adamany, "School Reform in Detroit and Public Act 10," 33–35, 133, 137, 147. For a good description of some of the political wheeling-and-dealing prior to the final passage of the bill see Bess Keller, "Takeover Plans for Detroit Shift Gears," *Education Week*, 24 March 1999.

38. This comparison draws heavily on Taylor and Wittmann, "Extraordinary Measures," 11–22, and Meinecke and Adamany, "School Reform in Detroit and Public Act 10," 16–19, 33–42. Other sources include Senate Fiscal Agency, "Bill Analysis of Senate Bill 297 [Public Act 10 of 1999]" (Lansing, Mich.: Senate Fiscal Agency, 31 March 1999); Arthur E. Ellis to State Board of Education, "Senate Bill 297/Detroit School Intervention" (unpublished memorandum dated March 25, 1999 [in my possession]).

39. Pete Waldmeir, "Archer Hits Ground Running in Reforming Detroit Schools," *Detroit News*, 29 March 1999. Mario G. Ortiz, "Takeover Challenge Announced," *Detroit Free Press*, 29 April 1999; Darci McConnell and Mario G. Ortiz, "Suit Thwarts Board Plan," *Detroit Free Press*, 7 April 1999.

40. The original board members were: Pam Aguirre, CEO of Mexican Industries; William Beckham, President of New Detroit, Inc.; Marvis Cofield; a community activist and former teacher; Frank Fountain, Vice President of Daimler Chrysler; Freman Hendrix, deputy mayor of Detroit; and Glenda Price, president of Marygrove College. Engler appointed Arthur Ellis, state superintendent of instruction. Beckham, Cofield, Hendrix, and Price were African American; Aguirre was Mexican American; and Ellis and Fountain were white. "Newly Appointed Board Members," *Detroit Free Press*, 2 April 1999; Darci McConnell, "New Board Hopes to Get Closer to the Public," *Detroit Free Press*, 10 April 1999. Later Ellis was replaced by Mark Murray, another white male, who also served as state treasurer. Peggy Walsh-Sarnecki, "Engler's Man Bars New School CEO," *Detroit Free Press*, 19 January 2000.

41. Adamany's appointment was not without controversy. The original takeover law stipulated that the CEO receive a unanimous vote from the board. However, after Marvis Cofield made clear his intention to vote against Adamany, the Michigan House and Senate quickly revised the bill to allow for a divided vote. Opponents of the takeover saw this as an additional insult to the people of Detroit. On this change see Dawson Bell and Mario Ortiz, "Detroit Schools Pick New Leader," *Detroit Free Press*, 13 May 1999; Peggy Walsh-

Sarnecki, "Adamany Considered for Schools," *Detroit Free Press*, 17 April 1999; Peggy Walsh-Sarnecki, "Adamany Ready for Challenge," *Detroit Free Press*, 14 May 1999; Peggy Walsh-Sarnecki, "Adamany Won't Shy Away from Fight for His Goals," *Detroit Free Press*, 6 September 1999. See also Kerry A. White, "Detroit Board Names Interim Schools Chief," *Education Week*, 19 May 1999.

42. Mario G. Ortiz, "New Chief of Schools Outlines His Early Plans," *Detroit Free Press*, 19 May 1999; Emilia Askari, "School Board Gets Viewed with Caution," *Detroit Free Press*, 24 May 1999; Mario G. Ortiz, "New Team Finds Old Problems with Schools," *Detroit Free Press*, 27 May 1999; idem, "Adamany Team Gets New Faces," *Detroit Free Press*, 10 June 1999; idem, "Better Wages Lure Teachers," *Detroit Free Press*, 21 June 1999; Peggy Walsh-Sarnecki, "More Black Firms to Repair Schools," *Detroit Free Press*, 24 June 1999. Adamany's team also revamped payment practices to insure timely payment to contractors. The old board's consistent failure to pay its bills on time convinced many minority contractors to stop bidding on school projects. Since these firms had smaller cash reserves than larger, white-owned firms (and thus needed timely payments to survive), the old board's incompetence led to fewer contracts to minority businesses. As a *Detroit News* exposé pointed out, this fact alone belied the claims of opponents of the takeover that the old board was more supportive of Black businesses. Besides identifying massive incompetence and waste in the building program, the *News* also reported that more than half of contracts signed by the old board went to companies that had donated heavily to board members. Claxton and Hurt, "Bad Management, Cronyism Waste School Repair Money," <http://www.detroitnews.com>.

43. Peggy Walsh-Sarnecki and Mario G. Ortiz, "Hiring, Repairs Seen as a Start," *Detroit Free Press*, 29 June 1999; Janet Naylor, "No. 1 Issue: Overcrowding," *Detroit News*, 1 September 1999.

44. There was some question about whether the 1994 anti–teacher strike bill was enforceable. According to Professor Greg Saltzman, a labor researcher at the University of Michigan and Albion College, "Under the law, the Michigan Employment Relations Commission would have to hold an individual hearing for each teacher who struck. It would be impossible for [the commission] to handle the workload of hearing from 10,000 strikers." Brian Harmon, "Detroit's Teachers Talk Strike," *Detroit News*, 4 August 1999; Naylor, "No. 1 Issue: Overcrowding"; Mario G. Ortiz, "Planning for Change," *Detroit Free Press*, 4 August 1999.

45. Geralda Miller, "Detroit Teachers' Union Rejects Contract Extension," *Detroit Free Press*, 30 August 1999; Tracy Van Moorlehem, Mario G. Ortiz, and Peggy Walsh-Sarnecki, "Strike a Study in Division," *Detroit Free Press*, 1 September 1999; Peggy Walsh-Sarnecki, "Small Union Faction Holds Much Power in School Dispute," *Detroit Free Press*, 1 September 1999; Ann Bradley, "Detroit Teacher's Strike Bedevils New Regime," *Education Week*, 8 September 1999.

46. Mario G. Ortiz, "Teacher Talks at Key Stage," *Detroit Free Press*, 3 September 1999; Jim Suhr, "Legislators Plan to Intervene if Teachers Don't Return

to Work," *Detroit Free Press*, 5 September 1999; David Migoya and Peggy Walsh-Sarnecki, "Teachers Accord Close at Hand," *Detroit Free Press*, 6 September 1999; Peggy Walsh-Sarnecki, "No Strike Legislation Disappoints Lawmakers," *Detroit Free Press*, 7 September 1999.

47. Corey Dade, "Teachers Ratify Contract," *Detroit Free Press*, 25 September 1999; Peggy Walsh-Sarnecki, "With Strike Over, All Sides Ready to Resume Reform," *Detroit Free Press*, 9 September 1999.

48. Dade "Teachers Ratify Contract"; Walsh-Sarnecki, "With Strike Over, All Sides Ready to Resume Reform"; Brian Harmon and Cameron McWhirter, "Outlook Brightens for Change in District," *Detroit Free Press*, 8 September 1999; Associated Press, "Detroit Teachers Vote to End Strike and Return to Work," *Detroit Free Press*, 3 September 1999; Ann Bradley, "Detroit Schools Open Following 10-Day Strike," *Education Week*, 15 September 1999.

49. Mario G. Ortiz, "Practice Raises MEAP Scores," *Detroit Free Press*, 30 September 1999; Mario G. Ortiz, "Schools Get Millions to Experiment," *Detroit Free Press*, 13 October 1999. Brian Harmon, "Perform or Fail, Kids Told," *Detroit News*, 13 October 1999. David Adamany, *Report to the Detroit School Reform Board, 1999–2000* (Detroit, 2000), 8–9, <http://www.detroit.k12.mi.us./ceodoucments.htm>.

50. In 1988, principals in Chicago lost tenure in the first, non-mayor-centric reform legislation. Meinecke and Adamany, "School Reform in Detroit and Public Act 10," 44–7, 82. Chris Christoff, "Adamany's Bill Goes to Senate," *Detroit Free Press*, 30 September 1999. See also idem, "Bill Aims at Principals," *Detroit Free Press*, 13 October 1999.

51. The representative and the principal are quoted in B. G. Gregg and Brian Harmon, "House Vote Brings Racism Charge," *Detroit News*, 1 December 1999. Bess Keller, "Mich. Bans Unionization for Some," *Education Week*, 15 December 1999; Meinecke and Adamany, "School Reform in Detroit and Public Act 10," 44–46.

52. Kim Kozlowski, "School Chief Race Pared to 2," *Detroit News*, 13 December 1999; Brian Harmon, "School CEO Finalists Quizzed," *Detroit News*, 16 January 2000. Hendrix is quoted in Brian Harmon, "Schools [sic] Search Starts Over," *Detroit News*, 19 January 2000. The county commissioner is quoted in Walsh-Sarnecki, "Engler's Man Bars New School CEO."

53. Darren A. Nichols and Brian Harmon, "Detroit Schools Pick CEO," *Detroit News*, 5 May 2000. Peggy Walsh-Sarnecki, "High-Energy Educator," *Detroit Free Press*, 10 May 2000. Catherine Gewertz, "New Detroit Chief Welcomes A Difficult Job," *Education Week*, 17 May 2000.

54. Peggy Walsh-Sarnecki, "Head of Detroit's Teachers Union Won't Run Again," *Detroit Free Press*, 26 October 2000. Alan Richard, "Suit Challenges Detroit's Takeover of Schools," *Education Week*, 22 September 1999. Tracy Van Moorlehem, "Lawsuit Calls for a Halt to School Reform," *Detroit Free Press*, 14 September 1999. Edmunds is quoted in Andrea Cecil, "Legality of Detroit School Board Upheld," *Detroit Free Press*, 26 October 2000; Chastity Pratt, "Court Upholds Schools Takeover," *Detroit Free Press*, 13 June 2002. A comprehensive overview of the legal challenges to Public Act 10 can be found in Meinecke and Adamany, "School Reform in Detroit and Public Act 10," 50–87.

55. Keith Bradsher, "Detroit Mayor Says He Won't Seek Third Term," *New York Times*, 18 April 2001.

56. Id. "Mayoral Hopefuls Oppose Return of Elected School Board," *Michigan Report* 40:155 (13 August 2001): 3.

57. Jodi S. Cohen, "Detroit Schools Boss Rattles Complacency," *Detroit News*, 5 July 2001, idem, "Firm to Finish School Audits," *Detroit News*, 26 October 2001; Chastity Pratt, "Detroit's Schools Improving," *Detroit Free Press*, 17 January 2002.

58. Jodi S. Cohen, "Detroit Schools Share $1.5 Billion," *Detroit News*, 11 April 2002; idem, "Detroit Schools Boss Rattles Complacency."

59. Jodi S. Cohen, "Critics Blast Burnley, Layoffs," *Detroit News*, 21 January 2002; idem, "Detroit Teachers Get Early Contract," *Detroit News*, 3 July 2002.

60. Cohen, "Detroit Teachers Get Early Contract"; Jullie Blair, "City Schools Feel Pain of Fiscal Bites," *Education Week*, 23 January 2003.

61. Jodi S. Cohen, "Detroit School Enrollments Drop," *Detroit News*, 3 October 2001; idem, "Critics Blast Burnley, Layoffs"; Sherly James, "Education in Detroit: Schools Chief Put To Test," *Detroit Free Press*, 22 January 2002; Karla Scoon Reid, "Wary Detroit Board May Limit Access," *Education Week*, 13 March 2002. Besides the departure from Detroit of families with school age children, the growth of charter schools in Detroit has also led to declining enrollments in the Detroit Public Schools. On this trend see, Peggy Walsh-Sarnecki, "Education: Charter Schools Growing," *Detroit Free Press*, 10 September 2002.

62. Chastity Pratt, "Detroit School Chief's Review Not Tarnished by MEAP Scores," *Detroit Free Press*, 20 June 2002.

63. Jodi S. Cohen, "Detroit Toughens Classroom Standards," *Detroit News*, 16 April 2002. On other efforts to improve student achievement in Detroit see idem, "Summer School Size Doubles," *Detroit News*, 11 June 2002; idem, "Detroit Spends $12 Million on Reading," *Detroit News*, 12 June 2002.

64. Cohen, "Detroit Toughens Classroom Standards."

65. The survey was funded by the Skillman Foundation of Detroit. It examined attitudes of Detroit residents and those in Wayne, Oakland, and Macomb counties. Non-Detroit residents were more positive about the reforms than Detroiters but not by particularly wide margins. Jodi S. Cohen, "Metro Residents Support Detroit School Reform," *Detroit News*, 29 April 2002; Pratt, "Detroit School Chief's Review Not Tarnished by MEAP Scores."

66. There are several good books on the old model of mayoral control in Chicago. Two of the best are Paul Peterson, *School Politics: Chicago Style* (Chicago: University of Chicago Press, 1976), and Julia Wrigley, *Class Politics and Public Schools: Chicago, 1900–1950* (New Brunswick, N.J.: Rutgers University Press, 1982).

67. Meinecke and Adamany, "School Reform in Detroit and Public Act 10," 12; N. Scott Vance and Ron Russell, "Young Again Suggests City Control of Schools," *Detroit News*, 6 January 1989.

68. In September 2002, Kilpatrick removed Glenda Price, president of Marygrove College, and declared he planned to replace two or three more board

members. He argued he wanted a new mix of board members. Chastity Pratt, "Detroit Schools Trustee Ousted, *Detroit Free Press*, 10 September 2002.

69. Boyd et al., "Teachers Unions in Hard Times," 177; Mirel, *The Rise and Fall of an Urban School System*, 432–33.

70. Boyd et al., "Teachers Unions in Hard Times," 198.

71. Meinecke and Adamany, "School Reform in Detroit and Public Act 10," 88.

72. David Adamany made similar suggestions in his final report to the reform board calling for his successor to consider "revising curriculum standards and preparing standardized lesson plans." Adamany specifically called for the district "to align its curriculum standards more closely with the state's curriculum standards and with those that guide national tests of academic performance." Peggy Walsh-Sarnecki, "With Strike Over All Sides Ready to Resume Reforms"; Adamany, *Report to the Detroit School Reform Board, 1999–2000*, p. 19, <http://www.detroit.k12.mi.us./ceodoucments.htm>.

73. On the virtues of a "common, coherent curriculum" see the Summer 2002 issue of *American Educator*, particularly the following articles: David Kauffman, Susan Moore Johnson, Susan M. Kardos, Edward Liu, and Heather G. Peske, "Lost at Sea: Without a Curriculum, Navigating Instruction Can Be Tough—Especially for New Teachers," *American Educator* 26:2 (summer 2002): 6, 8, 46; William Schmidt, Richard Housang, and Leland Cogan, "A Coherent Curriculum: The Case of Mathematics," *American Educator* 26:2 (summer 2002): 10, 12–26, 47; David Cohen and Heather Hill, "The Case of California," *American Educator* 26:2 (summer 2002): 23–24.

74. Teachers teaching in areas that they are not trained or certified in is a national problem, but one that is particularly acute in school districts serving large numbers of disadvantaged student. See "1 in 4 Teachers Not Trained in Field," *New York Times*, 22 August 2002.

75. Adamany *Report to the Detroit School Reform Board, 1999–2000*, p. 24. See also David Adamany, *School Improvement Plan* (Detroit 2000), 3–5 <http://www.detroit.k12.mi.us/ceo/dpsplan>.

Chapter Six

Cleveland: Takeovers and Makeovers Are Not the Same

WILBUR C. RICH AND STEFANIE CHAMBERS

THE HISTORY OF CLEVELAND is filled with colorful politicians. A series of highly visible mayors including Carl Stokes, Dennis Kucinich, and George Voinovich have led the city by the lake. Each of these mayors became nationally known. Indeed, while the mayor's office is a political dead-end for many, each enjoyed a career in public service that extended beyond his term in office. None of them made public school reform the centerpiece of his administration. While each was drawn into school politics at least peripherally, their involvement was limited and they could claim few, if any, substantial reforms to show for their efforts. In this they are like many of the earlier generation of mayors discussed in the preceding chapters. Like Richard Daley, Sr., W. Donald Schaefer, and Kevin White, Cleveland's mayors have tended to shy away from the highly charged arena of school politics.

In 1989, Michael White, a former city councilman and Ohio state senator, defeated former city council president George Forbes, one of the most powerful Black politicians in city history. White entered office as a self-described pragmatic idealist with a reputation as a maverick Democrat whose governing style focused on the elimination of waste and the creation of a business climate that would attract jobs and stimulate the local economy. He promised to upgrade Cleveland's overall image and the reputations of its public schools.

During his first year in office, White ran an ad in *Fortune* magazine reading "Cleveland–Open for Business," signifying Cleveland's decision to overcome its image as "the mistake on the lake." This new business-friendly image brought national attention to the city and to the young reform mayor (Cohen 1997). Aside from trying to change the image of Cleveland (e.g., "The New American City") and attempting to lure back businesses, White made headlines by his support of the construction of new sports facilities and the Rock and Roll Hall of Fame (Miller and Wheeler 1997, 193). Mayor White brought the same pragmatic and upbeat attitude to his commitment to improve Cleveland's public schools.

Although the mayor's promise was initially met with plaudits, reforming the public schools proved to be a more enervating and difficult task than the downtown development component of his agenda. This chapter examines former Mayor White's efforts to reform Cleveland's public schools and how his direct control of the school board and its chief executive affected other school politics stakeholders. In order to conduct a meaningful analysis of Cleveland's public schools and its overall struggle for school reform, we looked at the turbulent years between 1980 and 2002. These two decades included fiscal crises, busing/ desegregation suits, state receiverships, and a mayoral takeover of the school administration. In a series of interviews with former and current board members, union leaders, foundations leaders, school activists, and the superintendent or chief executive officer, we were able to map the city's school district political terrain.

The Cleveland case is instructive for several reasons. First, former Mayor White represents something of a mixed bag compared to some of the mayors discussed elsewhere in this volume. Slower to link his identity to schools than was Baltimore's Kurt L. Schmoke, but less hesitant and reluctant than Detroit's Dennis Archer, White may represent a "balanced portfolio" approach that is more sustainable in the long run than a governance strategy that puts either all its money or none of it on improving city schools. Second, while he followed the lead of other mayors by garnering elite support within the business community and state legislature, Mayor White also aggressively experimented with a grassroots mobilization strategy, built around large education summits attended by a cross-section of stakeholders. Third, given the personal investment of the White Administration in public school politics and the high expectations he may have stoked, the Cleveland case calls into question the sustainability of mayor-led reform across administrations. The jury is still out on whether White's successor, Jane Campbell, can plot a new strategy without undoing much of the White legacy.

White's high profile involvement in public education raised several questions. Did his early efforts to establish and nurture a broad base for reform pay-off in later success, as the literature on civic capacity in urban education reform might lead one to project? Although his initial approach relied on informal politicking rather than formal institutional restructuring, in 1998 the Ohio State Legislature granted Mayor White overall administrative control of the public school system. Consistent with the "Chicago model," the new Cleveland superintendent would be called the chief executive officer (CEO). White was also given broad oversight of the school district's finances and the ability to hire (and fire) the CEO. Cleveland is particularly interesting because whereas Chicago residents were not given an opportunity to vote on mayoral control of the schools, Cleveland voters were. The overwhelming majority of Cleveland voters favored mayoral control over an elected school board. While only 30 percent of eligible voters cast ballots, 70 percent voted for retaining the school system's appointed board of education (Okoben and Townsend 2002). What is the impact of such a built-in citizen veto? Can structural reforms along corporate lines alter the way schools operate, or was the White era an interregnum during which the entrenched interests only appeared to acquiesce to city hall, biding their time until the mayor lost interest or lost office?

Background: The Shape and Scope of Cleveland's Public School Crisis

As in other northern industrial cities, white students once dominated Cleveland's public school district. Black students were segregated in neighborhood public schools within predominantly Black sections of Cleveland, such as Glenville, the boyhood neighborhood of Mayor White. Then came busing, and Cleveland saw the student population change drastically. In a *New York Times* article, Cleveland was ranked sixth among American cities for the highest concentration of segregated neighborhoods. Since 1990, the city has experienced a nine percentage point increase in segregated neighborhoods (Schmitt 2001). "White flight" to the suburbs (Galster 1998), combined with the lure of private and parochial schools, drew most of the white students from the city's public schools (Orfield and Yun 1999). In 1950, whites made up nearly 85 percent of the city's population; by 1990, they had lost their majority status. While the drop-off has been sharp, among the cities considered in this volume only Boston retains a larger white resident population (see Chapter 2).

Today Cleveland enrolls over seventy-six thousand students in its public school system. The overwhelming majority of students (seventy-one percent) are Black. Hispanics make up about 8 percent of the public school population. Less than one in five students is white and non-Hispanic. This is well-below the percentage in the pre-busing days and substantially below the proportion of whites in the population as a whole. Nonetheless, perhaps because of the segregated residential patterns, Cleveland has managed to retain a larger white student population than the other case cities discussed in this book. The current budget of the public school system is approximately $600 million and its teacher/student ratio is 25–1.

School performance in Cleveland is generally poor. The average ACT Assessment® score is 16.5 and the median SAT®1 score is 841. In 2001, 53.4 percent of Cleveland twelfth graders were classified as proficient in reading on Ohio's statewide test; this compared to 74.1 percent for the state as a whole. In math the performance was even more disappointing: 33.8 percent of Cleveland students were proficient, compared to 61.9 percent in the state (Council of Great City Schools, 2002:80). The system has a graduation rate of only 33.7%.[1]

Given these statistics, it is understandable why Clevelanders might be alarmed by the quality of their schools. Some of their concerns became manifested in mistrust and unwillingness on the part of many citizens, politicians, and businesses to invest more funding in a system they perceived to be ineffective and riddled with waste. This contributed to a fiscal crisis that came to a head in 1981, when the state took the extreme step of putting the public school district in receivership for three years. This and other steps, such as the state's establishment of the Cleveland Education Fund, helped stabilize finances for a little while. But debt continued to knock at the district's door.

The City Responds: Mayor White and School Politicians

Because of this record, particularly the high dropout rates and low achievement scores of its students, the City of Cleveland undertook a massive, high profile effort to reform its public schools. Mayor Michael White played an important and increasingly central role in crafting the city's response. While the mayor-centric approach is predicated on assigning new formal powers to the mayor, White's initial approach was to rely on more informal strategies of coalition building. Proponents of mayoral takeover often adopt a confrontational approach to school reform; the "old guard" in the education establishment often prove to be adept opponents. But White's first attempt at school reform involved an invitation to all concerned citizen groups to attend a citywide forum on education.

Michael White did not create the city's eagerness to address the public school crisis, but he understood it and responded to the issue with a politician's sense and sensibility. In May 1990, White launched the Cleveland Summit on Education. His strategy involved mobilizing some of his own electoral base and transferring its energy to the education arena. It entailed bringing together a large, diverse group of community activists and school stakeholders in the hope that a more open discussion would lead to a more coherent, collective vision.

In 1991, Mayor White provided important support to the "Four

L-Slate Reform Coalition" — so named because all of the candidates' names started with the letter "L"[2] — that propelled them to school board election victories in 1991 and 1993. Despite having a reform board, the school system continued to drift educationally and to experience fiscal and administrative problems. Like their counterparts in Detroit's HOPE team, the Cleveland reform board was not very successful in changing the culture and the politics of the public school system.

As was pointed out in *Black Mayors and School Politics*, mayors are considered outsiders in the politics and the culture of public school systems (Rich 1996). Given the structural distance between the school board and city hall, mayors who believe that they have a mandate for change have to decide whether to support or confront the extant public school policy stakeholders. Whether mayors take a cooperative or confrontational approach, the stakeholders will test their commitment.

The Cooperative Approach

Cooperative mayors collaborate with the extant educational establishment and attempt to include all the stakeholders in the quest for change. This is consistent with a *civic capacity* approach to school reform (Stone 2001, 1998; Ingram 1991). Clarence Stone states that civic capacity "refers to the mobilization of varied stakeholders in support of a community wide cause" (Stone 1998, 15). This massive mobilization effort should include everyone interested in schools, especially the business community, the minority communities, teachers, and administrators. The assumption is that none of these groups, particularly the minority communities, acting alone can generate enough civic capacity to make school reform work. Because of its role in the local economy, the business community is a critical stakeholder. Without the financial resources of the business community and nonprofit foundations, the cost of mobilization (e.g., staffing, publicity, rental space) could not be met. Based on a reading of the civic capacity literature, three propositions are possible:

1. The greater the inclusiveness of a citizen mobilization scheme, the greater the possibility for school reform.
2. The higher the level of consensus among stakeholders regarding the goals of school reform, the more targeted the citizens' demands, the greater their ability to overcome divisions as the reform process unfolds.
3. To the extent that mobilization means more resources, teachers, administrators, and their unions will welcome citizen participation.

A leader, in this case the mayor, who takes the cooperative approach assumes that, in the long run, the civic capacity method of public school reform will triumph; the stakeholders will come together and stay together for collective action. Such an approach requires the mayor to convince the public that victory is not only possible, but that it is simply a matter of perseverance and consensus building. In other words, the extant educational establishment is viewed as an ally in a largely cooperative enterprise. Accordingly, the overall future interest of the public schools will transcend the particular interests of the current school policy stakeholders.

Advocates of increased civic capacity or enhanced citizen participation were very optimistic about the public school reform prospects for cities like Cleveland. The fact that the first Cleveland Summit on Education attracted seven hundred parents, students, business leaders, teachers, and community leaders to discuss issues such as early childhood education, academic achievement, and school and community relations was significant (Good 1999, 7). With each subsequent Summit, attendance increased, as did the interactions among the stakeholders. Conveners and sponsors of these events claimed that people from all walks of life met to discuss a single issue, public school reform (Good 1998, 8).

Organizing a city forum may generate publicity, but it does not follow that such a meeting can facilitate change. Theoretically, a cooperative mayor can achieve symbolic interaction among groups without changing the status quo. This is why some mayors prefer a confrontational approach.

The Confrontational Approach

A confrontational mayor opposes the extant education establishment, attacking its leadership and their interests. This usually takes the form of rallying the public against the extant school leadership and ancillary stakeholders, and replacing them with new people. The existing educational establishment, or what has been called the *public school cartel*, will fight to protect its interest. Public school cartels constitute "a coalition of professional school administrators, school activists and union leaders who maintain control of school policy to promote the interests of its members," (Rich 1996, 5). Public school cartels (PSCs) are not cartels in the pure economic sense, but their behavior is "cartel-like." Most members of the cartel shy away from any term that implies the PCS has total control of the public school decision-making process and prefer to describe themselves with less-loaded terms, such as "people concerned about the schools."

A confrontational approach implies less confidence in the amenability of the PSC in general, and in citizen mobilization schemes in particular. A mayor who takes this approach understands that overcoming the institutional realities of school politics — including state laws, interest group agreements, and bureaucratic inertia — requires a full commitment to replace the extant education leadership with new laws, new people, and a new attitude. Simply put, the confrontational strategy presumes that the PSC cannot be trusted to make changes or engage in meaningful cooperation. Aside from enjoying power, it is also wedded to old ideas, and frozen into long-standing relationships within the school politics network.

PSCs can be understood as by-products of an institutionalization of school governance that allows a self-regulating, self-serving, and self-aggrandizing cluster of school professionals and politicians to emerge and take root. Labor contracts and state school board laws help the local cartels to solidify their preemptive positions in public school decision making. Protected by the widely shared belief that school affairs should be "left to the professionals" and buffered from "political interference," PSCs gained substantial control over the governance of American public schools, especially those in large central cities.

The cartels in Rust Belt cities seem most effective when the following conditions are met: a high degree of de-industrialization; one-racial-group domination of the electoral system; highly politicized education interest groups; and a school board governance structure with an extensive policy scope (Rich 1996).

A high degree of de-industrialization refers to a situation in which there are few, if any, manufacturing jobs left in the local economy. The remaining service economy provides low-wage and low-skilled jobs, but they are not adequate replacements for the lost manufacturing jobs (Bluestone and Harrison 1982). Without such jobs, the city operates with an inadequate tax base. One-racial group domination of the electoral system refers to a situation in which one racial group has a voting and/or office-holding majority.[3] Highly politicized education interest groups are organized around political institutions in order to minimize the impact of *ad hoc* or new groups. Extensive policy scope is defined as the school board having overall legislative power over matters relating to public schools. In this type of city environment, several propositions are possible:

1. The higher the level of de-industrialization, the more important school budgets are to the local economy.
2. If a single racial group can control electoral outcomes, it is more likely to do so in public school board elections. (In the case of appointed boards,

the majority on the board will reflect the dominant racial groups in the
public schools.)
3. The more state funding is involved in the local district, the more likely
   the stakeholders will be forced to divide their attention between city hall
   and state house politics (Rich 1997, 6).

Proposition #1 captures the fact that public schools are a major employer in a de-industrialized urban economy. The higher the level of
de-industrialization, the more important the school budget is to local
economy. Proposition #2 suggests that public school politics reflects
race-conscious politics. In such an environment, there will be less incentive for multiracial coalitions and bargaining. Proposition #3 underlies
the fact that interest group politics usually cluster around legislative
bodies, either at the state or local level.

Our review of the last decade of Cleveland school politics suggests
that Mayor White took a hybrid approach to public school reform,
using elements of both the cooperative and the confrontational approaches. Through its citywide summits, co-existence with the teachers
unions, racial politics, and governance structures, Cleveland provides a
good test of the propositions outlined above for both civic capacity and
the cartel rejoinder.

Mayor White's Hybrid Approach

Although Mayor White's cooperative approach also entailed working
with state officials, the PSC, and other stakeholders, the centerpiece of
White's legacy for the Cleveland public schools were the summits. For
Mayor White, the citywide summits were a successful mobilizing and
attention-getting mechanism. This is not to say they were all inclusive.
Since the inception of the summits, the recruitment of participants was
carefully monitored. The president of the Cleveland teachers union
characterized the attendees:

> There were targeted invitations. [The summits included] people who had par-
> ticipated before and had shown a level of interest. We physically asked indi-
> vidual schools to send some individuals, so that every school would have at
> least one person who could report back to the school on what the Summit
> had to say or what it suggested doing. . . . I believe it was kind of unique in
> the sense of being so broad, bringing virtually everybody in the community,
> even people who had nominally no connections with school districts were
> brought in and willingly so. The schools are plums embedded in the pudding
> of society. Society is not going be successful . . . unless the schools are success-
> ful (DeColibus 2001).

On the one hand, this targeting of invitations was clearly done to build citizen support and consensus for public school reform. On the other hand, it precluded surprises and gate crashing by disruptive outsiders. With each summit, there were more attendees and more opportunities to enhance the social capital of the city (Orr 1999). Aside from restoring public confidence in the public school reform movement, the summits became a vehicle for promoting Mayor White's desire to center the effort in city hall. Clarence Stone observed: "The concerns of parents and other stakeholders are highly fragmented; the occupational and career concerns of educators themselves sometimes loom larger than concern about achievement for children . . . The political test of reform, then, lies not in accumulating endorsement for an appealing idea, rather it is the challenge of how to fold the particular and lasting concerns of diverse stakeholders into a general effort to bring about change" (Stone 1998, 17).

Did organizing the summits create the civic capacity Stone recommends? Were there disagreements among summit participants? Did educators seek to defend their professional prerogatives? Were the reports generated by the summits incorporated into the school decision-making agenda? Did the summits provide an opportunity for many voices to be heard? Did the summits meet Stone's political test? These important questions are addressed in the sections that follow.

Whither the Summits?

Bringing such a disparate group together to discuss public school reform was a testimony to Mayor White's ingenuity. Touted as being one of the new breed of Black mayors (Mahtesian 1996), Mayor White moved quickly into school politics with his summits on education, the first of which adopted a vision statement with a set of ten-year goals. The summit mission, adopted May 1990, reads: "to initiate an ongoing process by which the community and the schools articulate a common vision, develop shared goals and begin to identify and implement an action agenda which results in public school improvements that guarantee every student in Cleveland a quality education," (Summit 1990).

At first glance, the mission statement reads like a preamble. However, in this case, the leaders of the first Summit wanted to formulate a statement that reflected the concerns and aspirations of the seven hundred assembled leaders, parents, and teachers. This was no easy task, as each set of stakeholders arrived with separate agendas. Many were parents seeking answers about the failing public schools and their children's performance in them. Others were community activists using the forum to get visibility for their agendas. Still others came to the summit just to hear what the new mayor and the superintendent had in mind for the public school system. In 1991, the second summit drew one thousand people and produced another set of twenty-seven policy initiatives. While this effort defined an agenda for change, it did not in itself provide the muscle needed to push reform into practice; few if any of the proposals were implemented by the public schools.

Meanwhile, having apparently lost confidence in the incumbent members of the board, Mayor White backed a reform slate for the school board elections. He reasoned that a new group of board members who shared his views would make the necessary fundamental changes in public policy. As we suggested earlier, PSCs rarely take such reform boards seriously. To the "old hands" within the system, reformers appear to be neophytes who lack the will, inside knowledge, and stamina to bring about genuine, lasting change. Like George Washington Plunkett of New York's Tammany Hall, members of a public school cartel tend to deride reformers as "morning glories," and tactically sit back to wait until they lose their bloom.

In 1993, the third summit attracted one thousand four hundred participants. This summit focused on implementation of the Vision-21 Plan, a comprehensive education action plan (Vision 21 1993). This plan, designed to prepare Cleveland's public schools for the twenty-first century, was Superintendent Sammie Campbell Parrish's effort to put her stamp on the system. Four hundred people organized into twenty-four working teams to implement the Vision-21 Plan (Summit 1993), which predicted that, by the year 2000, the Cleveland Public Schools would be recognized nationally for academic excellence. To achieve this goal, the system would require a total commitment from the local community and massive financial resources. The Vision-21 Plan did not survive Parrish's tenure, which ended in 1995.

The early summits of 1990–1994 are fascinating examples of citizen mobilization. They generated several documents that not only outlined goals, but also allowed the participants to interact with a wide spectrum of stakeholders. The steady increase in attendance and support is consistent with the civic capacity proposition number one: the greater the level of citizen mobilization, the greater the possibility for school reform. The high profile of school reform as an issue in city politics had alerted everyone to how important the public schools were to Cleveland's future. However, it is not clear whether the recruitment of summit attendees delved deeply into the ranks of ordinary Cleveland residents. Organizers hoped that the participants would include a representative sample of parents, but most of the attendees were "targeted invitees," meaning school administrators, teachers, business people, community activists, and foundation leaders. Still, the scope of the involvement, reaching two thousand attendees at its peak, was extremely impressive, and it is likely that the breadth of involvement was increasing over time as well.

Regarding civic capacity proposition number 2 — increased stakeholder consensus leads to targeted citizen demands and increased ability to overcome internal divisions — the results were more problematic. Internal disputes among Black political elites suggest that, while there was a general consensus on the need for school improvements, that consensus did not extend to the question of who should lead the reform. The dispute between Mayor White and his critics can be interpreted either as a reaction to the mayor's new appointment powers or as a real disagreement about the saliency of citizen input in public school governance. Some of the disputes were philosophical; others rooted in tactical political maneuvering. Because mayoral appointment of the school board robbed other Black politicians of a chance to achieve visibility, some politicians joined the call for a return to the elected board. The NAACP also opposed the takeover and challenged mayoral control in federal court. This divergence of opinion and class cleavage within the Black community made mobilization for school reform even more difficult (NAACP 2001).[4]

By 1994, Mayor White began taking a less visible role in the summit. The 1996 summit, which drew two thousand attendees, marked a watershed in the structure and the function of the summit (Butler 1997, 1–4). Mayor White was away on business, yet the summit went on without him, indicating that this institution had a life beyond the mayor's vision. In his absence, state-appointed superintendent, Richard Boyd, presided over the summit. Site-based management, i.e., more autonomy for the building staff, was one of the primary ideas promoted at the summit. Although a few studies showed that this approach would improve the morale of teachers, others claimed that it placed more demands on teachers without changing their authority over policy (Dondero 1993; Hess 1998). The parents at this meeting complained about the teachers, the lack of books and computers in the schools, and the conditions of the public school buildings (Jones 1996). This debate over the conditions of the schools came as the federal courts ended court-ordered busing in Cleveland. Busing was supposedly draining energy and resources from the schools. The new order allowed stakeholders to focus once again on the operating problems of the district.

During the citywide summits, Mayor White was careful not to alienate the teachers union leadership. Albert Shanker, president of the American Federation of Teachers, was invited to be one of the featured speakers at a summit. Throughout the summits, relations between city hall and the teachers union improved. The 2000 contract negotiations went well and the union was a strong supporter of school levies and bond issues. On fiscal issues, cooperation improved the utility of all the stakeholders without disadvantaging any of them.

This cooperation provides partial support for the civic capacity proposition number 3: mobilization is supported by teachers, administrators, and unions because it can lead to more resources. Mobilization educates the public about the intricacies of budget planning, and the impact of unexpected expenditures. The more the public understands about the process, the more amenable it will be to proposed levies.

Two observations are possible after reviewing the six summits. First, because the summits generated and consolidated support for experimental school reforms, the increasing turnouts posed a potential problem for city hall. Even if the group maintained its vigor and focus, there was a risk that some members would grow restless about the slow pace of reform and subsequently challenge the assembly's sponsors for control over the agenda. Alternatively, the multiple voices might dissipate into a cacophony, with the group becoming a disruptive force. Managing such turnouts required energy that could conceivably have been better utilized to make much-needed administrative changes.

Second, perhaps because he sensed these risks, Mayor White began disengaging and the nature of the summits began to change. The meetings first evolved into a general forum for public school leadership. Subsequently, when these open forums became unwieldy and the difficulties of moving from ideas to action became of greater concern, the citywide assemblies were replaced by small working committees made up of the traditional school policy stakeholders. Retaining the name of the summit, it now functions as a small non-profit organization. As Marva Richards, the Executive Director of the summit put it, "We serve the role of pulling people together for the conversation" (Richards 2001). There are no plans to convene another citywide summit in the near future. The Cleveland Summit on Education, however, continues to be supported by business and local philanthropic organizations (Dempsey 2000).[5] Although the summits attracted attendees, they did little to address the serious fiscal problems of the public school system.

The Mix of Summits and the Fiscal Crises

No one was more aware of the mix of summits and the fiscal crises than Mayor White. Aside from the summits, his school agenda included building public confidence in the fiscal integrity of the system, a frailty that had plagued the system prior to his tenure. A decade before Mayor White's election, the state had taken the district into receivership for three years, but fiscal troubles kept haunting the district. In 1992, Superintendent Frank Huml resigned, in part because the board refused to place a 9.8 mills operating levy on the ballot. Dr. Sammie Campbell Parrish became superintendent, making her the third school head since Mayor White had taken office. Parrish was also unsuccessful in placing a 12 mills operating levy on the ballot and an 8 mills levy on the ballot two years later.

In 1992, the state approved a $139 million loan to keep the district from being again placed in receivership. Despite the best intentions of fiscal managers, "red ink" continued to flow and a $51 million deficit forced the District to make an $18 million budget reduction. The cuts ranged from teacher's cutbacks to school supplies.

The deteriorating conditions and the proposed desegregation settlement prompted the board to place a 12.9 mills operating levy on the ballot. In May 1994, voters rejected the levies. The second $16 million levy was voted down the following November. During the 1994–1995 school year the district overspent its $500 million budget and was $125 million in debt. Implementation of the Vision-21 Plan got a mixed reception from Dr. Parrish's appointed evaluation committee, and she lost the confidence of the mayor. In February 1995, Parrish resigned.

The Parrish resignation, the failed levy efforts, and new debt added more uncertainty to the ongoing fiscal firestorm of the district. In March 1995 Judge Robert P. Krupansky of the U.S. Sixth Circuit court of Appeals, ordered the state to takeover the schools. Judge Krupansky called the Cleveland Public Schools "a rudderless ship mired in mismanagement, indecision and fiscal irresponsibility," (Miller and Wheeler 1997, 196).

Obviously, the reform boards, supported by the mayor, did little to extinguish the fiscal firestorm. The high turnover in superintendents (ten times between 1980 and 1992) also undermined efforts to restore public confidence in the district. Although Mayor White's school board candidates won in the 1991 and 1993 elections, the 1995 election would be different. Seventeen candidates entered the race. Board president Lawrence Lumpkin, and members Adrian Maldonado and Tony Cuda decided not to run for reelection. These decisions, coming after the court-ordered takeover (Stephens 1995a), were a sign that, with state receivership, membership on the board would be meaningless, and White's strategy of changing school policy through a reform board had failed.

The Search for an Alternative Solution

The school reform discourse changed in 1995 as many school activists began to watch the developments surrounding Chicago's mayoral takeover of the school system. Cleveland community leaders, such as Rev. James Lumsden, of Westside-Eastside Congregations Acting Now (WE-CAN), suggested that Mayor White takeover the schools (Stephens 1995b). Such support for a takeover within the African American and church-based communities was not typically the case in some of the other cities discussed in this volume. This suggests that Mayor White's prior involvement in a cooperative, mobilization-oriented strategy may have made mayoral control less threatening and symbolically charged. The idea of mayoral control was one of the most interesting topics of the 1996 summit.

After six years in office the mayor became more amenable to an appointed board. The mayor's elected reform board had not turned the school system around in terms of either finances or student performance. The summits, though well attended, were also not enough to persuade the mayor that they should be continued or be seen as a reliable vehicle for school reform.[6] The mayor slowly became convinced that elected reform boards do not work and that more direct city hall involvement was needed. This was clearly a more confrontational approach to the PSC, if not the beginning of a showdown.

In his 1996 State of the City address, Mayor White called for a new law that would allow him to appoint the school board. He used a medical analogy: the Cleveland school system was a sick patient. He suggested that, if nothing were done, the city's tombstone might read: "Here lies Cleveland, a city that betrayed its children, a city that killed its future" (Draper 1996). Interestingly, the Republican-dominated state legislature was quite willing to hand over control of the schools over to the Democratic mayor. It was two Republican state legislators (Senator William G. Batchelder and Representative Michael Wise), representing districts outside of Cleveland, who introduced a "Chicago-style" takeover of the schools. The bill was introduced without consulting the education leaders. Steven Minter, Executive Director of the Cleveland Foundation and longtime stakeholder in the school politics, asserted, "No one talked to us [about the bill] (Minter 2001)." The two legislators acted alone.

The idea of a mayoral takeover had been discussed in the 1996 summit, but the mayor nonetheless felt that the bill was premature and asked the legislature to delay it until he could appoint a commission to study the idea. Meanwhile, the mayor and Superintendent Boyd signed a "Memorandum of Understanding," creating a Cleveland-School Community Covenant. The Covenant also restructured the Summit Convener Group into a Summit Strategy Council, chaired by the mayor and the superintendent. The Summit Strategy Council was further divided into a group of 125-member work teams, or stakeholders, that met every month to discuss school policy. The entire process had a defined timetable with expected completion dates ("Memorandum" 1996).

For our purposes, the most important section of the Covenant was section H, establishing a Governance Task Force. The mayor appointed Steven Minter, executive director of the Cleveland Foundation, and David Bergholz, executive director of the Gund Foundation, as co-chairs of the Advisory Committee on School Governance. After three months of research and debate, the committee produced a widely circulated and discussed report recommending a mayor-appointed school board. There were also legislative hearings in Cleveland and Columbus on the proposed changes in the school governance structure.

In September 1997, the state legislature passed House Bill 269, granting the mayor control of the schools. The new legislation also included a 2002 referendum on whether to retain the appointed board. The public discourse that followed the enactment of the new law created some confusion about the timing of the referendum and the mayor's day-to-day role in the schools.

In a letter to the *Plain Dealer*, the mayor tried to correct two misconceptions about the governance proposal. He asserted that the law did not provide for a referendum before the new administrative changes would begin, nor did it provide for the mayor to directly manage the schools. White asserted, "That is the job of the CEO. . . . If the new governance system is approved, the responsibility that the mayor will inherit is sobering, but I will not shrink from it. I have the fortitude, patience and unyielding confidence in our children to see it through" (White 1997).

The plight of the schools became the central issue in Helen Smith's primary challenge to Mayor White's 1997 reelection. After the *Plain Dealer* wrote an editorial supporting the takeover, George Forbes, a critic of the mayor, wrote an editorial supporting the NAACP suit against the takeover. During the campaign Smith also wrote an editorial attacking the mayoral takeover plan. She asserted, "My goal is to have the school governance issue on the ballot for the May 1998 primary election" (Smith 1997). Smith made the runoff, but White defeated her with 55 percent of the vote.

The pending 1998 mayoral takeover was met with several lawsuits. Stanley Tolliver, former president of the school board, filed a suit in Cuyahoga County Common Pleas Court on behalf of resident parents, claiming the takeover violated the city charter. Toliver explained: "There's no question that it was unconstitutional. . . . You have to remember that this was a Republican-led legislation that put the Cleveland Public Schools under the jurisdiction of the mayor. Without the votes of the people. . . . What's so sneaky about it is that this is the same mayor, along with other people, who persuaded the voters to pass one of the biggest tax levies for the schools and then turned around and denied those same people the right to elect their own school board. There's no question that the mayor wanted control because of the financial incentives" (Toliver 2000).

In addition to the suit filed in Common Pleas Court by Toliver, the Cleveland Teachers Unions and the Service Employees International Union Local 47 filed a federal suit. Clearly, this case suggests that former members of the PSC and their allies were opposed to a mayoral takeover. They lost the case in federal court, as the judge ruled that the takeover law was constitutional.

In 1998, Mayor White appointed the Reverend Hilton Smith chair of the newly created nine-member school board. The mayor then appointed Barbara Byrd-Bennett, a former New York City school administrator, as the new CEO of the Cleveland school system. She came highly recommended to the mayor and the board and even received an endorsement from the vice president of New York State United Teachers, a federation of more than nine hundred local unions. Nevertheless, a local reporter also warned CEO Byrd-Bennett about the politics of Cleveland. He asserted, "You're here to make White look good. You may be running the schools, don't forget he is running the show," (Afi-Odelia 1998). By all accounts, the new CEO and Mayor White had a good working relationship. In interviews with board members and others in the city, the consensus was that CEO Byrd-Bennett was making positive changes in the administrative structure of the schools.[7] Some even suggested that the new CEO—not the board—was "running the system." One former school board member noted: "I think that there is more stability in the Cleveland schools since the mayoral takeover. He [Mayor White] brought in Dr. Bennett, a professional educator, and since then he keeps his hands off the day-to-day operations of the schools, it's a good marriage. Dr. Bennett is very much her own person and she will not be dictated to in terms of carrying out her responsibilities," (Pinkney 2000).

In addition to the fact that the new governance structure appears to have created a good working relationship, the school board has tended to be virtually unanimous on all decisions, from high-level decisions on budgetary matters, to mid-level decisions involving day-to-day management issues (Community 2000). Rev. Smith, the Chair of the Board, went so far as to say that there were "no politics on the board. It is just like any other board . . . [except] no one is running for office," (Smith 2001). Notwithstanding Rev. Smith's assurances of nonpartisanship and lack of political ambitions by his fellow members, what they decide *is* political.

At first glance, it appears that the PSC has ceded control to the mayor and new CEO. The lack of voting cleavages on the school board indicates that the PSC has little or no objection to what the mayor and his CEO are attempting to do. Although White had encroached on their turf, the changes he made were not yet institutionalized. For the PSC, the publicity from a successful mayor/CEO experiment could facilitate more resources for the system. The PSC understands that CEO Byrd-Bennett is an employee. Her tenure is limited, and they can wait her out if necessary. PSCs rarely criticize superintendents or CEOs until they plan to get rid of them, and Byrd-Bennett hasn't (yet) done anything to merit dismissal. Indeed, she has even received praise from the some of the mayor's staunchest opponents. The perception that she is running the show makes it easier to fire her and blame failures on her. Leaders of the PSC can be expected to promote the notion that all bad things happen because of the superintendent.

One of CEO Byrd-Bennett's first acts was to reduce her cabinet from twelve to five key members and to hire a new chief financial officer. She also assumed a very high-profile presence in the schools with a series of "Conversations with the CEO" (Abdulhaqq 2001). After a year on the job, she issued a report entitled *Educating Cleveland's Children*, essentially a list of changes she had made, including a summer school program, improvements in the computer system, and the establishment of Sylvan Learning Center® labs in ten high schools (Educating 2000). She also reorganized the system into six regions with superintendents who "are my eyes, ears and voice in the schools day-to-day." She is trying to unify a system with "fiefdoms" that look like "too many castles with moats around them" (Byrd-Bennett 2001). Unifying the school system and trying to get everyone to work together has not been an easy task. Despite all the problems, the CEO received relatively good reviews from the press, education and community leaders. A *Plain Dealer* editorial concluded, "Byrd-Bennett survived a rocky start arriving November 1998, overcoming near-unprecedented levels of organizational disorder by dint of her charisma and passion" (Sheridan 2000).

Nevertheless, Mayor White felt compelled to defend the new board and CEO repeatedly. White asserted in his 2000 State of the City address that "this is the best board of education we've in more than 30 years. Byrd-Bennett is everything I had hoped that she would be, and she is more. She is an educator, a visionary and an administrator" (Sheridan 2000). This support was necessary to reassure the public that something *was* being done about schools, but the new leadership needed more time. White's speech fed the soaring popularity of the CEO.

Popular school leaders are not uncommon but it does raise a series of questions: What does the popularity of CEO Byrd-Bennett tell us about the efficacy of the public school cartel (PSC)? Can a popular school executive with strong mayoral support override the PSC interest? Does this signal the loss of the preemptive power of the PSC? In order to understand the relation between Cleveland's PSC and school politics, it is important to understand how this entrenched group gained power in the first place.

The Preemptive Powers of PSCs

In *Black Mayors and School Politics*, public school cartels were described as having preemptive power because, once the cartel is entrenched in the policy process, it will remain dominant regardless of opposition to its policies (Rich 1996). They were a part of what the public policy literature calls the *issues networks*, *policy community*, and *attentive public*. The PSCs have gained preemptive power because they have worked at it. One facilitating factor is that, at least within congruent PSCs, members have accepted the notion of a unitary interest that transcends the particular needs of the members they represent. Internecine battles do occur, but members are taught that public disagreement decreases control, invites unwanted attention, and encourages interlopers. Accordingly, group socialization is a very important part of keeping members committed. Members are also taught that patience has its rewards. PSCs have won many battles by simply waiting out their opponents. More importantly, PSC members are taught to keep their eyes on the prize, i.e., control over school policy.

In addition to socialization, PSCs get support from state officials. State governments are willing partners in local control. Indeed, local control is defended in the name of democracy and tradition. Nevertheless, it is the informal arrangements between states and local districts that enable a PSC to protect its turf. A state and its local PSCs seem to make a set of tacit bargains (Rich 1997, 8):

1. Inner city school politicians have agreed, implicitly, to temper their demands for school integration in exchange for control of school resources. State officials have agreed, again implicitly, to funnel more resources to the district in exchange for silence on the growing education advantage enjoyed by white suburban districts.

2. Since state and accreditation officials only require a minimum offering in the curriculum, education issues are rarely a part of the bargaining process. Both parties have accepted the notion that low achievement scores of inner city students are not grounds for state intervention. The tacit agreement is that state will intervene only if there is massive

fiscal mismanagement and scandal (e.g., the 1981 and 1996 state takeovers of the Cleveland Public Schools).

In examining Cleveland according to these tacit bargains, strong evidence emerges in terms of state/PCS bargains. One example is Cleveland's 1976 desegregation order that established a court ordered busing program and guaranteed $276 million in state and local money to provide equal resources for all students.[8] One of the reasons the state was forced to intervene was because it was named as a defendant in the case. After twenty-four years of federal court supervision, the desegregation consent decree ended in July of 2000. Although the plaintiffs in the case fought the end of the desegregation order, administrators supported the end of oversight (Spector 2000). Since the decree was lifted, state intervention in the Cleveland schools has lessened considerably. Because the state devolved oversight of the district to the mayor in 1998, there certainly appears to be less talk about school integration. The conditions of tacit bargain number one seem to hold for the exchange between integration and political control of schools, but it is not clear whether this has yielded a fiscal windfall for the district.

Tacit bargain #2 involves the circumstances under which the state will intervene. The State of Ohio has become involved with the Cleveland schools during fiscally tumultuous times, but has remained less aggressive in the student achievement crisis. This is readily apparent when considering that the Cleveland schools, despite the fact that they are relatively solvent, still have not made dramatic progress in student achievement. Yet, the state chooses not to intervene under these circumstances. This is consistent with its second tacit bargain with the PSC.

The Cleveland PSC

The Cleveland version of the educational establishment, or the PSC, operates like its counterparts in other cities. Operationally speaking, members of the PSC have been able to preempt the decision-making process in school districts and effectively monopolize the provision of educational services for students who remain in the public schools. In some cities, this cartel-like group plays a deciding role in the selection of superintendents, school board elections, the agenda at board meetings, and how the budget is spent. However, superintendents are temporary employees and, as such, they are not members of the cartel. Richard DeColibus, president of the CTU describes the role of the superintendent. "What normally happens in most urban school systems, a new superintendent comes in with some flashy new plan and says I got the plan; here it is. Everybody do it. That's fine. Everybody goes through the motions. The olive [plan] doesn't work. The guy leaves. The next superintendent comes in with I got a great new plan, here it is; let's do it. It is simply cycled over and over again. The end result is that none of the changes are really institutionalized or internalized. They tend to be simply cosmetic things and have no real impact on the educational process" (DeColibus 2001).

The high-profile activities of superintendents or CEOs such as Bryd-Bennett often cloak the fact that very little is happening at the administrative and classroom level. Although the media focuses on the superintendent as the chief actor in school policymaking, this is not always the reality. In most inner cities, the school chief executive's tenure is so short that much of their projects are rarely fully developed. There are so many state laws and rules that the most a superintendent can do is play a small part in the larger drama.

If the Cleveland PSC had preemptive power, why didn't it just dominate the situation and not allow the mayor to carry out his structural changes? Aside from including the PSC leaders in the summits and skillfully building support before going public with a policy change, White was careful to avoid the perception that he was micromanaging the school system. He allowed CEO Byrd-Bennett to get the visibility and the credit for change. Taking a supportive role also facilitated relations with the PSC. The fact that the Cleveland PSC members were divided over elected board issues made mayoral encroachment less difficult.

Schisms are not uncommon among PSC members. Such PSCs are called *conflictual*. In conflictual public school cartels, internecine battles do occur and sometimes become public. This is often the case when a member is expelled or dismissed from the group (e.g., members of the old Cleveland elected board such as Stanley Tolliver and Gerald Henley). This is in contrast to *congruent* cartels. "Congruent public school cartels have accepted the notion of a unitary interest that transcends the particularistic needs of the interest groups they represent," (Rich 1997, 7). They stay together on public issues. This was not the case during Cleveland's elected-board era. The comportment of the appointed board has helped the image of system, an image that was in need of improvement.

Remember that Cleveland's school district constituencies may be limited to local voters, but its audience includes the state government and foundations (Wilson 1969). Cleveland is still a major city in Ohio, and candidates for statewide elections are not anxious to be seen as bashing a city that has mobilized its citizens around its failing schools. Besides, the district is not currently in receivership. The foundations have kept a watchful and supportive eye on the system. So far, things have gone relatively well. Does this mean the PSC has acquiesced to mayor-centered school reform?

On its face, state intervention and the institution of a mayoral-appointed board might be seen as a sign of a collapsing PSC, but a closer examination suggests that the Cleveland public school cartel is intact. The teachers union was a player in the organization of the summits and the school bond elections. The summits were discontinued with little fanfare and old stakeholders became ensconced in the new summit organization. Byrd-Bennett's reorganization of the district into regions did not change what happened in the classrooms. Teachers got a new contract and school activists did not blame the teachers union for the plight of the public schools. So far as the teachers were concerned, Cleveland's public schools remained the way they were before advent of the CEO/appointed board. A review of the PSC propositions supports the resiliency of the PSC.

PSC proposition #1 concerns the inevitability of one group dominating the board. Nevertheless, the appointed board is composed of five Black voting members, four white voting members, and two ex-officio, nonvoting members.[9] Although white students make up 20 percent of the public school population, white members occupy 44 percent of the board seats. There is no Hispanic representation on the board. The overrepresentation of whites on the board is not surprising if one considers the city's interest in maintaining white identification with the school district and its efforts to discourage "white flight." White board members can also be useful as "honest brokers" in the ongoing political conflict among Black leaders. White board members, as well as foundation leaders, can also be useful to in mayoral lobbying efforts with the state legislature.

According to PSC proposition #3, state funds tend to make the central PSC interest group, the teachers union, pay almost equal attention to state and city politics. The State of Ohio has been very involved in the funding of the Cleveland school system and currently provides 52.7 percent of the district's revenue (State 2000).[10] On the occasions when state receivership was necessary, the oversight regimes were not particularly onerous. Richard Boyd, the last state-appointed superintendent, was very helpful in returning the district to city control. Having a former mayor (George Voinovich) as governor may have also reduced potential tensions between the state department of education and the district.[11]

In sum, the Cleveland PSC has remained intact despite state and mayoral takeovers. A weak tax base and poor fiscal management exposed the PSC to state auditors and state-appointed administrators. In the latter case, the state-appointed superintendent must have been an embarrassment for the PSC. However, as noted earlier, superintendents are not part of the cartel and have limited impact on the system. At the same time that the state took control of the superintendency, school board elections continued as scheduled. Although the board's powers were certainly limited by state intervention, the PSC presumably maintained a level of control over the system. Specifically, it was during this period that the $13.5 million operating levy was passed, generating additional funds for the school district. The teachers union was able to negotiate new contracts throughout the takeovers. The central office remained intact until the arrival of CEO Byrd-Bennett. Although reduced in size, its staff has apparently adapted to the high-profile management style of the new CEO. Yet the polls show a continuing low level of confidence in the school system. A survey of Clevelanders by the Triad Research Group identified an increase in the percentage of people who perceive the schools as excellent or good from 11 percent in 1996 to 25 percent in 1999 (Clevelanders 1999). However, those are not exactly good numbers. The rest of the survey also suggests that parents wanted higher standards and that they felt welcome at the schools. This may mean the mayoral takeover has moved the school survey numbers along, albeit at a glacier-like pace.

More important than attitude surveys is the history of voting behavior on school levies. The Cleveland PSC has supported these levies but voters have not always followed their lead. In the recent bond campaign, the public wanted assurances that the money would be spent wisely. This concern explains Mayor White's decision to establish a twenty-three-member Bond Accountability Commission before the successful May 8, 2001, vote. This commission will oversee spending and hold regular public meetings. Simply put, the district needs more public trust in order to raise more money. The success of the 2001 bond issue and levy suggests that school officials are achieving that goal.[12] The election yielded a $335 million bond issue and a $46 million maintenance levy, with a $500 million state match for school facilities. With a strong turnout in the predominantly Black east side wards, 60 percent of voters approved the bond issue. However, a new levy will not change the power relations within the system because the PSC is more of a political, rather than a financial, nexus.

Despite all of the praise for the work of the CEO, attitudes toward the mayor-centered reform have not changed. A 2000 *Plain Dealer* poll showed 80 percent of Clevelanders wanted to end White's control of the schools (Stephens and Frolik 2000; van Lier 2001). A poll taken in November 2001, but released in 2002, showed 41 percent wanted the board members appointed by the mayor. Mayor Campbell stated her preference to retain the present system. Byrd-Bennett has stated that she will not work for an elected board, and the November 2001 poll showed her with 64 percent approval rating (Okoben 2002a).[13] She took the lead in the fight to retain the mayoral appointed board (Okoben 2002b) and received a mandate from the voters to retain the current governance structure.

Predictably, the Cleveland school district still looks like any innercity school system. The conditions that incubate and nurture a PSC are still in place. The disinvestment in the city explains a part of the plight of its schools. Between 1950 and 1990 the city lost thousands of manufacturing jobs. Manufacturing jobs in Cleveland peaked in 1969, and the decline in such jobs contributed to the mass exodus of residents to the suburbs and outlying areas (Stuart 1978). Cleveland became a classic case of disinvestment in a Rust Belt city (Swanstrom 1985). The social pathologies associated with unemployment and poverty is exacerbated (Chow 1992). For example, the increased number of single-parent households, crime and drug abuse has made the job of the schools even more challenging.

Former mayor White's efforts to reverse the city's fiscal predicament and turn the city schools around achieved only partial success. The school budget still accounts for too large a portion of the city's employment base. In 1999–2000, the Cleveland operating school budget was $583 million. The district is one of the largest employers in Cleveland with 9,217 employees, 4,796 of whom are teachers. This finding supports PSC proposition number one: school budgets become an important part of the city economy as a result of deindustrialization. The inevitable consequence of a weak economy is the continuing fiscal teetering of the school district.

Most of the district's fiscal problems can be traced to using property tax as a primary source of revenue. A declining tax base left school budgets with several fiscal shortfalls.[14] The disparities among suburban and urban (and rural) districts have been challenged in the courts.[15] In a 4–3 ruling the Ohio Supreme Court ruled in *DeRolph v. State (1997)* that the state's system of funding schools was constitutional, but that the state must spend more to rectify disparities between the rich and poor districts. The court did not specify a deadline for rectifying the disparities, but it did indicate that it will become involved with education funding if any of the districts that filed the original suit request such action. Until a more equitable funding formula is negotiated, the Cleveland schools will remain largely dependent on a limited tax base for funding their schools.

The Cleveland school district has been on a fiscal roller coaster for decades. In 1981, the district was placed under financial receivership for three years. The State of Ohio then established the Cleveland Education

Fund to help stabilize the district. However, the city could not stay out of debt, so in 1991, and again in 1992, the state made short-term loans to the city to prevent another receivership. The loans were for $44 million and $75 million, respectively. In 1994, the voters expressed their dissatisfaction with the district by voting against a school levy.

By 1996, the district was in fiscal hot water again, as it faced a $152 million deficit. It was obvious to state officials that the district was a cauldron of fiscal mismanagement. The state auditor declared a fiscal emergency and placed the district under the supervision of a Financial Planning and Supervisory Commission. The voters responded with a $13.5 mills operating levy that generated $67 million annually, and was the first approved in twenty-six years. Since the levy's passage and the mayor's takeover of the schools, the district has reached financial stability with a cumulative surplus of approximately $158 million. Despite this fiscal recovery, there are numerous areas where improvements in the schools still remain necessary. This is why the recently approved bond issue and its maintenance levy are so important.

The 2001 bond issue victory also highlights a more perplexing problem facing the schools, that is, the changing political demographics of Cleveland. Black voters on the east side overwhelmingly supported the levy, but voters on the predominately white west side were less supportive. This was consistent with previous levy votes. Nevertheless, CEO Byrd-Bennett spent considerable time explaining the need for the bond issue in west side communities and framing the issue as a vote for all of Cleveland's children. As a result, the west side opposition was less strident than in previous times. This does not mean, however, that race is disappearing as a significant factor in the city's school politics.

Race as a Factor in School Reform

Race continues to be a factor in school reform because of the high percentage of Black children in the Cleveland public schools. School reform has become a racial progress issue. Who gets what, when and how is a very salient school policy issue for the African American community. For many low-income inner city parents, effective schools are seen as escape portals for their children. They want change and will accept a structural transformation if it means improved public schools. For African American teachers and school administrators, the entire public school reform process is often regarded as an assault on professional autonomy. Like any professionals, they are leery of lay encroachment.

The school demographics are changing faster than the overall population. Although African Americans represent 51 percent of the city's population of 478,403, African American voters have needed white voters' support to pass school levies or bond issues. Although the white population continues to decline, it is still a factor in school-specific initiatives.

The growing population advantage of the Black community sometimes masks class and ideological cleavages. Black voters and Black leaders do not always agree. Former Mayor White was not universally admired in the Black community. Among a few Blacks he was even known as "White Mike." This moniker was the result of the concessions he made to the predominately white business community. It can also be traced to his first race against George Forbes. Forbes received 90 percent of his support from Blacks. White received only 30 percent of his support from the Black community, and 90 percent of the white vote. Clearly, there remains some fallout from that race.[16] In addition, there were power brokers in the Black community who routinely challenged White on issues such as the end of the desegregation order, the legality of the transition to mayoral control of the schools, and the levy initiatives. Three such individuals — Councilwoman Fanny Lewis, attorney Stanley Toliver, and George Forbes, now with the NAACP — were vocal critics of the former mayor. Despite the political differences within the Black community, Blacks are still the largest racial or ethnic group among Cleveland's adult population. They cannot be safely ignored in any future school-related election.

With the election of Jane Campbell, a white woman, new dynamics now animate school politics. So far, she has continued the White reform initiatives. Retaining Byrd-Bennett was a master stoke in term of her transition to office. It is not clear what Campbell plans to do about the schools. The fact that the teachers union endorsed her so quickly suggests they know her views and believe they have little to fear. However, the leadership in the Black community has apparently taken a wait-and-see attitude toward the new mayor.

Summary

There are several lessons to learn from using citywide summits as a vehicle for public school reform. First, laymen are at a disadvantage when afforded an opportunity to compete with professionals for control of a citywide school agenda. The professionals can simply refuse to engage them on pedagogical issues or terminate the meeting, which is what happened in Cleveland. Lacking continuity between summits, a new agenda was created at each meeting. Several of the recommendations of the summits were never implemented. Since there was no survey of attendee expectations and reactions to the summits, it is difficult to explain why they kept attending the assemblies without a discernible change in school policy. The PSC is notorious for creating reports, binding them in attractive covers, and ignoring them. Second, the professionals saw the summits as an opportunity to showcase their leadership skills. It was as though parents and school activists were ignored, as if the assemblies were operating with parallel agendas. Third, the abrupt termination of the citywide summits also suggests that they had served their purpose, and the mayor realized, or was convinced, that he needed a tightly organized, and full-time group to promote the new mayor-centered structural reforms. The relative ease with which Mayor White's structural reforms were accepted benefited from his initially taking a cooperative approach and then buffering his later confrontational tactics with softer rhetoric about "change." This hybrid approach suggests that cooperative and confrontational approaches are not mutually exclusive. This type of public cooperation among stakeholders brought a lot of attention to the schools and mobilized much-needed external support for reform (e.g. the success of the 2001 bond levy).

In terms of the institutional realities, the Cleveland school system is still struggling to overcome its history and precarious fiscal situation. This situation is not self-correcting, and requires the state of Ohio to legislate a new and more equitable system of funding for the schools. If the state legislators thought that giving the mayor control over the board would allow them to fiscally disengage from the system, they were wrong. Our review suggests that the district's fiscal dependency on the state may increase, not decrease.

Our review also highlights the importance of images to the success of mobilizing the public. Because former mayor White and his appointed CEO, Barbara Bryd-Bennett, were at the apex of this mayor-centered approach to school reform, all eyes were on the two personalities. The fact that the former mayor eschewed micromanaging the school system helped Byrd-Bennett's efforts to revitalize and modernize the administrative structure of the district. This constitutes a dramatic shift in White's strategy of getting very involved before the takeover and then keeping "an appropriate mayoral distance" or letting the experts run the system after the takeover. Although the appointed school board members were watched closely, they were also careful not to generate any negative publicity. One member said, "We decided as a group not to behave as previous boards" (Hopkins 2001). City hall, the central office, and the board were able to present a united front for the levy campaign.

Although the 2001 bond victory was a triumph for the coalition of city hall and educational leaders, it did not necessarily follow that the

PSC would support the retention of the appointed board or that the Issue 14 bond coalition would stay together for the elected board referendum in 2002.[17] Nor did it mean the PSC had locked itself into the structural changes White instituted. Union President DeColibus has stated that teachers support the appointed board because they like CEO Byrd-Bennett. In July 2002, DeColibus endorsed the mayoral appointed board on behalf of the union. The endorsement was based on popularity of Bryd-Bennett and the belief that the then-present leaders "have done a good job and deserve a good grade" (DeColibus 2001).

In Cleveland's 2001 mayoral race, public school reform and the future structure of the school board were key issues. New mayor Jane Campbell has built a new relationship with the PSC. This new relationship got off to a good start after the Cleveland Teachers Union endorsed Campbell in the primary. Both Raymond Pierce, her opponent, and Campbell strongly supported extending mayoral control beyond 2002. Both also stated publicly that they would retain CEO Bryd-Bennett. The decision by Campbell to continue White's reforms speaks well for continuity. In any case, there are lessons to be learned from the White administration. Clearly, Campbell must avoid confusing the current truce between the PSC and city hall as a permanent governing coalition. The popularity and longevity of CEO Byrd-Bennett is a story in itself. After being warned by reporters that Cleveland politics is different than New York City politics, she survived White and was persuasive enough to retain the CEO structure in November 2002. By endorsing Campbell and her subsequent pledge to keep Byrd-Bennett, the union leadership in the PSC has begun creating a new working relationship with city hall.

Before the 2001 mayoral election, a poll found that 62 percent of respondents did not support the idea of mayoral control of the schools. Among west side residents the margin was 72 percent, 53 percent for east side residents. Black respondents were evenly divided on the issue of an appointed board (Okoben and Townsend 2001). This poll showed an increase in support for the appointed board (the 2000 polls showed that 80 percent opposed the idea). Proponents of an elected board faced an uphill battle without the support of the new mayor. The same campaign team that led the bond issue, the Committee for Cleveland's Children, worked diligently to retain the mayoral appointed board in the 2002 referendum. Ironically, the dissident Black leadership's argument that an appointed board is undemocratic and disenfranchises the Black community did not resonate with the voters. Having a white woman as mayor and a relatively popular Black women as CEO probably complicated the campaign for an elected board due to the racial and gender symbolism. The departure of Michael White may have taken some of the emotions out of the debate about who determines the make-up of the school board. Mayor Campbell is not part of the leadership rivalry in the Black community. As of this writing, she has not inherited any of the angst and hostility previously directed toward White. Regardless of the fact that the city will retain the mayoral appointed board, the survival of the PSC depends on whether it stays deeply engaged in all aspects of school policymaking. The leadership of the PSC works best when it anticipates and participates in changes in the political environment. As this review suggests, the PSC has served its members well.

Finally, the question of the efficacy of citywide public assemblies or summits as a vehicle for citizen mobilization and school reform remains open. Although the Cleveland case is instructive, it does not completely answer the question of whether an annual meeting of citizens can be useful to public school reformers. The idea of citizen-led school reform remains attractive, but is also fraught with problems. Almost thirty years ago, Professor James Riedel warned citizen participation advocates that "officially sponsored citizen participation tends to be co-optation rather than representation" (Riedel 1972, 212). The summit members were never outsiders because the mayor had organized the group. With the institutionalization of the Cleveland Summit on Education as an in-house advocacy group, the public became spectators in the mayor's ongoing reform efforts. What is striking about the summits is that there has been little or no outcry about the decision to discontinue citywide assemblies. It is also interesting that no new organization emerged as an alternative to the sponsored summits. Yet the more important question is whether Cleveland schools' future policy options will result in fundamental improvements in the academic performance of Cleveland schools. After all, this was the original purpose of the school reform effort.

Notes

1. The 1999/2000 graduation rate data comes from the Center for Urban School Collaboration, Cleveland State University. They have plotted declines in graduation rates for five years.

2. Leon Lawrence, Susan Leonard, Lawrence Lumpkin, and James Lumden.

3. We are suggesting this pattern can be observed in white-led cities, particularly those meeting the other conditions. Blacks in such cities seem to be more politicized than their counterparts in Black-led cities.

4. The NAACP board changed its vote and finally endorsed the bond issue.

5. The foundations include the George Gund Foundation, the Cleveland Foundation, the Martha Holden the Jennings Foundation, and the Joyce Foundation.

6. Although not the subject of this paper, 1996 was also the year Cleveland began participating in an experimental voucher program that provided tuition for parochial and private schools.

7. Interviews conducted between the summer of 2000 and the spring of 2002.

8. *Reed v. Rhodes*, 422 F. Supp. 708 (D. Ohio 1976).

9. The two ex-officio members represent their colleges, Cleveland State University and Cuyahoga Community College.

10. This figure is based on the 1998–1999 data, which includes desegregation monies.

11. In 1998 Voinovich was elected to the United States Senate.

12. We were reminded by one of the reviewers of this chapter that some of the activists in the bond campaign are potential contenders for building improvement contracts. If they are seen as major beneficiaries of bond issue, public trust may be lost once again.

13. A poll taken in 2001 found that Cleveland's east side gave Byrd-Bennett a seventy-six percent approval rating whereas the west side gave her a sixty-nine percent approval rating; see also Naymik 2001.

14. White's attempt to lure more business with tax abatements may have had perverse effects on schools funding; see Lewin 1997.

15. *DeRolph v. State*, 78 Ohio St. 3d 193 (1997).

16. Queue-jumping by a younger generation leader is rarely forgiven, see Rich, ed. 1996.

17. CEO Byrd Bennett agreed that there is no linkage between the bond victory nor was it a referendum on Mayor White (Byrd-Bennett 2001).

References

Abdulhaqq, Rashidah. 2001. Telephone interview by S. Chambers. 30 April.

Afi-Odelia, E. Scruggs. 1998. "What Works in New York May Not Work Here." *[Cleveland] Plain Dealer*, 25 November.

Bluestone, Barry, and Bennett Harrison. 1982. *The Deindustrialization of America: Plant Closings, Community Abandonment, and the Dismantling of Basic Industry.* New York: Basic Books.

Butler, Esther Monclova. 1997. "The Changing Role of the Cleveland Public School Board (1965–1995): Should Urban Public Governance Be Restructured?" Ph.D. diss., Cleveland State University.

Byrd-Bennett, Barbara. 2001. Telephone interview by W. Rich. 9 May.

Chow, Julian Chun-Chung. 1992. "The Changing Structure of Neighborhood Social Conditions in Cleveland Ohio, 1979–1989." Ph.D. diss., Case Western Reserve University.

The Cleveland Public Schools: A Commitment to Action, 1996–1997 Strategic Plan and School Community Covenant. 1996. Cleveland: City of Cleveland.

Clevelanders Expect Better Schools. 1999. Cleveland: Cleveland Summit on Education and Cleveland Initiative for Education.

Cohen, Adam. 1997. "City Boosters." *Time* 150 (18 August): 22–25.

Community Oversight Committee. 2000. *Report #2: 1999–2000*. Cleveland: Cleveland Municipal School District.

Council of Great City Schools. 2002. *Beating the Odds II: A City-by-City Analysis of Student Performance and Achievement Gaps on State Assessments*. Washington, D.C.: Council of Great City Schools.

DeColibus, Richard. 2001. Interview. 23 April.

Dempsey, Louise. 2000. Interview by S. Chambers. Cleveland-Marshall College of Law, Cleveland, 19 August.

Dondero, Grace M. 1993. "School-Based Management, Teachers' Decisional Participation Levels, School Effectiveness and Job Satisfaction." Ed.D. thesis, Fordham University.

Draper, Lawrence. 1996. "Mayor White Outlines His Plan to Save City Schools." *West Side Sun News*, 8 February.

Educating Cleveland Children. 2000. Cleveland: Cleveland Municipal School District.

Galster, George. 1990. "White Flight from Racially Integrated Neighborhood in the 1970s: The Cleveland Experience." *Urban Studies* 27:385–99.

Good, Barbara. 1999. "A Dozen Years of School Reform." *Catalyst*.

Hess, Fredrick. 1998. *Spinning Wheels: The Politics of Urban School Reform*. Washington, D.C.: Brookings Institution Press.

Hopkins, Miggy. 2001. Telephone interview by W. Rich. 30 April.

Ingram, Booker T. 1991. "Citizen Participation: Analysis of Parent Participation in District Advisory's Councils in Three Ohio School Districts." Ph.D. diss., Ohio State University.

Jones, Patrice. 1996. "Summit on School Woes Draws 2,000." *[Cleveland] Plain Dealer*, 28 January.

Lewin, Tamar. 1997. "Tax Breaks Squeeze Schools in Cleveland." *New York Times*, 21 May.

Mahtesian, Charles. 1996. "Handing the Schools to City Hall." *Governing* 10(1):36–40.

"Memorandum of Understanding between Cleveland Schools Superintendent Richard Boyd and Cleveland Mayor Michael R. White." 1996. Cleveland Municipal School District, 11 March.

Miller, Carol Poh, and Robert A. Wheeler. 1997. *Cleveland: A Concise History, 1796–1996*. Cleveland: Case Western Reserve University.

Minter, Steven. 2001. Telephone interview by W. Rich. 1 May.

"NAACP Opposes School Levy." 2001. Associated Press, 6 April. Lexis Nexis Academic.

Naymik, Mark. 2001. "Voters Like School Boss, Split on Police Chief." *[Cleveland] Plain Dealer*, 4 November.

Okoben, Janet. 2002a. "Cleveland Divided on School Control, 41% Back Mayor Running, Poll Finds." *[Cleveland]Plain Dealer*, 17 May.

———. 2002b. "Mayoral Control of Schools OK'd." *[Cleveland] Plain Dealer*, 6 November.

Okoben, Janet, and Angela Townsend. 2001. "Mayor's School Control Unpopular." *[Cleveland] Plain Dealer*, 27 September.

Orfield, Gary, and John T. Yun. 1999. "Resegregation in American Schools." Cambridge: The Civil Rights Project, Harvard University.

Orr, Marion. 1999. *Black Social Capital: The Politics of School Reform in Baltimore. 1986–1998.* Lawrence: University Press of Kansas.

Pinkney, Arnold. 2000. Interview by S. Chambers. Cleveland. 15 August.

Rich, Wilbur. 1996. *Black Mayors and School Politics.* New York: Garland Publishing.

———. 1997. "Defining and Measuring Public School Cartels." Paper presented at the Eastern Educational Research Association, Milton Head, S.C., 19 February.

———, ed. 1996. *The Politics of Minority Coalitions.* Westport, Conn: Praeger.

Richards, Marva. 2001. Telephone interview by W. Rich. 3 May.

Riedel, James. 1972. "Citizen Participation: Myth and Realities." *Public Administration Review,* May/June, 212.

Schmitt, Eric. 2001. "Segregation Growing among U.S. Children." *New York Times,* 6 May.

Sheridan, Chris. 2000. "Is Barbara Byrd-Bennett's Plan to Turn Around Cleveland Schools Making the Grade?" *[Cleveland] Plain Dealer,* 6 February.

Sleeper, Jim. "The End of the Rainbow: America's Changing Urban Politics." *New Republic* 209 (November): 20–25.

Spector, Kaye. 2000. "The Future of Deseg Programs." *Catalyst,* March/April, 1.

Smith, Hilton. 2001. Telephone interview by W. Rich. 9 May.

Smith, Helen. 1997. "Who Will Run the Schools?" *[Cleveland] Plain Dealer,* 21 October.

State of Ohio. 2000. School District Report. Columbus.

Stephens, Scott. 1995a. "17 Seek Cleveland School Board Seats." *[Cleveland] Plain Dealer,* 25 August.

———. 1995b. "More Mayors Taking Control of Schools." *[Cleveland] Plain Dealer,* 29 October.

Stephens, Scott, and Joe Frolik. 2000. "Few Want Schools in White's Hands." *[Cleveland] Plain Dealer,* 29 May.

Stone, Clarence N., ed. 1998. *Changing Urban Education.* Lawrence: University Press of Kansas.

Stone, Clarence N., et al. 2001. *Building Civic Capacity: The Politics of Performing Urban Schools.* Lawrence: University Press of Kansas.

Stuart, Reginald. 1978. "Cleveland Crisis a Decade in Making." *New York Times,* 22 December.

Summit on Education, 1990 Report to the Community. 1990. Cleveland Summit.

Summit on Education, 1993 Report to the Community. 1993. Cleveland Summit.

Swanstrom, Todd. 1985. *The Crisis of Growth Politics.* Philadelphia: Temple University Press.

Toliver, Stanley. 2000. Interview. 30 September.

van Lier, Piet. 2001. "District to Ask for Levy." *Catalyst,* January/February.

Vision 21: An Action Plan for the 21st Century. 1993. Cleveland: Cleveland
Public Schools.

White, Michael. 1997. "Appointed CEO Will Focus on Children, Improvements." *[Cleveland] Plain* Dealer, 21 October.

Wilson, James Q. 1969. "The Mayors v. the Cities." *The Public Interest* 16
(summer).

Chapter Seven ————————————

Washington, D.C.: Race, Issue Definition, and School Board Restructuring.

JEFFREY R. HENIG

ON JUNE 27, 2000, voters in the District of Columbia (DC) narrowly approved a referendum radically altering the structure and mode of selection of the city's school board and giving the mayor a much stronger formal role in school governance. As in several other large cities that have moved in that direction, the rationale for restructuring was framed in terms of efficiency, effectiveness, and accountability—symbolically powerful values that have no a priori grounding in particular parties or demographic groups. The proposal to use institutional reform to jump-start systemic education reform was introduced into a community that had good reason to believe that something needed to be done.[1]

Given the racial and economic composition of the student population, the prime beneficiaries of any successful reform effort would inevitably be low-income, minority groups, primarily African American.[2] Most of the city's public and corporate elites—both black and white—supported the change. Yet the vote on the referendum closely followed racial lines, with African Americans much more likely than whites to oppose the change. The day after the referendum, Mayor Anthony Williams "acknowledged . . . that the outcome of the school board ballot issue has highlighted the District's racial divide and put him at odds once more with the city's African American community" (Cottman and Woodlee 2000).

This paper explores the DC school board restructuring campaign and its immediate aftermath. What arguments were offered for and against the change? What individuals and groups took leadership roles on either side? How and why did a proposal that was framed in racially neutral and generally apolitical terms stimulate such a racially defined cleavage? Why, in particular, did African Americans, the purported beneficiaries, mobilize so emphatically against the proposal? Was this a case of misguided loyalties to familiar institutions? Was it an idiosyncratic consequence of parochial issues and personalities? Or did historical experience and current conditions combine to inject objectively meaningful racial content into issues that mistakenly are portrayed in racially neutral terms?

I argue that the sharp racial cleavage exhibited in the vote had deep roots, some running through soil peculiar to the District's political history, some anchored in racial perceptions, loyalties, and calculations that are shared by other central cities with large minority populations (Henig, et al. 1999). It is too early to judge whether the long-term consequences of the structural reform will redound to the benefit of the schools or to particular subsets of the local community. But I will suggest that the racial polarization that became activated around the "birth" of this more mayor-centric system put it at greater risk, at least initially. While some of that framing may have been opportunistic, and some could have been avoided by more sensitive tactics on the reformers' part, I will also suggest that this was *not* just a case of image manipulation. Shifting power from ward-based elected boards toward at-large and mayorally appointed boards, like other formal changes designed to increase the role of mayors, has objective consequences beyond those associated with efficiency and managerial accountability. It also reconstitutes constituencies in ways that can affect the racial distribution of power, whether so intended or not. It is possible that the cleavages pricked by the structural change will prove short-lived, and that the mayor will be able to translate school reform successes into a broader coalition of support, but the near-term result has been some erosion in the mayor's political base, not only among grassroots elements that opposed the change, but also among elite interests concerned that he has not used his new powers quickly, surely, or effectively enough.

Two Puzzles

The results of the June 2000 referendum in the District present two puzzles. The first: Why was this so close? The second: Why were the results so racially skewed?

On the face of it, the proposal to restructure the school board would appear to have been a shoo-in for strong public support. The perception that the District's school system was dysfunctional was broadly shared, and almost no one regarded the sitting school board as a credible source for positive reform.[3] The referendum came in the wake of several years during which the oversight of the school system had been in the hands of the congressionally appointed Financial Control Board.[4] The Control Board's mixed record and high-handed manner sparked some sympathy, and mild nostalgia, for the largely disempowered elected board, but a very public and messy internal battle among the school board members during the summer of 1999 sharply reminded citizens of that body's weaknesses.

Elites in the city were unusually united in supporting the proposal for structural reform. Heading into the year 2000, the only disagreements appeared to be over the specific form that a restructured board would take. After an initial period of jousting, Mayor Williams proposed that he appoint a five-member board, while the superintendent and various city council members offered less dramatic proposals to make the board incrementally smaller and increase the proportion elected at-large instead of by ward. Most key elite groups lined up however behind a proposal for a "hybrid" board, including both appointed and elected members. Mayor Williams became the primary advocate, but he was supported by the majority of the council, including his major rivals in the prior election.[5] The Control Board supported the referendum. So did both the *Washington Post* and the *Washington Times*, rivals for local circulation with editorial stances often at odds. The business community, through such organizational vehicles as the chamber of commerce, the Greater Washington Board of Trade, and Federal City Council, was strongly in support.[6]

Although there was some opposition from interested stakeholders, most notably the citywide federation of PTAs,[7] these were out-gunned in financial and organizational terms. The primary fund-raising and organizational vehicle for supporters of the referendum was the New School Leadership Committee. During the period leading up to and immediately following the vote, it raised sixty-six times as much money as did the opposition group, the "Just Vote No! Campaign." The largest single donor to the pro-referendum group, a businessperson from Northern Virginia, gave $40,000, three other donors gave each $20,000 or more. In contrast, the two biggest donors to the opposition campaign gave $500 apiece (in one case $300 was "in-kind") and no one else gave more than $100.[8]

The involvement of the umbrella PTA organization did not indicate solid resistance among grassroots parent activists. Historically, the most visible, and arguably most effective organization representing parents in DC, has been Parents United, initially formed in 1980 as a vehicle for expressing the need to increase funding for the deteriorating public school system. The proposed referendum forced a split among some of the traditional leaders of Parents United, with some taking public positions on either side of the issue, and one of its most visible accepting the leadership position in the pro-referendum group. As explained later, the opposition within both the PTA group and subgroups within Parents United rested mostly on fears that this was another in a series of erosions of local democratic control.

On the face of it the two sides squaring off against one another were not sharply defined by race. At the elite level—where the issue was framed and most of the media attention focused—whites and Blacks could be found in prominent positions on each side of the issue. The mayor, probably the lead spokesperson for the restructuring, is African American. Within the "Just Vote No! campaign" organization, the president, treasurer, and largest single donor were white. A key February 7, 2000, DC Council vote in favor of the compromise proposal that became the core of the referendum revealed a split—the vote was narrowly approved by a 7–6 margin. But as Table 7.1 indicates, this cleavage had no discernible grounding in race, nor, for that matter, in party, socioeconomic status, or whether elected by ward or at-large. Black and white members of the council split as evenly as possible. From the two wards with majority white populations (Wards 2 and 3), one council member voted for, and one against, the measure. The representatives of the two wards with the highest percentage of residents who were Black also split their votes.

Despite the powerful elite push in favor of the referendum, it squeaked by with a margin of only 843 votes, just over 2 percent of the 40,179 cast. Despite the apparently biracial character of the coalitions at the elite level, at the voter level sharp racial cleavages were revealed. Figure 7.1 illustrates this by plotting the "pro" vote in relation to the racial composition of 140 precincts in the city.[9] The simple correlation between the two variables is an extraordinarily high $-.95$ (p $<$ 0001).

In the District, as in the United States generally, race and class are closely intertwined.[10] But compared to most cities, the District's African American population includes a sizable middle-class to upper-class component. Table 7.2 distinguishes precincts according to both race and economic class. This provides some insight into the extent to which the pattern in Figure 1 might reflect class rather than race. Four types of precincts are identified: (1) predominantly white precincts had populations that are majority white in a city in which the average precinct had fewer than 30 percent white in 1990; (2) mixed race precincts were predominantly nonwhite but fewer than 90 percent black; (3) Black high-income precincts had 90 percent or more black residents and median household incomes above the citywide median of $30,350; and (4) Black low-income precincts were at least 90 percent black and had median household incomes below the citywide median.

The results suggest that both race and class are related to the degree of support for the June 2000 referendum, but the sharper gradient appears to be associated with race. Precincts with more than 50 percent white populations supported the move to a partly appointed board at rates two-and-a-half times as great as did predominantly Black pre-

TABLE 7.1
Council Vote to Approve Partially Appointed School Board, February 17, 2000

	Panel A: Individual Members' Characteristics and Vote				
	Members' race	Electoral District	Party	% Black in Electoral Base, 1998	Median Household Income in Electoral Base, 1998
For					
Chavous	B	Ward 7	D	96.2	$32,952
Cropp	B	At-large	D	62.3	$43,011
Jarvis	B	Ward 4	D	79.4	$45,826
Ambrose	W	Ward 6	D	67.8	$45,999
Evans	W	Ward 2	D	31.1	$46,732
Graham	W	Ward 1	D	52.1	$38,533
Schwartz	W	At-large	R	62.3	$43,011
Against					
Allen	B	Ward 8	D	89.6	$27,937
Brazil	B	At-large	D	62.3	$43,011
Catania	W	At-large	R	62.3	$43,011
Mendelsohn	W	At-large	D	62.3	$43,011
Orange	B	Ward 5	D	87.7	$34,902
Patterson	W	Ward 3	D	4.5	$79,832

	Panel B: Vote Aggregated by Councilmember Characteristics				
	% Black	% Ward-based	% Dem.	Mean % Black in Electoral Base	Mean Income Electoral Base
For	43%	71%	86%	64%	$42,295
Against	50%	50%	83%	61%	$45,284

Source: Data on race and income prepared by the D.C. Office of Planning/ State Data Center.
<http://www.dclibrary.org/sdc/>. Council member characteristics coded by author.

cincts. Black high-income precincts had college graduation and home-ownership rates more than twice as high as the Black low-income precincts, but only one out of three voters in those precincts supported the referendum, just five percent higher than in the Black low-income precincts. One might reasonably argue that Black low-income precincts had the most at stake in the vote. Not only do they include the highest proportion of school-age children (Table 7.2), but their inhabitants also are least likely to be able to afford private school as an alternative to

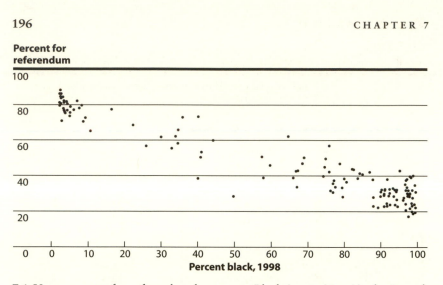

7.1 Voter support for referendum by percent Black in precinct. (Author's analysis of precinct results provided by District of Columbia, Board of Elections and Ethics)

unsatisfactory public schools. Yet support for the referendum was by far the lowest in these precincts, while it was highest in those with the fewest children and the greatest financial capacity to afford private schools.

Table 7.2 reveals something else as well. The proposal to restructure the school board passed overwhelmingly in the 39 precincts with a majority white population, but failed, on average, in each of the three other types, comprising 101 precincts. Why did the proposal pass despite this narrow geographic base of support? Part of the explanation lies in the large size of the victory margin in those 39 precincts, but another key element has to do with turnout rates, as indicated in Table 7.3. Although residents in predominantly white precincts were the least likely to have a direct stake in the public school system, their turnout rate was substantially higher than in the rest of city; turnout rates in the 44 Black low-income precincts were much lower. This is especially notable in light of the fact that this was a special election. No other offices or issues were on the ballot, so citizens with limited interest in schools had little direct incentive to go to the polls. Table 7.3 also shows what would have happened if all precincts had experienced the same turnout rate; applying the citywide average to the actual proportional votes in the precincts suggests that the referendum would have failed by a margin (1,866 votes) more than twice as large as the margin (843 votes) by which it was passed.

TABLE 7.2
Referendum Support by Precinct Type

	Precinct Type			
Precinct Type	Predom. White	Racially Mixed	Black, High	Black, Low
No. of precincts	(39)	(38)	(19)	(44)
Avg. % Black	12.5	74.6	94.3	97.4
Avg. % Hispanic	6.4	8.1	2.1	1.4
Avg. % College Grads	68.7	27.7	20.3	8.9
Avg, % Owner Occupied	47.2	36.0	67.5	32.0
Avg. % age 5–17 years	7.5	14.5	13.9	18.5
Avg. % FOR referendum	75.8	42.0	33.4	28.6

Source: Author's analysis of precinct results provided by District of Columbia, Board of Elections and Ehics.

Accounting for the Puzzles

Why did the proposal to restructure the school board, giving the mayor the power to appoint four of nine members, generate such a strong and racially patterned opposition? Why did it do so, especially, in light of the facts that elite support was bi-racial, that the mayor himself is African American, that the sitting elected board was widely disdained, that the pre-existing electoral structure frequently produced boards with substantial minorities of white members, and that the city council, which is elected on a mixed ward and at-large basis very similar to that of the pre-existing school board, had recently produced the first majority white council in the city's post–Home Rule history?

Political scientists recently have emphasized the important role that issue definition can play in the process of policy change. During periods of relative policy stability, policy subsystems like education can become dominated by a small group of insiders who benefit from the status quo and promulgate a vision of the scope and nature of relevant problems that legitimizes existing programs and policies and paints other approaches as infeasible, inefficient, counter-productive, and possibly dangerous. Challengers occasionally can unseat subsystem elites, and pave the way for nonincremental policy change by generating new framings of issue definitions that broaden and reshape the scope of political conflict (Baumgartner and Jones 1993).

I suggest that the evolution of the school board restructuring in the District of Columbia might best be understood as a case of dueling issue definitions. Two alternative "narratives" were available to account for

TABLE 7.3
"What If" All Precincts Turned Out at the Citywide Average Rate?

Precinct Type	Predom. White	Racially Mixed	Black, High	Black, Low
No. of precincts	(39)	(38)	(19)	(44)
Avg. registered voters (2000)	2488	2480	2364	2177
Avg. % turnout	14.6	12.2	13.4	7.9
Total votes cast FOR	10460	4917	2078	2188
Total votes cast AGAINST	3288	6354	3939	5214
Votes FOR IF turnout at citywide precinct mean (11.7%)	8520	4749	1773	3187
Votes AGAINST IF turnout at city mean	2724	6131	3398	7842
Result IF:				
FOR	18,229	47.6%		
AGAINST	20,095	52.4%		

Source: Author's analysis of precinct results provided by District of Columbia, Board of Elections and Ethics.

the nature and extent of the problems in DC public schools and to focus attention on a particular solution set. Both provide accounts of the cause of the District's education problems, and both provide accounts of why some solutions are more likely to work than others. In one version, race plays little or no role; the account centers on governance structures. In the other, race is the dominant subtext. Both narratives are intellectually coherent and consistent with generally known facts. But in the referendum campaign each resonated differently with different audiences. Which version rang truer depended on listeners' deeply held notions about how the world works, as well as their assessment of the trustworthiness of the speaker. Factors like personal economic success and length of time living in DC affected those preconceptions, but perhaps the surest and most consistent predictors related to political experience interpreted through a racial lens.

Setting the Table for Mayor-centric School Reform: The "A-racial" Narrative

The District of Columbia was once regarded as having a model urban school system (Diner 1982), but in the 1950s and 1960s things began to unravel, and by the late 1980s[11] it was apparent to most observers that a crisis had developed. Racially based events such as the Supreme Court's 1954 decision in *Brown v. Board of Education* and the riots following the assassination of Martin Luther King in 1968 undoubtedly delivered major shocks to the system,[12] but according to the "a-racial" narrative those impacts were absorbed more than three decades ago. In contrast, the school governance structure that Congress created for the District during this same period was not a one-time traumatic event, but a deeply engrained institutional parameter that continued to shape decision making for as long as it was in place.

Public schools were the first responsibility that Congress returned to local authority. DC's elected school board took office in 1969. Congress did not establish an elected mayor and council until 1973. The new school board structure imposed by Congress comprised eight members elected by ward and three members elected at-large.[13] The board was established as an independent agency, but without authority to raise its own revenue.

During the late 1960s and well into the 1970s, the school board was the setting for some highly visible political maneuvering and antics. Initially, the school board was the only major elected local office in the District, so it became the logical focal point for individuals and groups seeking to build a base for political power. The board's meetings often were raucous — occasionally requiring the presence of police to restore order — and its reputation for responsible governance was low (Diner 1982). Most education experts recommend that school boards focus their efforts on broad local policy decisions (Danzberger, Kirst, et al. 1992; Century Foundation 1992), but DC's early school board seemed at times to swerve in two wildly different directions. Like many urban school boards, the District's new elected board quickly allowed itself to get drawn into micromanaging, not hesitating to call upon individual principals to reassign teachers, accept a particular student transfer, or hire this-or-that acquaintance. More idiosyncratically, some early board members also took it upon themselves to address global policy issues as well. In one well-publicized case, a board member ran up costly phone bills in a misguided attempt to insert himself as a mediator who could resolve tensions between the United States and Cuba.

Although some observers wrung their hands over the situation, the problem stream did not develop into a torrent for quite some time. During the 1970s and early 1980s, two strong and capable superintendents[14] managed to keep the system functioning, and even to spur optimistic reports. Indeed, during that era, the prime worry, at least within the media and among local elites, was that the elected school board would make life unendurable for the superintendent.

Few thought the schools were working as well as they should be during this period, but neither was there a sense that matters were wildly out-of-control. Among those with a reform bent, various policy solutions were afloat in what Kingdon (1995) refers to as the "primordial soup." For the most part, these focused on such conventional notions as "more money,"[15] "better curriculum,"[16] or "better people," meaning efforts to elect more responsible members to the school board.

But the 1990s saw problems come to a head, and with the increased evidence of unsatisfactory school performance came a growing belief on the part of some local stakeholders that the problems went beyond questions related to the personalities or capabilities of the individuals in key offices. By the end of the 1980s, the elected school board included a reform-minded contingent and, while the quality and orientation of the board members were uneven, they were, for the most part, dedicated individuals who were committed to making the schools work for DC youth. Several members had come up through the ranks of the grassroots reform movement with backing from Parents United, the preeminent community voice on school issues. In 1989, the business community, which had been only an occasional and behind-the-scenes player in school issues since Congress established the local governance structure,[17] became more directly involved as the foundation of a new reform organization, The Committee on Public Education (COPE), which played a role in recruiting a new superintendent and setting a reform agenda. The new superintendent, Franklin Smith, was greeted with high expectations. He had had apparent successes as superintendent in Dayton, Ohio, and soon outlined a reform strategy for the District that incorporated many of the same ideas that had worked in Dayton and that were on the list of initiatives favored by COPE.[18]

When conditions failed to improve as swiftly and dramatically as reformers had hoped, some blamed Smith for being too timid or ineffectual, but the notion also began to germinate that the problems went beyond individuals, and could be found in the organizational and governance structure itself. One key structural element that was regarded as problematic included the separation of responsibility for raising revenue from responsibility for spending it. Such separation of authority struck some as irrational and an inevitable source of conflict and gamesmanship. School officials could evade responsibility by claiming that the council was shortchanging them; council members and the mayors could claim that the money they made available was not being used wisely or well. A second structural element that increasingly was seen as problematic was the large and heavily ward-based membership of the school board. Even when the individuals elected were reform-minded and well intentioned, the ward structure created strong incentives for them to interpret their role as constituent service, rather than broad policy setting. As later characterized in a *Washington Post* report chronicling the school system's downward cycle into crisis: "As divided and self-indulgent board members played ward politics and squabbled over office space, staff, and job perks, SAT scores plummeted, . . . almost half of all high school students dropped out . . . classrooms went without textbooks, and cafeteria food was terrible."[19]

Such a structural analysis was appealing to the business sector.[20] Corporations have few of the formal divisions of power characteristic of American government, and the notion that the problems could be solved by making the school system operate more like a business was hard to resist. Such a structural analysis also appealed to those schooled in public administration, where attention to organizational lines of authority and formal responsibilities is well ingrained (see Meier this volume). That is especially so for analysts without a deep familiarity with the local community and the ways past attempts to graft institutional arrangements onto local political culture and experience have misfired. In the normal course of events, the business and analytic sectors alone would rarely have the clout to act on their definition of the problem without first engaging in long and challenging efforts to draw others to their point of view. But the District's unique situation vis-à-vis Congress[21] provided leverage for more dramatic change.

On November 15, 1996, three days after it had declared that DC public schools deserved a grade of "an absolute F," the Financial Control Board that had been appointed by Congress to bring the city back from the brink of bankruptcy took dramatic action.[22] Declaring that, "in virtually every area, and for every grade level, the system has failed to provide our children with a quality education and safe environment in which to learn," the Control Board fired Superintendent Smith, hired retired Lt. Gen. Julius W. Becton Jr. to replace him, reduced the elected school board to primarily an advisory body, and transferred most of its authority to a new board of trustees.[23]

The story of the Control Board's adventures and misadventures in addressing the city's school problems is too intricate to relate here.[24] Most relevant is the fact that the Control Board's involvement was tied to a target date—June 2000—for returning authority to local control. By late 1998, at least one reform-minded group was paying attention to that date. DC Appleseed Center for Law and Justice, a relatively new nonpartisan nonprofit public interest organization "dedicated to addressing systemic management and financial problems of the District of Columbia," announced: "Because the Control Board is expected to return the schools to local control over the next two years, the District must consider how to improve its system of school governance, which in the past has failed to promote sound education for the District's children" (Appleseed Center, 1998).

Its resulting report, released in September 1999, served as a catalyst to the discussions that produced the June 2000 referendum. Appleseed's focus on systemic reform and its base of expertise — its director was a lawyer and many of its board and volunteers came from local law and accounting firms — drew it naturally toward problems and solutions related to formal institutions of governance. The authors speculated that structural change might previously have been kept off the agenda due to "concern that the disruptive effects of changing the governance structure would outweigh any benefits" and concluded that the "transition we are now in, however, provides a unique opportunity to consider and implement real, meaningful changes without unnecessarily disturbing the status quo" (Appleseed Center 1999).

The Appleseed report recommended reducing the size of the school board and also sketched out several alternative models by which a restructured board might be selected. If members were to continue to be elected, it recommended moving away from ward-based elections to a "hybrid" model that combined ward-based (or some other subcity unit) primaries followed by a citywide run-off election including the top two vote-getters from each of the ward elections. This structure, it argued, would ensure representation from all sections of the city,[25] fostering the kind of involvement and sense of connection promoted by ward-based campaigns. But, since all members would ultimately be selected at-large, it would "temper the micromanagement that accompanies the demand for constituent services" and create "an incentive for all board members to work together on issues common to all schools in the system" (22–23).

The report went on to discuss the advantages that might come from moving either fully or partially to an appointed board, with the "hallmark" of all appointed boards being "mayoral control." Mayoral control, it suggested, "can translate into a governance system with several strengths, including concentrated accountability, and the likelihood that public education will be coordinated with other government services for youth" (24). Recognizing that each structural change has advantages and disadvantages, and that there is "no silver bullet," Appleseed stopped short of endorsing any single change, with the exception of its strong recommendation that the size of the board be reduced.

Although the Appleseed report did not penetrate the consciousness of most DC residents, key stakeholders, including the business community, the Mayor, council leaders, and the control board, absorbed it and reacted accordingly.[26] During the months leading up to the report's release, local headlines had been filled with news of an embarrassing internal squabble among the sitting school board members (Strauss and Wilgoren 2000). One contingent attempted to unseat the sitting board president, charging her with various improprieties. For a body that hoped to convince Congress, the Control Board, and the public that it was up to the task of regaining its authority to run the schools, this publicity was devastating. According to those involved, this context gave the Appleseed report added momentum.

In the aftermath, Kevin Chavous, chair of the DC council's committee on education, announced a proposal to move to a smaller board of education — a partial response to the Appleseed report — but to have all of the positions continue to be elected. Mayor Williams initially had been reluctant to thrust himself into the forefront on this issue. Prompted by the Chavous proposal, though, and, according to some observers also prodded by the local business community, he announced in January that such timid measures would not suffice. Once in the game, Mayor Williams jumped in with both feet, coming out in support of an even smaller board that would be entirely appointed by the mayor. Going even further, he also argued that the mayor should select the superintendent of schools. Some on the council were willing to side with him, but others, including Chavous, argued that it was critical to maintain the democratic element provided by elections.

By now, the planned return of authority to the local board in June 2000 was looming, and the pressure was great to get agreement on a measure that could be submitted to the voters. Various compromise efforts were floated, mostly involving a mix of elected and appointed members, and retaining the board's authority to select the superintendent.[27] But mistrust between the mayor and the council led to a stalemate that appeared to be heading to a resolution that would have given voters the chance to chose among several options, including leaving things as they stood. This was an outcome that the Control Board and its chair, Alice Rivlin, thought should be avoided at almost any cost, lest competing proposals spark a racially based backlash that could end up maintaining the status quo and delivering the mayor and the Control Board a costly and embarrassing defeat.[28] Through a combination of persuasion and power, the Control Board engineered a compromise, in mid-February, behind which the mayor and a slim majority of the council united. It was that proposal that went to the voters on June 27 2000 (Williams 2000).

Alternative Issue Definition: Race, Power, and School Politics

Residents of the District had another framing of the issue available to them, one that to many resonated more deeply because its elements were familiar and consistent with their personal and political experiences, as they had come to understand them. As with the "a-racial narrative" that helped many business elites and analysts put the specific case of DC schools into a conceptual focus familiar to them and consistent with their prior training and professional beliefs, this definition of the problem placed school reform within a preexisting frame of reference that incorporated a much broader range of policy and political issues. This alternative frame of reference, however, put race and power, not organizational structure, at center stage. The public education system had a special role in this narrative, but less as an instrument for educating children than as a historically significant platform for democratic control, political clout, jobs, and social status within the local Black community. Thus, the basic themes of this broad frame were not specific to the schools. From the standpoint of citizens inclined to credit this narrative, the battle over the school board structure was just the latest installment in a long-running tale.

Although its historical roots run further back, this narrative, like the a-racial one, also has a natural beginning with the transition of Home Rule powers from Congress to the District. Prior to Home Rule, white segregationists from the Deep South controlled the House and U.S. Senate committees that oversaw DC affairs. Influential members of Congress, like South Carolina's John McMillan, who chaired the House DC Committee, displayed no sympathy for the desires of the District's Black residents. According to Charles W. Harris, "McMillan ruled the city as a kind of czar. He was viewed as the holder of ultimate authority over almost every aspect of life in the city."[29] Leaders of DC's black community accused the Congress of racism or, at the very least, of failing to appreciate the needs of a large urban Black population. Hence, as the Black Power movement swept the nation in the 1960s, there was broad resentment of Congress among DC's African American citizens and leaders.

Moreover, African Americans in D.C., like those in other major cities, were galvanized by the Civil Rights movement and mobilized by the civil disturbances that occurred in DC in 1968 and engulfed hundreds of communities from Gary, Indiana, to Los Angeles, California. Not satisfied with their "colonial" status, Blacks leaders demanded more authority in running DC government. In other cities, local black politicians learned over time how to play the game of electoral politics — how to balance the need to mobilize supporters with clear goals and big promises against the practical need to broker deals and make compromises with other powerful actors. Lacking both local electoral channels and formal representation in Congress, Black leaders in DC had a different type of training ground. Those who sought to build local support could champion idealistic positions and paint Congress as the enemy. Because they had no real power to get things done, their supporters

were unlikely to hold them responsible if these strategies failed to garner tangible gains.[30]

The institution of Home Rule removed the lid from a long-simmering
pressure cooker, and the transition to Black control of local offices was
immediate. In 1968, DC residents were allowed for the first time in the
twentieth century to elect representatives to a local governing body, the
school board.[31] After Congress passed the first Home Rule charter in
1974, DC voters elected the sitting appointed mayor, Walter Washington, as the District's first elected mayor in 1975.

Although the three decades between the initiation of the elected
school board and the June 2000 vote were eventful, only a few critical
points need to be highlighted here. During the first half of the post-
Home Rule era, Congress adopted a relatively "hands off" orientation
toward local governance. Individual members occasionally insisted
upon imposing pet concerns upon the local leaders, and broad constraints like the ban on taxing the income of suburban commuters remained firmly in place, but the sensitive racial environment made an
overwhelmingly white Congress wary of meddling too visibly as long as
the predominantly African American city appeared to be functioning
reasonably well under its elected leaders. This gave local leaders room
to gain and maintain control over the machinery of government (both
in the schools and elsewhere), including control over jobs and contracts.
One of the early acts of the elected school board was to fire the sitting
superintendent and appoint the first Black to the post; since 1970, each
of the nine superintendents has been Black.[32] Even during this era of
good feelings, however, minor skirmishes and Republican rhetoric kept
DC residents aware of Congress' continued formal power, and that, in
turn, meant that the emotional and symbolic legacy that associated
Congress with white control and elected local leaders with Black rights
and Black power, did not dissipate.

Indeed, a powerful strain in political thinking at the grassroots community level held that congressional acceptance of local Black rule was
a temporary concession, born in the turmoil of the sixties, and that the
"white power structure" (loosely incorporating Congress, the local
business community, remaining white residents, and the Maryland and
Virginia suburbs) had a long-term commitment and strategy to regain
political control. In local parlance, this is known as *The Plan*. As one
local activist told the *Washington Post*, "The general design for DC is
one of white takeover. . . . I think that this [changing the school board]
follows that general design and plan" (Blum 2000).

Perhaps reflecting the growing strength of conservative Republicans
in Congress and the White House, the 1980s and 1990s saw a reasser-

tion of federal muscle in the District, which had the effect of picking at
the wound of racial resentment. One major instance was the prosecu-
tion and imprisonment of Marion Barry for the use of crack cocaine.
Although Barry's personal transgressions were anathema to many in
DC's African American community, his powerful role as a symbol of
local Black power and authority led many residents and leaders—even
within the religious community, where the moral issues might have run
closer to the nerve—to view this as a racially motivated vendetta with
the goal of deflating a powerful opponent. Outside observers and interested parties in Congress expressed puzzlement at this tenacious local
loyalty to Barry, and many wrote it off as a reflexive and ill-considered
substitution of symbolic politics for the city's objective interests. From
the standpoint of the local loyalists, however, it was the outsiders who
were relying on symbols to interpret local events; in their minds it was
the demonizing of Barry—whom they knew to be a highly knowledgeable and often effective leader, able to build and sustain coalitions,
make pragmatic compromises, and demonstrate mastery of the technical aspects of local finance and administration—that was detached from
reality.

    A second seminal event was Congress' formation of the Financial
Control Board in 1995; a third was the subsequent Control Board takeover of DC's public schools. The fact that the Control Board itself was
racially mixed and initially headed by an African American had almost
no bearing at all on how it was perceived within the race-based narrative. In the view of many grassroots Washingtonians, the Control Board,
as an extension of Congress, *was white*. In the context of local political
history, as they understood it, some DC residents believed that the fiscal
problems and education problems cited by Congress were fictionalized
rationalizations for the long-anticipated reassertion of white control.
Others conceded that the problems were real, but believed that their
root causes lay in the constraints on democracy that Congress had never
relinquished, especially its prohibition of any income tax to be levied on
the Maryland and Virginia residents who worked within the city. Still
others conceded that the problems were real, and that local officials
bore a large share of the responsibility for them, but were nonetheless
convinced that racial factors accounted for the fact that similar problems in other cities did not lead Congress to trample on local democracy, and deny those citizens the opportunity to clean their own house.

    Finally, growing evidence of economic reinvestment and the increas-
ing size of the District's white population as a proportion of the total,
fueled a background hum of concern about gentrification, and its potential to unseat African Americans from the positions of power and dis-
place them from their neighborhoods. The white share of DC's popula-

tion dropped sharply from 1950 (65 percent) to 1970 (28 percent), but has been creeping upward (to 31 percent in 2000). That upward creep has been attributable entirely to the decline in total population — in particular the heavy movement to the suburbs by African Americans — but in the past few years there have been some indications of a small net increase in whites. When juxtaposed with other visible or symbolic changes, such as the selective gentrification of certain neighborhoods, and the election in 1998 of the first majority-white DC Council, this demographic trend has added fuel to concerns about *The Plan.*

Against this backdrop, the proposal to restructure the school board was seen by many as a direct assault on one of the institutions most closely associated with local democracy and African American control. And the referendum vote could be portrayed — and was explicitly portrayed by some — as a critical battle for those hoping to forestall a permanent transition of power from African Americans with deep roots in the local community to white newcomers, the business community, meddling outsiders, and their Black functionaries. While Mayor Williams declared that the referendum should be seen as a chance to "vote 'yes' for accountability, leadership, and change," one opponent argued that what those supporting the referendum "really favor is taking responsibilities from the board of education and giving them to — surprise! — themselves." Another argued that the proposal "not only fails to identify a remedy to reported inadequacies of our school system, it seeks to invalidate the vote of D.C. citizens" (*Washington Post*, 2000).

Preexisting Frames of Reference, Relative Trust, and the Credibility of Competing Narratives

After a long hiatus, social scientists have renewed their attention to the ways in which variable aspects of human perception affect behavior by influencing the processing of information and arguments. The assumption of *perfect information*, a concept borrowed from economics, had marginalized such concerns. Among social psychologists, this revival is manifested by expanding research on the heuristics that individuals employ when making decisions under conditions of uncertainty.[33] Among scholars interested in American political behavior, the same orientation is evident in revived attention to the dynamics of political persuasion as it affects mass opinion.[34] Among students of public policy, it shows up as growing attention to issue definition and the intersection between *bounded rationality* and policy change.[35]

For the most part, this literature has concentrated on cognitive or emotive tendencies that are exhibited across individuals and groups.

Baumgartner and Jones (1993), for example, establish that the battle between policy innovators and subsystem elites may hinge on the credibility of competing issue definitions. Since partisans on both sides of an issue are committed to the narratives they bring to the battle, the crucial audience will tend to be third parties or mass publics who are neither deeply invested in the issue nor informed about its intricacies. But relatively little is known about the factors that may influence particular third parties or when mass publics will be receptive to a new way of looking at things.

Moreover, the factors that have been identified as likely to be important to the viability of competing issue definitions generate mixed predictions in the particular case of DC school reform. Theories of bounded rationality and political socialization seem to predict a strong resistance to change. Because humans are boundedly rational and can focus only on a small number of issue attributes at any one time, they are inclined to rely on familiar assumptions and heuristics, especially when their direct stake is limited, uncertainty is high, or key decisions are discrete one-time adventures that are not part of an ongoing "game."[36] The issue definition associated with the reigning subsystem should be especially protected due to the elites' capacity to control instruments of socialization. But theories of nonincremental policy change highlight the way critical events can lead to perceptual realignments (Kingdon 1995), and theories of paradigm shifts in the sciences suggest that reigning frameworks can succumb to an accretion of anomalous findings (Kuhn 1996).

In the case of the DC school board referendum, the existing institutions were buffered from serious local challenge by a widely shared issue definition that focused primary responsibility on external enemies (Congress, Control Board, white businesses, and suburban interests). Even when this issue definition acknowledged shortcomings in local governance, it attributed those to personal foibles of incumbents who should, accordingly, simply be replaced. But the series of blistering reviews of the system leading up to the Control Board takeover, the failures of reform-oriented board members and a reform superintendent (Franklin Smith), and the fact that the five-year takeover had robbed the preexisting system of some of the normal tools for self-maintenance,[37] appeared to open a large window of opportunity for the challengers. In this instance, moreover, the subsystem challengers' were elites in their own right (although normally not actors in this particular subsystem) and had access to tools of persuasion (the major media, scholarly research, funding for advertising and public relations) more impressive on their face than those that could be mounted by the education community.

Critical to the DC story are insights about why certain issue definitions and frames of reference appeal differently to different groups, particularly groups that are racially defined. Using survey data incorporating experimental variation of question framing, Cobb and Kuklinski (1997) find evidence that Black citizens interpret policy messages differently, depending on whether they believe the source of the message is white (Ted Kennedy or George Bush) or Black (Jesse Jackson or Clarence Thomas). Their conclusion that white and black citizens may hear different messages even when exposed to the same arguments can help account for the political dynamics in DC. But the fact that there were white and Black spokespeople on both sides of the issue meant that race alone could not be the decisive factor.

What drove events, in the final analysis, was not the relative weight of the conventional political weaponry both sides brought to bear, as measured in some common metric. Nor was it the objective power of the facts, as judged by an engaged and discerning public. The key, instead, appears to lie in the credibility and trustworthiness of the message and messengers as differently judged by different sectors of the audience. And, while the race of the listeners was a powerful determinant of response, the race of the messengers ultimately was less critical than the extent to which their narrative aligned with familiar and compelling beliefs and the personal legitimacy they could claim by virtue of their own past records.

The reasons and analyses offered by proponents of reform were scrubbed clean of the racial and political history of the District.[38] This cool analytic framing of the issue was intellectually appealing to those highly schooled in such ways of thinking; symbolically appealing to those who accorded great respect to scholars, lawyers, and other claimants to relevant expertise; and emotionally appealing to those who hoped that wrenching issues of racial tension might be a thing of the past. In effect, this framing of the issue appealed disproportionately to the white community.[39] It also appealed to relative newcomers, both white and Black, personally unfamiliar with the historical particulars that this narrative excluded.

Black residents, particularly those who had grown up in the city, listened with a different set of ears and, also, to a large extent, to a different set of messengers. For them, a history of battles over local democracy and civil rights overwhelmed the specific elements of the school reform proposal. The school system was less important as an institution to prepare youth for work and college than as an institution that played both real and symbolic roles as a springboard for local self-rule and an important source of jobs and status within the Black community. Leaders with credibility included black ministers and others who had continually spoken out for DC statehood, and against congressional imposition of authority.[40] Against that background, the message of school reform associated with the Control Board was heard as one of racial disempowerment and the sacrifice of community-based jobs and institutions for the sake of corporate values (efficiency, lower taxes, managerial expertise). The interweaving of these various threads comes together clearly in the words of one Black parent leader who had a history of working within multiracial coalitions and was not normally quick to turn to race-based rhetoric. DC Black citizens, she told a reporter, "have no faith that white people will do what's necessary to help black children and parents in the schools. It wasn't the black community that came up with this issue. . . . Why should we believe it's in our best interest. . . . In the part of the city where people are worried about school closings, they don't want to see the white power structure get into the city. We don't want to feel like we're under somebody's heel. We don't know if we'll be listened to, and we think we won't"(Fears 2000).

That many of the messengers for reform, including the mayor, were themselves Black did not earn credibility for their arguments. This reflects two cross-cutting issues related to local roots and racial "style." The mayor is a relative newcomer to the District, as are many on his staff (many of whom are white). Many Black residents who were willing to support him in his 1998 election bid retain a "wait-and-see" stance about whether he warrants a long-term commitment of their loyalty and trust. Moreover, the "button-down" style of the mayor and his staff is regarded skeptically by some who questioned whether he "is black enough" to lead the city (Jenkins 1999). As one activist from the poorest and most predominantly Black precinct in the city put it, "The mayor's administration is made up of people who are white or people that are Black with more degrees than a thermometer" (Cottman and Woodlee 2000).

After the Change: Do Contested Structures Win Over the Doubters?

Variable perceptions, loyalties, and shared political experiences probably tell the main story of why the DC school board referendum was so close and so starkly racial in its pattern. But it would be a mistake to leave the story at that point. While they can be stubbornly persistent, subjective factors such as loyalties and shared beliefs can also be amenable to realignment and sharp change. Learned suspicion might fuel resistance to externally sponsored change in a context of uncertainty, but once the change is made — as it has now been in the District of Colum-

TABLE 7.4
Percent White in Public School Population vs. Total Population, Large Schools
Districts (100,000 +), 1990

	Predominantly White Pop.	Predominantly Nonwhite Pop.
Number of districts	(278)	(63)
1) % White: Total population	75.4	35.2
2) % White: School children	67.2	23.0
3) % White: Public school children	64.4	19.3
Ratio row 3/row 1	0.85	0.55

Source: U.S. Department of Education, National Center for Education Statistics. *School District Data Book for 1990 Census Data for 15,000 School Districts*; author's analysis.

bia — it is possible that experience could begin to win hearts and change minds. That could happen, for example, if the newly constituted school board managed to bring about a sharp decrease in dropout rates or clear improvements in standardized test scores and college attendance rates. Even if deeply rooted, the reticence that fueled the "no" vote could quickly fade, especially if such improvements clearly include the schools located in the least advantaged neighborhoods. If that becomes the case, the strategy of the structural reformers — to pull out all the stops to obtain a victory, even a narrow and divisive one — may prove to be both astute and in the long-term interest of the citizenry.

But lurking below the surface of competing issue definitions and symbolic politics are some objective consequences of institutional redesign that make a fairy-tale ending more problematic. Granting the mayor a stronger formal role in school governance means more than shifting authority into hands that may be more technically adept and less bound by the type of political constraints that tend to buffer the status quo. Shifting decision-making authority to a mayor, elected by the broad citizenry and accountable for the entire apparatus of local government, may empower a new constituency, one that may weigh public education lower on its agenda than did those traditionally moved to vote in school board elections, one that differs in race and class terms from the children who are the most immediate beneficiaries of educational reforms. As indicated in Table 7.4, the percentage of the general population that is nonwhite is considerably lower than it is for the school population, especially when one looks at public schools. And especially when one focuses on districts with substantial minority populations.

Regardless of their good intentions about meeting the needs of schools, then, mayors face constituencies that may pull them irrevocably to devote time and resources to competing priorities such as economic development, crime, and tax cuts. Elected school boards do not need to consider these competing priorities to nearly the same extent, and can serve as a more focused advocate for investment in the local schools. Regardless of their own race or ideological stance, mayors face constituencies that may make it difficult for them to redistribute resources, especially to target schools with large proportions of minority children. Elected school boards are subject to some of the same pressures to favor the more vocal and politically involved parents, but, especially when chosen by ward, they are likely to include at least some members with predominantly minority constituencies that mobilize around redistributory demands.

Adoption of mayor-centric governance structures, then, ultimately may generate real political pressures to reshape education reform in ways that emphasize efficiency, cost-cutting, and disproportionate attention to the needs of families who present the most credible threats of political retribution or suburban exit. Such tendencies may not be evident immediately after reform — while the forces that pushed structural reorganization onto the agenda retain the focus on schools that helped them push it onto the agenda initially — but they are more likely to show their face a year or two down the road, when the original reform coalitions lose their focus, and the competing demands on mayors and the public purse become more insistent.

While it is too soon to draw definitive conclusions, particularly about possible improvements in test scores and other educational outcome measures, the shift to a stronger formal mayoral role in the District of Columbia has failed to deliver the promised benefits as quickly and surely as some would have liked. Within a year it became apparent that the board was substantially overspending its budget — something it denied for months before finally acknowledging. Despite expectations that appointed and elected board members might constitute distinct and irreconcilable factions, on issues relating to funding the board has tended to speak in a relatively unified voice — and quite often that voice has been either implicitly or explicitly critical of the mayor's priorities. Shortly into its first year, the school board crossed swords publicly with the mayor, charging him with providing insufficient funding.

Anthony Williams retains considerable support based on his performance in handling the more routine tasks of urban governance — filling potholes, picking up garbage, and balancing the books. But public opinion polls indicate a sharp racial polarization in perceptions of his performance, with 73 percent of whites, but only 42 percent of blacks indicating that he "deserves to be reelected." The mayor attributes the poll results in part to political damage he suffered in the Black community due to his support for power to appoint the school board.

Rather than strengthening his reputation and electoral constituency, the mayor's involvement with the public school system so far seems to be an unambiguous liability. Asked to evaluate the mayor's performance on a list of twelve issues, all respondents (Black and white) gave Williams the worst scores for improving District public schools. Only 31 percent of respondents said he was doing either a "good" or "excellent" job; in contrast, 73 percent said he was doing well in improving the city's image and 60 percent indicated he was doing a "good" or "excellent" job at improving city services more generally (Timberg and Deane, 2002). While the *Washington Post* has generally been a strong supporter of the mayor, it has criticized him sharply for failing to come up with funds to maintain an aggressive summer school program. When Williams replaced a resigning school board member with a lesbian political activist, the *Post* interpreted that as a political ploy to build support in the gay community for his reelection bid — and a reneging on his promise to appoint only "the best qualified" candidates (*Washington Post* 2002).

Despite these "start-up" problems, Mayor Williams so far shows no signs of pushing school reform to the back burner. He admits that progress has been slower than he would like. "I'm not happy with the pace, but we're going to see the results now," he told the *Post* in June 2002. So far, however, his new responsibility for the schools has provided far more in political bruises than celebratory cheers. If the schools manage to make headway his support may well broaden. This is true whether or not school gains are attributable to his involvement, to other individuals, or to factors outside his orbit. If the school system falters, however, it is unlikely that he will be spared a goodly portion of the blame, even if it is other individuals or other factors that account for that failure. If that happens, future mayors and mayoral aspirants may be tempted to construct their electoral and governance coalitions around more malleable issues.

Notes

This chapter has benefited from suggestions from several sources. In addition to participants in the Russell Sage Foundation conference that gave birth to this edited volume, these include Lee Sigelman and Michele Moser of George Washington University and Jennifer Hochschild of Harvard University.

1. For example, on November 12, 1996, the financial control board appointed by Congress to bring Washington D.C. back from the brink of bankruptcy justified a takeover of the Washington schools based on the fact that the district deserved "an absolute F." In its report on *Children in Crisis: A Report on the Failure of D.C.'s Public Schools,* the control board declared, "In virtually every area, and for every grade level, the system has failed to provide our children

with a quality education and a safe environment in which to learn. . . . This failure is not of the students — for all students can succeed — but with the educationally and managerially bankrupt school system."

2. In the 1999/2000 school year, 85.2 percent of DC Public School System students were African American, 8.8 percent Hispanic, 1.6 percent Asian, and only 4.4 percent white. <http://www.k12.dc.us/dcps/data/data—frame.html> (3/9/01)

3. See, for example, Strauss and Wilgoren 1999. "'For 30 years, District residents have been pretty unhappy with the performance of the school board. Nobody ever says anything nice about it,' said Mary Levy, counsel for the education advocacy group Parents United."

4. The formal name for this body is The District of Columbia Financial Responsibility and Management Assistance Authority. I fall back, in this chapter, on the more colloquial "Control Board" label.

5. Kevin Chavous, who was his strongest challenger in the Democratic primary, and who by January 2000 was serving as chair of the council's committee dealing with education issues, and Carol Schwartz, his opponent in the general election.

6. Although the business leadership would have preferred the more radical proposal that Mayor Williams initially floated.

7. This organization, whose formal title is the DC Congress of Parents and Teachers, has only limited clout when it comes to affecting school policy.

8. Reports to the D.C. Office of Campaign Finance.

9. Racial composition is based on precinct breakdowns from the 1990 census. While there have been racial transitions in during the intervening years, the basic racial identity of precincts has been extraordinarily constant. I mapped census tract level estimates prepared by the DC State Data Center onto precinct boundaries in order to develop an estimate of precinct level racial characteristics at a time more proximate to the election. The correlation between that 1990 indicator and the official 1990 figures from the Bureau of the Census was .9811 ($p < .0001$).

10. The simple correlation between the percentage Black and the estimated median household income in the precincts, based on 1990 data, is -0.65 ($p < .0001$).

11. A reasonable point to date the public recognition of the problem is 1989, with the formation of the Committee on Public Education (COPE), a corporate initiated effort to form a broad-based reform coalition comprising business, civic leaders, and some educators and advocates.

12. Although decided alongside and on the same day as the more famous *Brown v. Board of Education*, the relevant case for D.C., actually was *Bolling v. Sharpe*. Unlike some southern jurisdictions, DC rapidly responded to the Court's order, immediately ending the dual system that had been in place (Henig 1997). In addition to *Brown*, the 1967 *Hobson v. Hanson* case, which successfully challenged racially discriminatory academic tracking, can be seen as a second major judicial intervention that had serious consequences for the local public school system.

13. There also was one non-voting student member.

14. The two superintendents were Floretta Duke McKenzie and Vincent Reed.

15. This was the initial platform of Parents United. The group, in fact, originally called itself "Parents United for Full Public School Funding." The name change was partly attributable to the evolution of a broader organizational agenda.

16. As superintendent, for example, Vincent Reed initiated a major revision of the curriculum.

17. For a more extended discussion of the business role in DC schools see Henig et al. 1999.

18. Including such things as cutting the central bureaucracy, establishing local schools, "restructuring teams," instituting public school choice. (See Henig et al. 1999.)

19. 13 March 1999.

20. The chair of the DC Chamber of Commerce Political Action Committee wrote: "Finding better candidates for the school board won't make a difference. The problem is that the board is too large and too balkanized; it is also too leaderless and too disconnected from other city efforts to succeed. . . . Putting the mayor and D.C. City Council on the hook for appointments also will increase their accountability for board performance" (Bolden 2000).

21. The difference between DC and other school districts should not be overstated. In many respects, Congress plays a role in the District that is analogous to that played by state governments in other school systems. State governments can and have displaced local school authorities, and the movement for them to do so has been increasing. Where DC *is* different, though, is in the fact that its residents have no voting representatives in the higher legislative body, so their ability to assert influence is minimal and their disenfranchisement potentially complete.

22. David A. Vise and Sari Horwitz, "Control Board Blasts System as It Readies Takeover Plan," *Washington Post*, 13 November 1996.

23. David A. Vise, "D.C. Control Board Takes Charge of Public Schools," *Washington Post*, 16 November 1996.

24. Suffice it to say that both General Becton and his appointers found that the challenges were much greater than they might have imagined. General Becton resigned after only seventeen months in office, and Arlene Ackerman, whom the control board named to replace him, resigned in the summer of 2000.

25. Significantly, the analysis of the costs and benefits of ward versus at-large election included virtually no mention of race, despite the fact that residential segregation gives most DC wards clear racial identities that are well ingrained in local perception and public dialogue. When community activists speak of "Ward 3" they are saying "white"; when they speak of Wards 7 or 8, they are saying "low-income Black"; when they refer to Wards 4 or 5, they mean Black middle- or working-class. The Appleseed Report instead refers blandly to the fact that "populations in different communities may have somewhat divergent educational goals, and schools in each ward may face different challenges" (22). There is one brief allusion to racial cleavages: "Those elected under the hybrid

system have an incentive to bring resources to the schools in their wards and can help ensure that the concerns of a minority-populated ward are represented" (23). But in the one instance in which it moves from abstract notions of representation to a concrete illustration, it chooses to frame the matter in terms of the possibility that one ward might have "a much higher percentage of non-English speakers than do others" (23) rather than frame the issue more directly in terms of conflicts between whites and Blacks.

26. Interviews with key actors confirm this.

27. In mid-January 2000, the D.C. Council was considering five separate bills. The mildest proposed maintaining the 11-member board, but having the public at-large elect the board president instead of having the president selected by the board members themselves as was the existing practice. The most radical, sponsored by Ward 3 council member Kathy Patterson, would have instituted a five-member board, all appointed by the mayor, who also would have power to hire and fire the superintendent. This was similar to the proposal then favored by Mayor Williams, although his proposal stipulated that candidates for the board would be nominated by a citizens' committee and that the mayor's choice would have to be confirmed by the D.C. Council. Mathews and Wilgoren 2000.

28. Although she may not have appreciated its full impact, Rivlin appears to have been quite sensitive to the deep racial differences in perception that lay just below the surface of DC politics — more so than was the mayor who, despite the fact that he was an elected official, was a relatively recent migrant to the city who, moreover, believed that such sentiments clouded reason and ought not be permitted to distract him from doing what was "right."

29. Harris 1995.

30. Other local leaders, interested in near-term, albeit incremental, gains, learned the art of directly lobbying those who did hold the reins of formal power, unchecked by the need to submit their performance to a public electoral test.

31. During the early 19th century, residents elected a city council and, for a briefer period, a mayor. In 1871 Congress replaced the local structures with a territorial form of government under which residents elected a House of Delegates but not the governor or other key local officers, which were appointed by the president. In 1874, prompted by local corruption and debt, Congress abolished established a community form of government with no locally elected members (See Harris 1995).

32. The nine includes the last three — Julius Becton, Arlene Ackerman, and Paul Vance — who were selected by the Control Board rather than the elected board it had temporarily displaced.

33. For an overview see Kahneman and Tversky 2000.

34. For instance, Sniderman, Brody, and Tetlock 1991; Kuklinski and Hurley 1994; Cobb and Kuklinski 1997.

35. For example: Baumgartner and Jones 1993; Rochefort and Cobb 1994; Jones 1995.

36. In an iterated game, individuals would have a greater incentive to invest in learning more about the issue and probing the competing issue definitions

more thoroughly. On the role of uncertainty and aversion to risk see, for example, Kahneman and Tversky 2000.

37. Such as control over budgets, jobs and patronage, and the power of inertia to give an edge to the status quo.

38. To some extent deliberately so. Race is widely regarded as a potent and potentially destabilizing force in DC politics; both white and Black elites devote considerable effort to avoiding language and actions that might stir the pot of racial polarization (Henig et al. 1999).

39. D.C. has an unusually highly educated African American population when compared to other cities or states, but its white population is disproportionately highly educated as well. In 1990, 36 percent of Black residents 25 or older had completed at least some college; the comparable figure for whites was 87 percent.

40. The precinct-level correlation between the percent of voters opposed to the June 2000 referendum and the percent who voted in favor of a Statehood Initiative twenty years earlier is .79 (p < .0001).

References

Appleseed Center. 1998. *1998 In Review: School Governance*. Washington, D.C.: DC Appleseed Center.

———. 1999. *Reforming the D.C. Board of Election: A Building Block for Better Public Schools*. Washington, D.C.: DC Appleseed Center.

Baumgartner, F. R., and B. D. Jones. 1993. *Agendas and Instability in American Politics*. Chicago: University of Chicago Press.

Blum, J. 2000. "D.C. Votes Revealing Old Divide." *Washington Post*, 30 October.

Bolden, A. S. 2000. Letters to the Editor. *Washington Post*, 19 June.

Century Foundation. 1992. *Facing the Challenge: Report of the Task Force on School Governance*. New York: Century Foundation Press.

Cobb, M. D., and J. H. Kuklinski. 1997. "Changing Minds: Political Arguments and Political Persuasion." *American Journal of Political Science* 41(4):88–121.

Cottman, M. H., and Y. Woodlee. 2000. "Mayor Sees Racial Divide in Vote." *Washington Post*, 18 June.

Danzberger, J. P., M. W. Kirst, et al. 1992. *Governing Public Schools: New Times, New Requirements*. Washington, D.C.: Institute for Educational Leadership.

Diner, S. J. 1982. *Crisis of Confidence: The Reputation of Washington's Public Schools in the Twentieth Century*. Washington, D.C.: University of District of Columbia.

Fears, D. 2000. "2 Voters, 2 Views across the District's Racial Divide." *Washington Post*, 9 July.

Harris, C. W. 1995. *Congress and the Governance of the Nation's Capital*. Washington, D.C.: Georgetown University Press.

Henig, J. R. 1997. "Patterns of School-Level Racial Change in D.C. in the Wake of *Brown*: Perceptual Legacies of Desegregation." *PS: Political Science and Politics* 30(3):448–53.

Henig, J. R., R. C. Hula, M. Orr, and D. S. Pedescleaux. 1999. *The Color of School Reform.* Princeton, N.J.: Princeton University Press.

Jenkins, A. 1999. "Black Enough? Some People Wonder Whether D.C.'s New Mayor Really Is. Here's One of Them." *Washington Post,* 17 January.

Jones, B. D. 1995. *Reconceiving Decision-Making in Democratic Politics: Attention, Choice, and Public Policy.* Chicago: University of Chicago Press.

Kahneman, D., and A. Tversky, eds. 2000. *Choices, Values, and Frames.* London: Cambridge University Press; New York: Russell Sage Foundation.

Kingdon, J. W. 1995. *Agendas, Alternatives, and Public Policies.* Boston, Little, Brown & Company.

Kuhn, T. S. 1996. *The Structure of Scientific Revolutions.* 3d ed. Chicago: University of Chicago Press.

Kuklinski, J. H., and N. L. Hurley. 1994. "On Hearing and Interpreting Political Messages: A Cautionary Tale of Citizen Cue-Taking." *Journal of Politics* 56(3):729–51.

Mathews, J., and D. Wilgoren. 2000. "A Model for D.C.'s Schools?" *Washington Post,* 14 January.

Rochefort, D. A., and R. W. Cobb, eds. 1994. *The Politics of Problem Definition: Shaping the Policy Agenda.* Lawrence: University Press of Kansas.

Sniderman, P. M., R. A. Brody, and P. E. Tetlock 1991. *Reasoning and Choice.* New York: Cambridge University Press.

Strauss, V., and D. Wilgoren. 1999. "The D.C. School Board, Troubled Still." *Washington Post,* 25 July.

Timberg, C., and J. Blum. 2002. "D.C. Mayor Restless for School Gains." *Washington Post,* 6 June.

Timberg, C., and C. Deane. 2002. "Williams Losing Support of Blacks." *Washington Post,* 26 May.

Washington Post. 2000. Letters to the editor. 19 June.

———. 2002. "Grading the Mayor on Schools." 4 June.

Williams, V. 2000. "D.C. School 'Hybrid' Approved." *Washington Post.*

Zaller, J. R. 1992. *The Nature and Origin of Mass Opinion.* New York: Cambridge University Press.

Part 3

THEORETICAL PERSPECTIVES

Chapter Eight

Structure, Politics, and Policy: The Logic of Mayoral Control

KENNETH J. MEIER

A DEEP-SEATED American belief is that we can solve fundamental problems of politics, policy, race, class, etc. by manipulating governing structures (Seidman 1997). A naïve political science (Weingast and Marshall 1988; Elster 1989) and economics (Williamson 1985) literature contends that institutional structures are simply efforts to generate efficiency, minimize transactions costs, and solve problems. A more realist approach (Knight 1992) holds that institutional structures are established and altered to create and protect political biases: in short, all structures benefit some interests and harm others. This chapter examines the six case studies from the viewpoint of structural change. I will first present the formal a priori logic on greater mayoral control over the public school system, that is, how and why it should work. The second section will then note the types of biases that greater mayoral control is likely to engender. The third section will use the case studies to demonstrate why structural reforms, in practice, might produce outcomes different from the theoretical predictions. The final section probes the relationship between structural reform and the performance of urban educational systems.

The Formal Logic of Mayoral Control

Within the full range of school districts in the United States, the six cities studied are structural outliers. The overwhelming majority of school districts in the United States are independent, with elected school boards that possess the power to levy taxes (within the limits of state law). In such districts mayors have no formal control over the school district, and their informal influence is limited by norms presuming the "nonpolitical" nature of education. Larger districts, particularly in the Rust Belt, frequently deviate from a purely independent structure to incorporate some degree of mayoral control. Quite clearly in the six districts covered here and other major urban school districts, mayoral control is a variable rather than a constant. Mayors vary in their appointment powers relative to the board, their control over the school district's budget, their formal control over top level administrators, and their interest in education policy.

In theory, greater mayoral control will affect three aspects of school district governance. It should centralize accountability, broaden the constituency concerned with education, and reduce the extent of micromanagement. Each merits discussion.

Centralizing Accountability

Efforts to increase mayoral control over school districts attempt to centralize accountability, moving it from a multi-member school board and superintendent to the mayor. Centralizing accountability simplifies the voters' task: one and only person is responsible for the state of the schools. Without such centralization, school board members can blame each other or the superintendent for failing to deliver positive results. Some might consider such arrangements more democratic, but mayoral control also eliminates some other forms of democratic control by focusing exclusively on "overhead democracy" (Redford 1969). School systems can also be democratic from the bottom up (rather than the top down); school board members represent constituents, and even school administrators and teachers can represent parents and others directly.[1]

Centralizing accountability also facilitates creating a governing coalition. Every chief executive of a school district needs to put together a governing coalition among school board members, administrators, and other stakeholders. Dissension among board members makes a governing coalition more difficult to maintain and is perceived to undercut efforts to improve urban schools. Because the mayor already represents a voting majority and can appoint school board members, a mayor faces fewer barriers to creating a governing coalition than does a superintendent. A mayor-dominated school district, however, does not automatically solve the problem of creating a governing coalition. A governing coalition, for example, was not established in Boston, Massachusetts, until 1995, three years after the structural reform (Portz this volume). Similarly, the Chicago mayor has always had substantial authority over the public schools, but until recently declined to exercise that authority to create a governing coalition for school policy (Shipps this volume).

Centralized authority should also make it easier for a school district to coordinate with other units of government. In theory, unified control will allow for easier and better cooperation between the school district and other city departments. Given the wide array of factors that affect school performance, including the local economy, crime, and service delivery patterns, the school district should find it easier to get on the agenda of other city agencies. In addition, city governments probably have better developed capacities to deal with other governmental units at the state and federal levels; lobbying these governments should be second nature. The school district, in such a situation, can use the expertise of the city in terms of intergovernmental actions.

Broaden the Constituencies

The shift from a more traditional school district structure to a mayor-dominant structure alters constituencies in two ways. First, school board members no longer represent districts; appointment by the mayor means the board represents the broader constituency that elected the mayor.[2] Second, the executive focal point is the mayor, rather than the superintendent. The career patterns for superintendents and mayors have different implications for governing a school district. Superintendents in large urban districts serve an average of two-and-a-half years (*Urban Educator* May 2001, 1), less than a single mayoral term. The career pattern of superintendents is to move from district to district, in effect leaving their constituents behind. Mayors, in contrast, take their constituents with them when they move to higher office since their new electoral district quite likely encompasses their city (Stein 1990, 86–7). A mayor's constituency relationships, therefore, are longer term than those of a school superintendent.

The constituencies of the mayor and the superintendent or school board also differ in other ways. Turnout is higher in mayoral elections, and with higher turnout the electorate is likely to be less well-informed. One result might be that the mayor's race will become a referendum on school performance, thus motivating the mayor to respond in popular, but not especially productive, ways. Simplistic solutions rather than policies designed to address the complexities of educational problems are possible under such circumstances.

The constituency relationships, as well as the differences in tenure, mean that mayors can have longer term time frames than superintendents. This longer time frame, in theory, means that mayors can avoid the policy churn phenomenon that affects many urban school systems (Hess 1999). Linking the mayor and the superintendent, however, could also add an additional factor to the high level of superintendent turnover. A new mayor would quite likely replace a superintendent, contracts notwithstanding (e.g., Barbara Byrd-Bennett in Cleveland).

Specialization: Pros and Cons

Superintendents are trained education specialists. Mayors are, by definition, generalists. In normal circumstances, a specialist would be preferred over a generalist as the primary policy maker. At the same time
the reform perspective identifies micromanagement as a potentially serious problem, particularly if authority is split between the superintendent and the school board. Because mayors are generalists they should
be accustomed to delegation and thus less inclined to micromanage. In
short, the centralization perspective views the dangers of micromanagement as a greater problem than lack of expertise.

In formal terms, therefore, an increase in mayoral control is designed
to create clearer accountability, an emphasis on longer term results, and
less micromanagement. This structural reform, however, takes place
within several trends in urban education policy that create both opportunities and constraints for the mayor. First, the role of state governments in public education has increased dramatically with states contributing a higher percentage of overall funding, setting higher standards,
creating statewide accountability systems, and, in some cases, centralizing finances (Elmore et al. 1996). With this increased role has come a
greater willingness of state officials to intervene in local school district
affairs. Second, the six case studies show that school districts are a major source of jobs, particularly middle-class jobs, in declining Rust Belt
cities. For some, protecting these jobs is the first priority. Third, race
remains a dominant urban issue and, for many, the central issue of education policy. Governing coalitions and policy disputes often are racially
polarized. Fourth, these changes take place within a national education
agenda that links quality education to economic development and competitiveness. Two key policy instruments in this national agenda are
higher standards and standardized tests. As a result, mayors, are likely
to focus on these instruments and have a narrower view of education
than a school board that may be interested in representation, equity,
specialized curriculum, and other similar issues.

Structural Changes and Politics

The most direct effect of increasing mayor control should be on the
politics of education policy (policy impacts are likely to be less direct).
The key constituency changes from the ward-based constituencies of
school board members to the citywide constituency of the mayor. This
change places a premium on majority (viewed in a numerical sense)

representation over minority representation. As such, this change has implications similar to changes from single member districts to at-large elections (Engstrom and McDonald 1981; Meier, England and Stewart 1989; Meier and Stewart 1991) and to the adoption of the initiative and referendum (Gamble 1997).

The distributional consequences of such changes should be obvious. Politics is how racial and ethnic minorities are able to get their issues on the educational policy agenda (see Meier and Stewart 1991). Politics in many cases, then, determines policy. To the extent that mayoral control limits or cuts off one or more avenues of access to either the agenda or policy makers, some groups are likely to benefit by the process and others harmed. The Chicago case (Shipps, this volume) clearly demonstrates how the burdens of change and testing have been levied on the African American population, which is not part of mayor Daley's coalition, and not on the Latino population, which is.

Distributional consequences need to be distinguished from symbolic consequences. Appointed boards tend to be highly representative in terms of race and ethnicity (Robinson, England and Meier 1985). At the same time, the mayor can carefully select board members to limit their substantive representation by tapping individuals who do not share values with the constituents that they symbolically represent. Polinard, Wrinkle, Longoria, and Binder's (1994) study of school boards and city councils before and after changes to district level representation demonstrates that district election systems produce different types of minority representatives, specifically individuals who reside in minority neighborhoods and act as delegates for their constituents. Mayoral control, therefore, has the potential of severing symbolic representation from substantive representation. Mayors in the six cities appear to favor a pattern of appointing Blacks and Latinos professionals rather than grassroots leaders. The school board will then look like, but not act for, the community.

The symbolic versus substantive representation distinction should also be applied to the "jobs issue," that is, to the school district as a source of employment. The mayoral control position holds that such concerns are symbolic, that jobs are merely patronage for various interests. In contrast, substantial literature demonstrates that the employment of minority teachers has significant consequences for the performance of minority students. Minority students attending schools with more minority teachers are less likely to be assigned to special education classes and more likely to gain access to gifted classes; they are less likely to be disciplined and more likely to graduate (Meier, England and Stewart 1989; Meier and Stewart 1991). These relationships are stronger for African American students than for Latino students. Similarly, minority students attending schools with more minority teachers are more likely to score higher on standardized tests; this relationship is stronger for Latino students than for African American students (Meier 1993; Meier and Stewart 1992; Meier et al. 2001). In short the employment of minority teachers is associated with positive educational consequences for minority students.[3]

Structural changes to permit greater mayoral control over schools also create obstacles that require resources to overcome. By creating essentially larger electoral constituencies (now one can only influence education policy by electing a different mayor rather than by electing a different school board member), money matters more. The average cost of an election campaign rises, and those with more resources are likely to gain better access, compared to those without resources. At the mayoral level, this change translates into greater business access. Rather than being one interest among many on educational policy, the business community becomes one of the most advantaged players in the educational policy arena.

The structural changes discussed in this volume affect the access of different groups of people in systematic ways. Access and politics quite clearly affects policy; both sides of the debate would accept that premise. Similar to the case study conclusions of Henig, Shipps, Rich and Chambers, mayoral control does not take politics out of educational policy, it merely lodges it in a different set of actors. Politics still determines who gets what, when and how.

Why the Formal Logic Might Not Hold in the Real World

Any structural design has to adjust to the situation where it is placed, the individuals who participate in the structure, the past history of the jurisdiction, and countless other factors. Efforts to create greater mayoral control over education are no exception to this rule. The individual case studies demonstrate that the logic of this structural reform can be altered in a variety of ways.

First, an increase in mayoral control has to adjust to the local politics. Henig demonstrates that conflict within the Black community is an important factor in adopting a policy of greater mayoral control. Past political disputes condition the current debate and obscure key issues. Linkages to the white community both in Washington, D.C., and Cleveland generated opposition in the African American community. As the Chicago case demonstrates, local factors can actually facilitate the structural change rather than retard it. Mayor Daley, with the Chicago tradition of strong executive action, had a relatively easy time exerting control over the school system. Any person recruited to be superintendent by the mayor must also face a similar political history.

Second, reformers assume goal congruence, that is, that everyone concerned is interested in improving education performance. While few would reject such a goal publicly, clearly individual actors also pursue other goals. The Cleveland reforms were pushed by a state government interested in resolving financial problems, rather than educational problems per se (Rich and Chambers, this volume). Governor Engler appeared to be concerned as much with breaking the teachers union as with any efforts to improve the Detroit Public Schools (see Mirel, this volume). To the extent that politicians are interested in goals other than education quality, mayoral reform is likely to produce results that do not affect the school system's performance or at best affect performance only indirectly, and with a higher probability of unintended consequences.

Third, simply changing a structure to provide for a larger constituency is no guarantee that the representative of that constituency is more competent — or less corrupt — than the representatives of the smaller constituency. Terry Moe (1989) argues that at the national level, the president's larger constituency will result in more attention to national interests and less to narrow, parochial interests. Moe's theoretical contention contrasts with the empirical reality that presidents frequently advocate narrow interests, knowing that they can be a source of political support. Just as presidents have advocated narrow interests at the national level, one can perceive similar possibilities at the local level. Historically, we have numerous examples of mayors found to be corrupt or incompetent including Marion Barry, Lee Alexander, and Richard J. Daley. Whether schools would have been better off with individuals like these in charge is a difficult position to maintain.[4] Because mayoral control centralizes authority with fewer checks on that authority, the skill and abilities of the mayor become paramount. Logic suggests that mayors, who win office based on electoral skills, might not have the optimal governing skills.

Fourth, mayor-dominated structures interact with the personalities and tactics of the specific mayor. William Schaefer in Baltimore, Maryland, for example, was unconcerned with issues of educational performance, as was Kevin White in Boston (Orr this volume, Portz this volume). Rich and Chambers (this volume) note that mayors might be either cooperative or conflictual in their approach to the public schools. A mayor who opts for conflict can cause a great deal of damage to a school system by opposing bond issues or advocating approaches that undercut public schools. Milwaukee Mayor John Norquist, for example, failed to support a major bond issue to rehabilitate the city's deteriorating schools and advocated vouchers rather than reform of the public schools (Hess 2002, 93). Opposition by powerful political figures such as a mayor could delay needed reform, even in a system where the mayor has no formal power over education. Thus, mayors, as a result, can be a source of greater problems rather than a source of solutions.

Fifth, in education policy, the sustained effort necessary to reform a school system might well be too long for any politician, even a politician with an extended time frame. Mirel (this volume; 1999) shows how the collapse of the Detroit school system took place over several decades. The drop in performance occurred concomitant with the exodus of the middle class to the suburbs, the decline in good paying jobs in inner cities, an erosion of urban social capital, the diversification of student populations, and several other deleterious demographic trends in major urban areas. The results of reforms, therefore, are likely to be incremental and slow in coming simply because the educational system faces such severe constraints. An estimate of ten years for turning around a school system is not unrealistic, especially if one considers the need to change such factors as crime, drug abuse, or a lack of jobs. Mayors, by definition, must move from issue to issue as the salience of various topics changes. Whether a mayor can maintain a high priority on education for sufficient time to generate measurable results remains an open question.

But Will It Work?

For a mayor-centered education reform to work, it will need to do more than simply provide more power for the mayor. The above discussion suggests that structural reform might not provide positive results for several reasons that are tied to either local situations or larger nonlocal forces. Greater mayoral control, by itself, accomplishes nothing in terms of educational reform. The reform must somehow also change how students are taught; that is, the change in structure needs to result in changes in education practice. For this to occur, two things need to happen.

First, the choices about education policy made by the mayor or the mayor's chief executive officer need to be good choices. Solutions to education problems are myriad. Many changes will work well in small scale trials, but getting these reforms to operate on sufficient scale to affect an entire school district is much more difficult (see Elmore 1996). Because mayors are not experts in education, the possibility always exists that the policies that they select will be less than optimal. The clear solution is for the mayor to select a chief educational officer/superintendent with expertise and administrative skills. The mayor would then provide the political support the superintendent needs to implement a reform agenda.[5] Unfortunately, politicians tend to favor magic bullets for education — simple solutions for complex problems. The probability of failure, therefore, is high.

Second, the policies adopted would need to be implemented. The gap between formal policies and policies at the street level, in this case the classroom, are often substantial. The implementation literature documents a large number of institutional, organizational, and human barriers to successful policy implementation (Mazmanian and Sabatier 1989; Goggin et al. 1990). School systems vest a great deal of autonomy in individual teachers; without their enthusiastic cooperation, successful implementation of any reform proposed by the mayor is highly problematic. In essence, the mayor needs to build up a trust relationship with teachers and school district employees, creating in the process social capital that can be invested in higher performance. The trust relationship is reciprocal, however, and must be reestablished whenever a new mayor is selected.

Conclusion

Structural changes that increase the mayor's control over urban school districts are intended to centralize accountability, limit the access of narrow constituencies, and reduce the level of micromanagement. Changes in structures, however, produce changes in politics; and these changes in politics are likely to produce important changes in public policy. Of particular interest are the distributional consequences of such changes which are likely to provide educational benefits for some at the expense of others.

In practice, structural reforms that provide the mayor greater influence in education policy can deviate from these theoretical expectations. The structural changes must adapt to local politics, consider the potential goal conflict among the various actors, realize that larger constituencies do not necessarily produce better decisions, understand how changes interact with the personalities of mayors, and deal with the long term nature of education reform. These practical limitations imply that structural reforms may not produce the benefits that advocates suggest. Exactly how these structural changes produce beneficial changes in the way that children are taught in the classrooms is also not clear. The relationship between greater mayoral control over education and the quality of education remains, at best, an empirical question, and at worst, a major risk.

Notes

1. The top-down or bottom-up forms of democracy come into conflict in a variety of other situations. The debate over the long (that is, for electing many state executives) versus the short ballot at the state level; the conflict between client participation and political control in the public administration literature; and the conflict between decentralized poverty programs and urban mayors in the 1960s are three examples.

2. Mayoral appointments are likely to represent the mayor's electoral coalition rather than the entire city. The general unanimity of appointed boards reflects this political make up. The important point is that the constituency represented is the mayor's rather than the entire city. An elected school board, particularly one elected by districts, is quite likely to represent a broader range of interests than will a single executive.

3. Some evidence suggests that Anglo students also fare better in schools with more minority teachers (see Meier, Wrinkle, and Polinard 1999).

4. The real question is whether in the long run education is better with mayoral control or school board control. While these urban school boards have not distinguished themselves in setting policy, nationwide there are a great many independent school boards that have produced excellent public education systems.

5. Why a mayor would be any better at selecting a superintendent than would a school board is unclear. Expectations for superintendents in major urban districts are exceptionally high. The number of individuals who have the ability to run an inner city district and reverse declines in performance are unlikely to be many.

References

Elmore, Richard F. 1996. "Getting to Scale with Good Educational Practice." *Harvard Educational Review* 66:1–26.

Elmore, Richard F., Charles Abelmann, and Susan Fuhrman. 1996. "The New Accountability in State Education Reform: From Process to Performance." In *Performance-Based Reform in Education*, ed. Helen F. Ladd. Washington, D.C.: Brookings Institution Press.

Elster, Jon. 1989. *The Cement of Society*. New York: Cambridge University Press.

Engstrom, Richard, and Michael McDonald. 1981. "The Election of Blacks to City Councils." *American Political Science Review* 75 (June): 344–54.

Gamble, Barbara S. 1997. "Putting Civil Rights to a Popular Vote." *American Journal of Political Science* 41 (January): 245–69.

Goggin, Malcolm, Ann Bowman, James P. Lester, and Laurence J. O'Toole. 1990. *Implementation Theory and Practice: Toward a Third Generation*. New York: HarperCollins.

Hess, Frederick M. 1999. *Spinning Wheels: The Politics of Urban School Reform*. Washington, D.C.: Brookings Institution Press.

————. 2002. *Revolution at the Margins: The Impact of Competition on Urban School Systems*. Washington, D.C.: Brookings Institution Press.

Knight, Jack. 1992. *Institutions and Social Conflict*. New York: Cambridge University Press.

Mazmanian, Daniel A., and Paul A. Sabatier. 1989. *Implementation and Public Policy*. Lanham Md.: University Press of America.

Meier, Kenneth J. 1993. "Latinos and Representative Bureaucracy: Testing the Thompson and Henderson Hypotheses." *Journal of Public Administration Research and Theory* 3 (October 1993): 393–415.

Meier, Kenneth J., Warren Eller, Robert D. Wrinkle, and J. L. Polinard. 2001. "Zen and the Art of Policy Analysis: A Reply to Nielsen and Wolf." *Journal of Politics* 63 (May): 616–26.

Meier, Kenneth J., Robert E. England, and Joseph Stewart, Jr. 1989. *Race, Class and Education: The Politics of Second Generation Discrimination*. Madison: University of Wisconsin Press.

Meier, Kenneth J., and Joseph Stewart, Jr. 1991. *The Politics of Hispanic Education*. Albany: SUNY Press.

————. 1992. "Active Representation in Educational Bureaucracies: Policy Impacts." *American Review of Public Administration* 22 (September): 157–71.

Meier, Kenneth J., Robert D. Wrinkle, and J. L. Polinard. 1999. "Representative Bureaucracy and Distributional Equity: Addressing the Hard Question." *Journal of Politics* 61 (November): 1025–39.

Mirel, Jeffrey. 1999. *The Rise and Fall of an Urban School System: Detroit, 1907–81*. Ann Arbor: University of Michigan Press.

Moe, Terry M. 1989. "The Politics of Bureaucratic Structure." In *Can the Government Govern?*, ed. John E. Chubb and Paul E. Peterson. Washington, D.C.: Brookings Institution Press.

Polinard, J. L., Robert D. Wrinkle, Tomas Longoria, and Joseph Binder. 1994. *Electoral Structure and Urban Policy*. Armonk, N.Y.: M. E. Sharpe.

Redford, Emmette. 1969. *Democracy in the Administrative State*. New York: Oxford University Press.

Robinson, Theodore P., Robert E. England, and Kenneth J. Meier. 1985. "Black Resources and Black School Board Representation: Does Political Structure Matter?" *Social Science Quarterly* 66 (December): 976–82.

Seidman, Harold. 1997. *Politics, Position and Power*. 5th ed. New York: Oxford University Press.

Stein, Robert M. 1990. *Urban Alternatives*. Pittsburgh: University of Pittsburgh Press.

Weingast, Barry R., nd William J. Marshall. 1988. "The Industrial Organization of Congress." *Journal of Political Economy* 96:132–63.

Williamson, Oliver E. 1985. *The Economic Institutions of Capitalism*. New York: The Free Press.

Chapter Nine

Mayors and the Challenge of Modernization

CLARENCE N. STONE

AFTER YEARS OF low civic priority, urban schools and their students have gained an increased measure of attention. The size of school budgets, the salience of workforce issues, and the link between the investment appeal of the central city and the quality of its schools have worked to give public education a new visibility. Thus urban schools have come under pressures to meet performance standards, supply workers for a changing economy, and cease being isolated institutions that give perfunctory service to a marginal population.

As civic leaders learn that writing off public schools has ill consequences, they begin to ask what mayors, as elected chief executives, can deliver — what part can they play in school reform? Foundations, the business community, nonprofit organizations, state officials, and other interested parties want to know that their own investments into the school reform process will be put to good use. Past disappointments have led many among these stakeholders to conclude that the existing governance arrangements produce unreliable partners. City hall on the other hand, once viewed as part of the problem, has gained new credibility due to the emergence of a seeming new breed of mayors that is pragmatic, proactive, and sensitive to reformers' interests in efficiency, high standards, and accountability for results.

The perceived needs to act forcefully and to give attention to mayors as allies have appeal to those who see themselves as thorough-going realists. In the modern era of globalization, cities cannot afford to disregard the critical role of schools as the major channels of human capital investment and as a foundation for local economic vitality. Today's mayors are in some ways better situated than school professionals to see and respond to those challenges. Analyses of civic capacity, for example, emphasize the need for school reform to be anchored in broad multisector coalitions (Stone and others, 2001, p. 112). Compared to the typical school superintendent or school board member, mayors are better situated to mobilize such coalitions and their skills may better fit the task of building community-wide coalitions.

It is important to understand that the performance of urban schools is no mere management problem to be mastered by strong executive direction. To be sure, particular moves that a mayor can make, such as taking on recalcitrant organizations of teachers and principals, may be warranted and helpful (cf. Bissinger 1997), but the challenge of sustainable school reform is greater than the burdensome inflexibility that union contracts sometimes impose. Weakly performing urban schools are rooted in history and closely tied to inequalities of race and class.

Acknowledging this is sometimes seen as risky. If the problems in schools are interwoven with societal flaws that are long-lasting and well-defended, it can be tempting to see the available options as consisting only of radical upheaval or fatalistic acquiescence. Neither of those options is likely to work as a base for building broad community support. But it is possible to reconcile a realistic appraisal of the enormity of the undertaking with a pragmatic and incremental strategy for improvement. Pretending that school reform is a nuts and bolts puzzle that can be solved simply by changing whose hands are on the policy levers purchases near-term optimism at the cost of longer-term disillusionment. If, as argued here, the performance of urban schools is hampered by the problem of uneven development, then simplistic pursuit of mayor-centrist approaches can exacerbate disabling political cleavages, divert energies and resources, steer able and well-intentioned local leaders into political booby traps, and render them less effective than they might be otherwise. It is important, then, to understand the full scope of the issue.

Ineffectual Schooling as a Problem of Uneven Development

While pedagogy, management, and governance each tell part of the story of why many central city schools are failing, the challenge also can be seen as a problem of uneven development. Today's urban school children are the progeny of households long tied to low-wage work and declining industries (e.g., share-cropping and other labor-intensive forms of agriculture, obsolescing factories in the Rust Belt, and border-area textile work). These children represent generations of social under-investment, particularly in their education. They also stand as a conspicuous example of society's failure to integrate all groups into its mainstream. Stereotypes of race, ethnicity, and class help perpetuate urban backwaters while a dynamic economy continues to evolve and place a premium on highly skilled and educated workers. In short, the performance of urban schools does not occur in a social and economic vacuum. Turning big-city education systems around requires facing the reality of years of uneven development.

Accumulated Disadvantage

The social and economic isolation of children from lower-income households has much to do with color and class. Both current residential patterns and a past employment history in which workers of color were relegated to marginal and often low-paying occupations clearly have a racial foundation, but class also plays a large part in the perpetuation of uneven development. For a complex of reasons, the nation has a long history of underinvesting in children and youth from lower socio-economic families. Public policy has played a large role in that process, but the backbone of under-investment has to do with channeling opportunity through the private household. An immense gap separates the opportunities that attach to growing up poor from those linked to a middle-class upbringing. While many low-income parents, like their middle-class counterparts, provide care and encouragement to their children, it is nonetheless a stubborn social fact that life chances vary with position in a system of stratification. The difference, I want to emphasize, is not about values. It is about capacity to provide opportunities.

Consider what we know about life chances. Middle-class children receive better health care and, in some cases, better nutrition than those from lower socioeconomic-status households (Rothstein 2000). Middle-class parents tend to be better educated and therefore better able to expose their children to the kinds of materials and experiences that promote learning readiness of an academic kind among young children, and that reinforce academic skills as children develop. For example, middle-class children are more likely to have computers at home and to be offered special opportunities, such as summer camps oriented toward science and math.[1] In advance of college, they are more likely to be enrolled in "prep" courses for SAT® tests. Middle-class schools tend to have more resources: for example, they don't have the textbook shortages that continue to plague some inner city schools; science labs are newer and better; and they have more and better-trained counselors for college placement. Even when a school district tries to assure equity in the allocation of resources, differences in the strength of PTAs and other parent groups produce significant differences in what schools can draw on (McAdams 2000, 60–61).

Equally, or perhaps more important, than resources is the development of expectations and aspirations.[2] Starting from a position of advantage and rich opportunity, middle-class children grow up in an environment that evokes high expectations and nurtures the motivation to achieve academically. Lower-class students tend to get less exposure to motivation-building experiences. Moreover, these factors are cumulative. Academic success and motivation in the early years provide a foundation for further academic success and continued motivation in later years. By contrast, lagging academic achievement in the early years weakens motivation and undermines a foundation for effort and academic success in later years.

Because advantage is clearly stratified along class lines, schools, on their own, cannot simply override all those considerations embedded in family and neighborhood conditions. This was a lesson of the Coleman report, although it should not be overlooked that its findings indicate that the school experience has more importance for children from lower socioeconomic households than for the children of the affluent classes (Coleman 1966; also Jencks and Phillips 1998, Ferguson and Ladd 1996). Thus school factors are by all accounts of great importance. Still, it is inescapably the case that schools build on what comes from the informal foundations and social supports that family and the larger society provide. As put in a study of school reform in Chicago: "Student achievement is jointly constructed out of the efforts of school professionals, students, their parents, and the communities of which they are a part" (Bryk, et al. 1998, 296).

Beyond the "Village" Metaphor

If schools are to succeed at a high level they need help from what one writer described as an infrastructure of support (Rich 1993; see also Oakes 1987, and Waddock 1995). This term refers to a wide range of programmatic efforts that encompass everything from early childhood initiatives to postschool transition to work or college. It includes efforts to enable parents to contribute more effectively to the education of their children and reinforce academic achievement for them. This may involve efforts to bring parent and school into a collaborative relationship, and to bridge the gap between school and community. After-school programs and special tutoring play a part, along with the use of mentors and other ways of exposing students to a large realm of possibilities. In some cases, apprenticeships play a part and, in all cases, there is a need to prevent the youth culture from becoming a totally autonomous force, disconnected from the adult world of opportunity and responsibility.

Thus, formal schooling is nested in a much wider set of experiences. This is why the "village" can contribute to educational achievement. The allusion to the fact that it takes a village to educate a child has been widely promoted, and its core connotation is legitimate. While perhaps necessary, however, a village is not sufficient when it is, itself, debilitated and isolated. If the wider society is not mobilized to provide an appropriate set of experiences and encouragement, social and economic inequalities extending beyond individual children and their parents will handicap the classroom learning of children and also make teaching in such classrooms less attractive to teachers in search of professional fulfillment. Middle-class children have their own, richer villages from which to draw sustenance. For non-middle-class children, disadvantages at the community level can be piled onto disadvantages at the family level, leaving the classroom less able to overcome what other forces have set in motion (Furstenberg 1993).

That a portion of society is weakly connected to today's technology-driven economy is not, then, a self-correcting problem. Indeed, as argued above, market dynamics, especially when played out through the private household, tend to magnify both the advantages of the affluent and the disadvantages of the non-affluent. In this sense, uneven development is a natural outcome in a market-based society. The reform task is to overcome that implanted tendency, and the leverage of the public sector — including its capacity to allocate resources and regulate private behavior — is a necessary component.

This is a task to which mayors most certainly can contribute. As the focal point for general local governance, they have the capacity to protect and expand local investment in schools, insist upon greater coordination between schools and other agencies, and use their bully pulpit to mobilize public support for the education enterprise. It is for exactly these reasons that many reformers are anxious to put the mayors at center stage.

But the fact that mayors potentially *can* do these things does not mean that they will be inclined to do so. After all, mayors gravitate toward initiatives that offer visible results in a short time frame. The logic of their position does not predispose them to take on intractable issues. Embedded problems, such as weak academic performances by lower-income students, require a long-term effort, and they call for interventions that can alter the community environment. Although education reform might well start in the classroom, at some stage it must broaden into a process of community change and that is a process many mayors may be reluctant to engage.

At its foundation, urban school reform is about much more than changing classroom practices or managerial techniques. The challenge is one of integration through modernization — that is, lessening the degree of uneven development. We are accustomed to thinking about education as a pathway to the mainstream economy. We are less accustomed to thinking about household position in the economy as a key to educational opportunity and performance. Past weaknesses in economic position get passed on from generation to generation unless bold actions are taken. Academic performance is rooted in a context, which itself must be addressed if lasting improvement is to be achieved. A critical question regarding city hall leadership in school reform is whether mayors, tied to a reelection cycle (and, in some cases, term-limited), can mount the kind of extraordinary and extended effort needed.

A Community Development Perspective

Structural reforms such as mayor-centrism that formally integrate educational decision-making into broader governance arrangements may well be desirable in the modern age. But the simple fact that such reforms may be desirable does not ensure that they can be smoothly injected into ongoing civic and social arrangements, that they will find latent constituencies within the communities to embrace and protect the initiatives they launch, or that their technical advantages can be realized if they are met with indifference or distrust at the grassroots level. Substantially improving schools in deeply disadvantaged communities means more than throwing the right seeds on the ground. It requires preparing the ground. And occasionally it requires adapting the seeds to local conditions.

Like European imperial forces regarding the societies they colonized or Progressive Era reformers peering down their noses at the immigrant urban masses, contemporary proponents of structural reform may be too quick to conclude that the "pre-modern" arrangements they encounter in the inner city simply reflect social disorganization bucked up by patronage and parochial loyalties. Central city school systems may be enmeshed in a more complex, functional (for some purposes), and resilient set of loyalties, norms, and interlocking interests than is widely appreciated. This has broad implications for externally driven or top-down efforts to move towards mayor-centrism. First, it suggests that resistance may be more unyielding than typically presumed. Second, it raises the possibility that imposing abrupt institutional changes risks bruising and possibly destroying indigenous networks and leaders that could be promising agents for education reform.

Recent studies of Industrial Areas Foundation (IAF) organizations in Texas make a strong case for linking school reform to community development (Shirley 1997; Warren 2001). Organizing for community development calls for educating citizens in how to come together and find their own voice, how to negotiate with centers of power, and how to create a different set of expectations, both within lower-income neighborhoods and among those actors who deal with such neighborhoods. Community development also involves getting parents and other community members to see how they can become proactive participants in problemsolving, and thereby become attractive allies in larger community efforts to address community needs in today's changing world (Cortes 1993).

Students of the IAF are not alone. Civil rights hero Robert P. Moses is another advocate of community organizing. He sees his Algebra Project as a new phase of the struggle for equality (Moses and Cobb 2001). Advanced math skills, Moses argues, are the entryway to the contemporary economy and, without that entry, equality cannot be realized. In a foreword to a book about the Algebra Project, David Dennis connects the project to the earlier struggle for voting rights in the Deep South. He observes that Black students have a long history of being steered away from the academic paths that led to advanced math courses: "They're being told that algebra is not for them just as sharecroppers and Black people were told voting was not for them" (vii).

Although the Algebra Project has made some headway against ingrained practice, Moses' account of his experience with the project is not fully reassuring. He documents official resistance in both the rural South and the urban North, from Cambridge, Massachusetts, to the Mississippi Delta. For example, in New York City a superintendent questioned how much demand there was for the Algebra Project (the specific issue concerned pre-algebra classes for fifth-graders). When Moses, with the superintendent's initial cooperation, demonstrated a large demand, the superintendent backed away and responded: "I've got too many letters. I cannot meet this demand" (150). The apparent openness to the project proved to be limited, and what Moses hoped would be a transforming step was instead translated into a few pilot classes.

Moses' account of his experience with seeking pre-algebra classes illustrates two vital points. One is that children in poor communities can be motivated on a large scale to take on academic challenges. In case after case, Moses shows readers that weak motivation, far from being an innate characteristic of the poor, is a reaction that is situationally promoted, and it can be reversed by altering the situation. Specifically, Moses shows that strong academic motivation can be evoked by an organized effort. The second point is that demands for opportunity encounter resistance from established decisionmakers. Often, resistance takes the form not of an absolute "stone wall," but rather the form of limited concessions. Again, in both North and South, education officials declined to reallocate resources on a scale that would encourage community-wide a higher level of academic performance by children from lower-income neighborhoods. As Moses assessed the tactic, "The system does not meet all of your demands but gives you something if only to keep you quiet" (151). The overall reform lesson is clear. Demonstrating that a program yields results is not enough. A political effort may be essential in altering established patterns of action. Community organizing meets a political need for local communities to press their case.

For school reform, the resource issue is fundamental. Conservative critics of urban schools see the problem as one of "cultural values, character, and family breakdown" (Will 1993). Such critics often point out that some individuals "make it"; they succeed in entering the mainstream, thereby supposedly demonstrating that individual effort is the key.

What this argument conveniently overlooks is the full context. Ron Suskind's book about Cedric Jennings, a student who goes from Washington, D.C.'s Ballou High School (in an inner city neighborhood) to Brown University, provides a useful insight into the larger picture. Even in schools regarded as academically weak, students like Cedric Jennings do receive significant forms of assistance. However, such help is selective. Suskind describes "a sort of academic triage that is in vogue at the tough urban schools across the country." The idea, Suskind says, is: "save as many kids as you can by separating top students early and putting a lion's share of resources into boosting as many of them as possible to college. Forget the rest" (Suskind 1998, 7).

The Algebra Project involves a totally different strategy. It is to bring students *en masse* onto the path to academic achievement. That means more than high-stakes testing. It means organizing among parents and children and, through organizing, seeking to radically widen opportunities. This does not mean downplaying obstacles, but stressing the fact that the barriers are external. In Mississippi, in promoting pre-algebra classes, Robert Moses said to prospective students: "Society is already prepared to write you off the way sharecroppers up in the Delta have been written off. They say you don't want to learn. You can change that and *you* have to decide whether *you* want to do it. I can't do that for you" (Moses and Cobb 2001, 150). Identifying external resistance, thus, does not mean talking about helplessness. Far from depicting students as powerless victims, Moses attributes to them a capacity to forge their own aims and pursue them.

The struggle, however, turns on more than inspiration to struggle. Organizing always has to contend with counter-moves. In the Mississippi experience Moses recounts, demand for pre-algebra rose to the level of five classes. Then teachers asked the students to take a test and "decide again whether or not you think you should take algebra" (Id. 150). Enrollment dropped to three classes. Resource constraints, including the number of committed and willing teachers, clearly affect how wide the gate of opportunity is open. Despite such partial setbacks, Moses sees his goal as a transformation of expectations within lower-income communities of color. As he put it, the aim is one of "establishing a culture of math literacy in the targeted population" (173).

Disconnection from the significance of math in today's economy is one of the results of uneven development. When Moses talks about "a culture of math literacy," he has in mind much more than what someone would say if asked about the value of math. Everyone would acknowledge its importance as a matter of abstract principal. Moses, however, is talking about math literacy as part of everyday life, and he wants to see advanced math as an integral part of the curriculum for all students, starting at the elementary level so that algebra is a natural culmination to what has already taken place.[3]

Algebra should not be regarded as a special opportunity for a few, or as something to be rationed out to selective classes. Moses wants to see math literacy, along with academic achievement generally, supported by peer pressure among school children — and, of course, also reinforced by parent support.

Imagine the reaction if a school district in an affluent, middle-class community were to announce that the five algebra classes for which students had signed up could not be provided — only two or three classes could be put into operation. The protest would be enormous. The middle-class has a strong sense of entitlement to the course offerings that position their children for college and for subsequently assuming a place in the modern economy. It is unthinkable that such course offerings would be unavailable. Not so in many inner city neighborhoods.

We can think of non-modernized settings as places of scarcity, and scarcity perpetuates itself. When resources are tightly rationed, that rationing has consequences for how people think and act politically. People become less oriented toward working together to achieve and protect their rights, and a different outlook takes hold. A revealing account of social organization in Chicago's public housing shows how, as conditions began to deteriorate and maintenance resources were cut back, tenant organization around collective issues declined, and patronage and other individual concerns gained ground (Venkatesh 2000; cf. Putnam 1993; and Reed 1999).

As places of scarcity, lower-income neighborhoods are more readily organized around pressing personal and individual concerns (Henig 1982). Pessimism is widespread. Often the order of the day is "get what you can now." That makes patronage a stronger force than collective aspirations. Even where there is "hope in the unseen," it may, as in the case of Cedric Jennings, rest more on a "triage" process for rescuing a few than on community efforts for reaching the many (Suskind 1998).

Scarcity comes into play in other ways as well. Professionals often see the world as neatly divided into discrete problems, best identified and addressed by specialists. Thus educators have a tendency to regard school reform as "running programs" rather than as an overall process of development (Bryk, et al. 1998, 278). Parents, even if engaged, may find themselves drawn into the same outlook. Moreover, "running programs" can evolve into meeting particularistic demands or the distribution of individual benefits to a worthy few. Nevertheless, organization around collective concerns is an achievable process. It is, however, something best done as part of a general movement toward community development, rather than something centered exclusively on school reform (Warren 2001; Shirley 1997; Medoff and Sklar 1994).

None of these comments is intended to suggest that group solidarity and group-based actions are at present totally missing from inner city neighborhoods or other places where uneven development is in evidence. Group solidarity is very much a part of traditional societies across time, no less so in "non-modernized" segments of the contemporary United States. However, when marshaled on behalf of protecting a supply of scarce goods, group solidarity functions differently than when it is working on behalf of collective aspirations for growth and development. In day-to-day operations, protective solidarity readily breaks down and gives way to a zero-sum mentality. A scramble over scarce benefits can ensue. By contrast, solidarity around growth and development builds upon a "positive-sum" mentality, and may for that reason be easier to maintain in day-to-day operations. At least in part, community organizing is about a positive-sum outlook within the group. Modernization itself can be regarded as a process of replacing scarcity and zero-sum thinking with a focus on growth and positive-sum thinking. In other words, one manifestation of uneven development is that part of society is saddled with a scarcity mentality while other parts see themselves as part of a condition of prosperity. That difference spills over into how people act politically. Meager resources, hostile media coverage, and resistant public officials can make community development a difficult strategy to pursue.[4] This means that, though city hall cannot assume a solo role, it can play an important part in creating an environment through which community development can be pursued.

The Mayor and Modernization

As seen by extraordinary participants like Robert Moses, urban school reform is a matter of transforming a situation of uneven development. It means more than changing classroom practice, but it includes changing the classroom. It means more than altering union contracts, though it might include that step as well. It means more than the use of high-stakes testing to hold educators and students accountable, but it does not preclude measuring classroom performance. And it certainly means more than an efficient use of existing resources, although efficiency is always welcome.

Reform as modernization means confronting the fact that a sizeable segment of the population has experienced a high degree of social and economic isolation. How can such isolation be overcome? A scattering of pilot programs and "triage" won't do it. Robert Moses' answer is to launch a new phase of the civil rights movement. The counterpart pursued by IAF affiliates is to promote collective action around concrete and specific issues as a means to further leadership development and to foster a fresh outlook. Community-based action aims to instill new expectations among students and their parents by organizing them around a cause. From past experience, we know that, commendable as it sounds, this approach is not inherently appealing to elected officials (Moynihan 1969; Jackson 1993). It carries with it too much political uncertainty. Mayors cannot be realistically expected to embrace community organizing with much fervor. That phase of reform is best conducted by advocacy groups outside the corridors of officialdom.

But there is another phase of reform to which mayors might contribute, and that has to do with building a network of community and social supports. Early childhood programs, after-school programs, family resource centers, and related measures can go far in overcoming isolation, changing expectations, reinforcing academic skills, and providing expanded channels of opportunity (Stone, et al. 1999). Again, this needs to be done on a mass scale, not just a few demonstration projects here and there.

The mayor's office is well positioned to treat education as part of a broad concern with families and children. Under Mayor Willie Brown, with a large boost from that city's Children's Institution, San Francisco has put in place a wide range of programs, from early childhood to youth-development activities for adolescence (Harder + Community Research. n.d.; San Francisco Department of Children, Youth and Their Families. n.d.). The city's Department of Children, Youth and Their Families has worked with the philanthropic community, the nonprofit sector, and the school system to build an expanding network of programs. This is a strategy of increasing social investment in those areas to meet those needs when private household investment falls short. Private efforts give the children of the affluent a large boost toward early childhood learning readiness, academic reinforcement for school-age children, and successful entry into the mainstream economy. But children do not choose the households into which they are born. Life

chances are unequally distributed. Still, those in lower-income households stand a good chance of successfully navigating academic channels
and entering into today's economy when they are supported by a full
range of community-based programs that enjoy public and voluntary
support. Here is where the mayor's office can play a useful role as
booster and coordinator.

Local Democracy

The mayor's role in school reform is often debated in terms of an elected school board versus one appointed by the mayor. Mayoral leadership is often defended on the grounds of clear accountability. It is generally agreed that the mayor's office makes a good target for popular
discontent, and, as argued above, the mayor's office is in a position to
see that non-school departments, such as parks and recreation, play a
useful supporting role. Yet, none of this guarantees that mayors are a
promising path to genuine school reform.

Opponents of mayoral appointment charge that education is too important to be entrusted to those who practice "politics as usual." After
all, electoral politics sometimes focuses more on patronage and the
"spoils of office" than on policy responsiveness (Ferman 1996). However, as the Civic Capacity and Urban Education study, along with
others, shows, elected school board members are not necessarily para-
gons of democratic practice (Stone, et al. 2001). Constituency service
and treating election to the school board as a stepping stone to the city
council or other local office underscore the kinship between education
and the more general realm of local politics. At the state level, Kentucky
recently ended the practice of electing the state school superintendent in
order to extricate the position from a widespread system of patronage
politics. Elections specifically for education officials are, then, no barrier
to the flourishing of "politics as usual."

Viewing urban school reform as a problem of modernization puts the
issue of local democracy in a broad perspective. It suggests the need for
a more robust form of democracy (cf. Barber 1984; Warren 2001). To
restrict democracy to electoral accountability is to reduce the role of
citizen to a passive role of signaling thumbs up or thumbs down. Noted
reformers like Robert Moses and the IAF's Ernesto Cortes see a more
active role for citizens. A network of community and social supports
rests on a highly engaged citizenry. The concept of civic capacity is itself
recognition that something as complex as school reform is likely to happen only with active involvement by major sectors of the community in
the process.

The current social science concern with social capital and civic engagement is perhaps itself a recognition that an election-centered notion of democracy is inadequate. Elections can, of course, become a means through which citizens mobilize to bring about changes in key positions of public authority, whether they be in city hall or in a separately chosen school board. But if change is to reach deep enough to alter education practice and performance so that they match citizen aspirations, then citizens, through their various group and institutional voices, need an ongoing form of engagement. Periodic elections alone are, as Benjamin Barber (1984) might say, an anemic form of democracy. Thus a formal shift from elected to appointed, or appointed to elected, school officials misses the point. If real school reform is to take place and meaningful engagement of the populace is to occur, then change in the school-community relationship will have to go much further than a simple switch in the method of selecting school officials. Democratic politics, genuinely practiced, turns on something more far-reaching than that.

There are no shortcuts. Some policy analysts see the key to change in quantitative benchmarks and formal evaluations. Important as such assessments may be, they are no panacea and, contrary to the assumptions of some, not even a sure path to innovation. Preoccupation with measurement contains its own dysfunctions. Community activists point out that focusing on short-term indicators discourages risk taking and works against the pursuit of longer-term strategies (Walsh [1998]). There is good reason, then, to regard formal modes of assessment as, at best, mixed blessings, with limited contribution to the aims of democratic accountability and social change. Community development, in particular, may be ill served by the use of quantitative techniques of program evaluation (Sheaff 1997, 149). A mayor who relies mainly on such techniques serves well neither the cause of democracy nor the process of social change.

Conclusion

Those who take on the task of improving city schools cannot simply launch a new initiative. They face practices that have grown up around a long history of social and economic inequality, practices that are embedded in a past not easily discarded. Even some members of minority communities see themselves as beneficiaries of the status quo. That they may see a system as unjust is no guarantee that they will favor change in the particular practices that most directly affect them. What is already in place affords modest benefits to some, and an occasional significant opportunity to a fortunate few. Moreover, to those who have experienced the world as an ungenerous and inhospitable place, the prospect of a new order, teeming with possibility, may well appear doubtful. For those accustomed to life on the margins, interpersonal networks of mutual protection have strong appeal, and such protection is not easily abandoned for the uncertain promise of reform.

Even the households of children badly served by past school practices may be wary. With a history of marginality and neglect, families sometimes see what is new as "experimenting" with their children (Raywid 1996). It is not clear that most mayors possess the combined will and skill needed to lead a far-reaching process of change, at least not in such a way as to bring minority children fully into the contemporary world of educational and economic opportunity. The move toward modernization is a large one and the resistance faced is substantial.

The term modernization might imply something certain to take place. Experience suggests the contrary. Far from being inevitable, modernization — especially inclusive modernization — poses a severe test for political leadership. Consider the six cities examined in this volume. In Baltimore, with Kurt Schmoke, a mayor willing to take on school reform, that effort evolved into a state-city partnership, and informally the local impetus for reform shifted toward community-based organizations. In Washington, D.C., Mayor Anthony Williams soon found himself confined to a narrow role of appointing a minority of the membership of the school board. A broader city hall initiative has yet to take hold. In Detroit, reform has come mainly from state action, with the mayor's office put largely in a reactive mode. School reform in Chicago started with a coalition including Mayor Harold Washington and neighborhood groups. However, after Washington's death and the later election of Mayor Richard M. Daley, school reform has been largely top down, focused on management issues and of dubious impact for the city's African American population. Only in Boston and Cleveland has the mayor's office been a force for school reform, with an agenda broader than management improvements. In none of the six cities is school reform part of a comprehensive city hall policy addressing uneven development.

Instead of putting mayors at the center of the reform process, it may be more realistic to accord them an important contributing role. An effective and sustained reform movement will require a foundation broader than the mayor's office. Still, mayoral political skills can contribute to reform in significant ways. Most mayors are accustomed to navigating cross-currents, and they can serve to reassure those who feel threatened by reform that their concerns will not be disregarded. Mayors can serve as conveners, bringing diverse players together and enlisting the participation of those who are reticent. Mayors can connect their cities to state funds and other external resources. But the shortcoming of the electoral arena means that mayors are unlikely architects of community development and democratic revitalization. Reform from the top down has inherent limitations, and the office of mayor is no exception to that rule. If reform is to be far-reaching, it will require a grassroots foundation as well as supporting actions by city hall.

Notes

1. A recent survey found that children living in households with annual incomes at or above $75,000 were more than twice as likely to have access to a computer and more than three times as likely to have access to the Internet as children living in households with incomes under $25,000 (Annie E. Casey Foundation 2002).

2. Of course, facilities and other resources along with setting help shape expectations and aspirations. See the telling column by King 2001. Another vivid account of how the conditions of the schools in Washington, D.C., affect community morale can be found in Fisher 2001.

3. El Paso's experience is relevant. El Paso has an NSF grant to promote math and science in the curriculum; its experience points to significant success in implementing a more rigorous curriculum, particularly in math and science (Navarro and Natalico 1999; Navarro and Bogart 2000).

4. Again, the public housing experience is instructive—Venkatesh 2000; and Popkin et al. 2000.

References

Annie E. Casey Foundation. 2002. *Kids Count Snapshot*. Baltimore.
Barber, Benjamin. 1984. *Strong Democracy*. Berkeley: University of California Press.
Bissinger, Buzz. 1997. *A Prayer for the City*. New York: Vintage Books.
Bryk, Anthony S., Penny Sebring, David Kerbow, Sharon Rollow, and John Easton. 1998. *Charting Chicago School Reform*. Boulder, Colo.: Westview.
Coleman, James S. 1966. *Equality of Educational Opportunity*. Washington, D.C.: U.S. Government Printing Office.
Cortés, Ernesto, Jr. 1993. "Reweaving the Fabric: The Iron Rule and the IAF Strategy for Power and Politics." In *Interwoven Destinies: Cities and the Nation*, ed. Henry G. Cisneros, 294–319. New York: W. W. Norton & Co.
Ferguson, Ronald F., and Helen F. Ladd. 1996. "How and Why Money Matters." In *Holding Schools Accountable*, ed. Helen F. Ladd. Washington, D.C.: Brookings Institution Press.
Ferman, Barbara. 1996. *Challenging the Growth Machine*. Lawrence: University Press of Kansas.

Fisher, Marc. 2001. "Strip-Search Is Just One of Many Indignities." *Washington Post*, 7 June.

Furstenberg, Frank F., Jr. 1993. "How Families Manage Risks and Opportunity in Dangerous Neighborhoods." In *Sociology and the Public Agenda*, ed. William J. Wilson, 231–58. Newbury Park, Calif.: Sage Publications.

Harder + Community Research. [2000?]. *Making a Difference for San Francisco's Children: The First Nine Years of the Children's Amendment*. San Francisco: Coleman Advocates for Children and Youth.

Henig, Jeffrey R. 1982. *Neighborhood Mobilization*. New Brunswick, N.J.: Rutgers University Press.

Jackson, Thomas F. 1993. "The State, the Movement, and the Urban Poor." In *The "Underclass" Debate*, ed. Michael B. Katz, 403–39. Princeton, N.J.: Princeton University Press.

Jencks, Christopher, and Meredith Phillips. 1998. *The Black-White Test Score Gap*. Washington, D.C.: Brookings Institution Press.

King, Colbert I. 2001. "A Tour the Mayor Should Take." *Washington Post*, 28 July.

McAdams, Donald R. 2000. *Fighting to Save Our Urban Schools . . . and Winning!* New York: Teachers College Press.

Medoff, Peter, and Holly Sklar. 1994. *Streets of Hope*. Boston: South End Press.

Moses, Robert P., and Charles E. Cobb. 2001. *Math Literacy and Civil Rights*. Boston: Beacon Press.

Moynihan, Daniel Patrick. 1969. *Maximum Feasible Misunderstanding: Community Action in the War on Poverty*. New York: The Free Press.

Navarro, M. Susana, and Joanne Bogart. 2000. "The El Paso Collaborative for Academic Excellence." *Instructional Leader* 13 (November): 1–2, 10–11.

Navarro, M. Susana, and Diana S. Natalicio. 1999. "Closing the Achievement Gap in El Paso." *Phi Delta Kappan* 80 (April): 597–601.

Oakes, Jeannie. 1987. *Improving Inner-City Schools*. Monica, Calif.: Rand.

Popkin, Susan J., Victoria E. Gwiasda, Lynn M. Olson, Dennis P. Rosenbaum, and Larry Burton. 2000. *The Hidden War*. New Brunswick, N.J.: Rutgers University Press.

Putnam, Robert D. 1993. *Making Democracy Work*. Princeton, N.J.: Princeton University Press.

Raywid, Mary Anne. 1996. "The Wadleigh Complex." In *The Politics of the New Institutionalism*, ed. Robert Crowson, William Boyd, and Hanne Mawhinney, 101–14. Washington, D.C.: Falmer Press.

Reed, Adolph L. 1999. *Stirrings in the Jug*. Minneapolis: University of Minnesota Press.

Rich, Dorothy. 1993. "Building a Bridge to Reach Minority Parents." In *Families and Schools in a Pluralistic Society*, ed. Nancy Chavkin, 235–44. Albany: State University of New York Press.

Rothstein, Richard. 2000. "Finance Fungibility: Investigating Relative Impacts of Investments in Schools and Non-School Educational Initiatives to Improve Student Achievement." 18 October. <http:www.financeproject.org/achievement.htm>.

The San Francisco Department of Children, Youth and Their Families. 2000–

2001. "Background Information on San Francisco Youth Development Initiatives." San Francisco: Department of Children, Youth and Their Families.

Sheaff, Mike. 1997. "Urban Partnerships, Economic Regeneration and the 'Healthy City.'" In *Transforming Cities*, ed. Nick Jewson and Susanne MacGregor, 141–52. London: Routledge.

Shirley, Dennis. 1997. *Community Organizing for School Reform*. Austin: University of Texas Press.

Stone, Clarence N., Kathryn Doherty, Cheryl Jones, and Timothy Ross. 1999. "Schools and Disadvantaged Neighborhoods: The Community Development Challenge." In *Urban Problems and Community Development*, ed. Ronald F. Ferguson and William T. Dickens, 339–69. Washington, D.C.: Brookings Institution Press.

Stone, Clarence N., Jeffrey R. Henig, Bryan D. Jones, and Carol Pierannunzi. 2001. *Building Civic Capacity*. Lawrence: University Press of Kansas.

Suskind, Ron. 1998. *A Hope in the Unseen*. New York: Broadway Books.

Venkatesh, Sudhir Alladi. 2000. *American Project*. Cambridge: Harvard University Press.

Waddock, Sandra A. 1995. *Not by Schools Alone*. Westport, Conn.: Praeger.

Walsh, Joan. [1998]. *The Eye of the Storm*. Baltimore: Annie E. Casey Foundation.

Warren, Mark R. 2001. *Dry Bones Rattling*. Princeton, N.J.: Princeton University Press.

Will, George. 1993. "Still Sick of Government." *Washington Post*, 21 January.

Chapter Ten

Concluding Observations: Governance Structure as a Tool, Not a Solution

JEFFREY R. HENIG AND WILBUR C. RICH

THE MOMENTUM BEHIND efforts to put mayors in the middle of the school governance reform process is powerful and the notion is appealing. Major structural changes in formal governance responsibilities, it is important to remember, are relatively rare in a system, like ours, more typically characterized by incrementalism and the politics of veto groups. Yet one by one many of the largest urban school systems have been proceeding down this new path. Sometimes they have done so on their own initiative; sometimes reluctantly. Supporters of a mayor-appointed school board believe that it will undo years of internal board bickering and incoherent administrative policy making. Almost always there has been local resistance due to instinctive traditionalism, loyalty to valued institutions and processes, wary skepticism, narrow self-interest, or committed belief that the proposed changes are wrong-headed or ill intentioned. Often, race has been a defining element of the cleavage along which lines of support and opposition have been drawn.

The momentum behind the mayoral takeover movement is understandable for a number of reasons. First, there is the broadly and sharply felt imperative to "do something." Many central city school systems are floundering. Granted, there are legitimate disagreements about the extent and cause of the problems faced by central city school, but there is also growing consensus change is indicated. Some portray city public school systems as being in free fall (Lieberman 1993; Coulson 1999); others suggest that the "rhetoric of crisis" is overplayed for tactical political reasons (Henig 1994; Berliner, Biddle, et al. 1995; Rothstein 1998). Some argue that responsibility for the problems can be laid squarely on the shoulders of educators, local public officials, and the governance structures through which they operate (Chubb and Moe, 1990; Lieberman, 1993; Rich 1996); others see the causes as rooted in basic attributes of American national institutions, including inequality of wealth, suburban exclusion, intergovernmental funding inequities, and racial discrimination (Kozol 1991; Anyon 1997). But it is not necessary or desirable to put off meaningful reform efforts until such deep debates are resolved. Those who can agree that there are important problems (even if they disagree about their magnitude) and those who can agree that local governments have the capacity to make things better (even if they disagree about whether they have the capacity to eliminate root causes) constitute a majority among the relatively interested and informed actors, and they make a responsive audience for mayor-centric proposals.

A second reason for the momentum behind this approach is that there are sound theoretical and empirical reasons to think it might work. The institutional logic in favor of having a centralizing focal point for policy integration and democratic accountability is laid out in this volume (Henig and Rich; Meier) and elsewhere (Kirst and Bulkley 2000; Wong 2001), and while this volume suggests that this logic may be less than ironclad and complete, there is no gainsaying its basic coherence and pedigree. Moreover, while the empirical record remains germinal and largely anecdotal, the conventional wisdom that mayoral control has leveraged significant improvements in Chicago — its showcase city — gains persuasive power when judged against the landscape of frustration and disappointment that more typically describes urban school reform undertakings.

Finally, the momentum behind mayor-centrism is understandable because the approach, and its rationale, align nicely with the interests and preconceptions of groups that are politically ascendant in our time. The "impulse to emulate business and impress business elites" (Tyack and Cuban 1995, 112) is one of the constants in the history of American school reform. As each of the case chapters in this volume indicates, corporate elites have been primary instigators of the mayor-centric approach. To corporate leaders, a structure in which there is integrative management culminating in a chief executive officer is familiar. Corporate leaders also feel culturally more comfortable and more confident of capturing the ear of today's "modern mayor" than they do with school board members, many of whom are steeped in the language and ideas of the education community, and many of whom are accountable to ward-based constituencies whose views business leaders consider parochial and particularistic. At the national level, the language of managerial efficiency also neatly aligns with the broad themes favored by those orchestrating a new coalition for the Republican Party.

Of course, business interests and Republicans are not the only influential forces on the American political scene. But to some grassroots and traditionally Democratic interests mayor-centrism also has appeal. The political dynamics of coalition building in particular states have made it possible for central city leaders to trade support for mayor-centrism for the commitment from state legislators to invest much more money into their districts. And for others, mayor-centrism has appeal primarily as a far less threatening alternative to other reform approaches, such as vouchers and privatization, which would much more certainly push them to the margins of local influence.

In light of the need to do something, it might seem churlish, short-sighted, or reactionary to raise objections to one of the handful of reform ideas that combines the capacity to mobilize enthusiasm from key stakeholders with credible prospects for success. Indeed, some of the arguments commonly raised — institutions don't matter; the underlying problems are too great for local government to make any difference; mayor-centrism is a racial conspiracy — strike us as dubious and evasive. Although the individual contributors and the chapters we have assembled here do not toe a single line on this issue, the overall tenor of the contributions suggests a stance of wary skepticism. Especially in light of the gung-ho, full-steam-ahead orientation of many of the boosters for mayor-centrism, we think such voices of skepticism are important to introduce into the public debate. But that does not mean ill-considered skepticism, self-serving skepticism, or skepticism for its own sake.

In this final chapter, we offer our own assessment of mayor-led school systems and their prospects. It is a position that is more nuanced, more contingent, and less assertive than those typically heard in the contemporary debate. We are sensitive to the need to take action, and therefore resistant to the temptation to let "the perfect be the enemy of the good." Our interpretation is grounded in the notion that society and its problems exhibit complex and contingent causal relationships, and we are therefore willing to "settle" for approaches that do not pretend to explain everything all of the time. Hence, we stand foursquare on the belief that collective commitment to solve social problems is both limited and fragile, and we are therefore wary of the corrosive effects of both ingrained pessimism and air-headed optimism. Most importantly, ours is a position that takes seriously the role of governance institutions in influencing how democracies define their agendas despite imperfect information, fluid value priorities, conflicting interests, and shifting majorities. If individual school districts or we as a society were confident, consistent, and internally united about what we want from public education, the case for integrated school governance structures with mayors in a central role would be almost incontrovertible. But choosing governance structures is not simply a question of arranging ourselves so as to best pursue an unproblematic agenda. The two tasks of setting policies and implementing policies are not neatly distinguished in our political system, and it is doubtful whether they could be. Putting mayors at the fulcrum of school governance, therefore, will change what urban school districts choose to do, as well has how they go about it. And it is on this side of the equation — where some values are given greater weight than others; where some groups' interests are elevated and some marginalized — that the complications emerge.

When and How Governance Structure Matters

> • *Structure matters, and that is why battles like this continually reemerge and why they can be so heated.*

Political science as an academic discipline has ebbed and flowed over the years in the attention it gives to formal political institutions. The behavioral revolution of the 1950s and 1960s was in large measure a reaction to the emphasis on formal laws and institutions that had characterized the field until that time. Laws and formal institutions are idealized notions about how things are supposed to work, the behavioralists argued. The real story of politics has to do with what politicians, individual voters, and organized interest groups actually do. More recently, the tide of thinking has turned again, with increasing numbers of scholars associating themselves with what has been labeled the "new institutionalism" (March and Olsen 1989). Probably most contemporary political scientists would agree that there are senses and times in which collective institutions function both as shapers and reflections of society. But the precise extent to which institutions should normally be regarded as independent variables versus dependent is still an issue of contention, with some camps sticking to relatively strong assertions of the priority of one view over the other.

The stance that "formal institutions don't matter, or at least don't matter much," is at least provisionally defensible on intellectual and even empirical grounds. Governance arrangements, it is clear, sometimes operate quite differently in practice than one would anticipate based on their formal characteristics. For example, elections for mayor and council in Chicago are formally nonpartisan, meaning that party labels cannot appear on the ballot. Nonpartisan elections are generally presumed to lead to weaker parties, yet contrary to its formal status, Chicago's elections stood for many years in many observers' minds as the ultimate expression of machine politics and (Democratic) party control.

In the specific instance of urban school reform, some opponents of structural reform argue that shifting authority and control from box to box on the organization chart will prove to be little more than window dressing. Not all of those who see teachers unions as powerful reactionary forces, for instance, believe that shifting the venue of decision making to city hall will curb their influence. Some reason that teachers and their union leadership will simply adjust by refocusing their campaign and lobbying efforts, and that the same concentrated efforts that made them an effective veto group within school board politics will enable them to exercise leverage over any mayors who find themselves at center stage in education policy (see, e.g., Rich and Chambers in this volume). To the extent that power is transferable from one venue to another, the policy consequences of structural rearrangement may prove minor and short-lived. Those who believe that the real root of the urban education crisis lies in economic inequality, and the ability of the wealthy to use their wealth to defend their interests politically, also have reason to doubt the efficacy of changes in governance structures. To the extent that government, in general, is weak and dependent, tinkering with its design is unlikely to alter outcomes of any importance.

Despite their wariness about overinvesting in the model of mayor-led school reform, however, the authors in this volume reject the position that governance institutions do not matter. Indeed, we would go so far as to say that most of the contributors take structural change more seriously than do the current proponents of that approach. They do so not by according it a stronger or more independent causal role in determining how policy is carried out, but by paying more attention to the role governance structure plays in shaping the policy agenda in the first place.

- *Structure, in fact, matters in more ways than many of the proponents of mayor-led school districts realize, or at least acknowledge.*

While the proponents of mayor-led districts zero in on the role of governance structures in shaping and implementing policy, the authors in this book pay at least equal attention to the role of those same structures in shaping and allocating relative influence to various constituencies with competing values, visions, and needs. In that sense, they see more at stake and (we believe) can better account for the level of resistance and particular lines of cleavage that emerge.

Americans' commitment to public education has been so strong and consistent that many have considered support for public schools to be immune from the partisan and ideological bickering that typically characterize the political agenda. Wirt and Kirst (2001) refer to this as the "apolitical myth," and show how early twentieth-century school reformers used it to wrest control of schools from urban political machines. To the Progressive Era reformers, apolitical consensus emerged from scientific methods and professional expertise. The contemporary version of this apolitical myth sees the external pressures of a global economic competition, not the technical know-how of reputed experts, as the primary vehicle for uniting disparate groups in a common commitment to education as a pathway to economic growth. According to this view, local governance regimes face a common set of challenges, and regardless of whether the coalitions that elected them are dominated by liberals or conservatives, public officials inevitably end up stressing education reform as a tool for economic development if they want any chance at all of steering their community to more prosperous times.

But political responses to efforts to introduce mayor-centrism reveal that deep divisions remain within cities about the direction in which public education should be moving. Some of these divisions may rest on high-minded, intellectualized philosophies of education and governance. Some rest on more emotional and intuitive senses of what and who is familiar, safe, and worthy of trust. And some undoubtedly rest on narrower, more materially based notions about who may win and lose jobs, contracts, influence, and power if policies really are changed. In any event, the divisions are real. Structural changes in decision-making institutions prick at those divisions precisely because institutions determine the rules of the game that confer advantages in access and leverage to some groups at the expense of others.

What Can We Legitimately Expect from Mayors?

> • *Giving mayors a stronger central role and decreasing the power of, or even eliminating, school boards has the potential to accomplish some very desirable ends, most notably jump-starting reform in places with calcified institutions intensely defended by people and organizations who fear that change will pass them by or run them over.*

The typical school governance arrangement — an independent elected school board — is not so flawed or dysfunctional as to have lost its credibility throughout most of the country. Some — indeed most — of the public school systems that stand out as excellent by the same measures by which central city systems appear so wanting, still operate under these arrangements. In high-achievement suburban school districts like Fairfax, Virginia; Palo Alto, California; Montgomery County, Maryland; Scarsdale, New York; and Newton, Maine, parents elect their school board representatives. Neither the broader local community nor the states have the will or inclination to change that.

Nonetheless, it is apparent that in some cases elected boards have not adequately met the challenges facing them. Some are simply amateurish and ill informed. Some assert themselves as micromanagers while failing to set broad policy objectives. Some have been "captured" by core constituencies — frequently the educators and parents who are the most motivated to become involved and who can exert substantial political leverage against the backdrop of low interest and low voter participation that is the norm in school board races.

Where independently elected school boards are failing, why do reformers not simply rally the public to unseat incumbents and elect a new school board more willing or able to do the job? In principle they can, and this alternative stands as a major challenge to those who call for redesigning the governance structure instead. The historical record in large city central cities shows that such electoral challenges to ineffective school boards are difficult but not at all impossible to undertake and that reform slates can be elected and gain control (for example, HOPE in Detroit, see Mirel in this volume; see also Henig, Hula, et al. 1999). But the reform slates often falter once in office, as the problems prove more obstinate, and the public's level and reliability of support more fickle, than envisioned.

When the existing arrangements are stagnant and reform efforts have sputtered and died, the danger grows that the public and others will simply lose hope. When that happens — when corporate interests throw up their hands, parents with the resources to do so exit to private schools or the suburbs, and state legislatures become convinced that investing more resources would be a waste of good money — the spiral of decline can become deep and swift. Critically, though, no matter how far the system declines, many families and their children cannot escape. Granting formal power to the mayor in such situations can provide a spark of hope, and a rallying point for another concerted effort.

- *But mayor-centrism is far from a panacea.*

This is partly because the policy outcome consequences of structural change almost always turn out to be less dramatic than reformers expect. Our political system is highly fragmented, both vertically along the hierarchy of federalism and horizontally due to separation of powers among the various branches of government. The result is multiple veto points that tend almost always to delay and dilute even very serious efforts at bringing about change. But mayor-centrism's limitations as a cure-all go beyond the simple fact that the consequences it engenders are likely to be incremental.

- *The outcomes of efforts to put mayors in the middle of school reform are likely to vary widely, depending*

upon context, personalities, and the tactics and capac-
ity of opposing groups, generating a risk that they may
push to the side or directly undermine alternative ap-
proaches to school reform with better prospects for
long-term success.

The contemporary faith in the inclination and capacity of mayors to solve education issues is somewhat ironic. Early in the twentieth century the much more commonly stated belief was that mayors' inclinations were not to be trusted. Seen as partisan "politicos", mayors were presumed to be more interested in patronage, power, and petty graft than in improving the lives of their constituents. By the end of the century, mayors were more likely to be portrayed as well meaning but essentially powerless. In a classic treatment, Douglas Yates explained why forces of modernization were leaving cities "ungovernable," with mayors locked into a cycle of crisis management and resorting to symbol and rhetoric as a compensation for their lack of real capacity (Yates, 1984). We do not believe that mayors are either untrustworthy or inherently ineffectual, but we do believe that they operate in the midst of constraints and cross-pressures that are quite real, and quite powerful. The needs to find issues on which they can "deliver the goods" to those who elected them and maintain the allegiance of other stakeholders whose cooperation they need to govern effectively are just as likely to steer mayors away from meaningful education reform as towards it.

Granting a stronger formal role to mayors is likely to reshape the school reform agenda, but precisely how it will do so depends upon numerous factors; under some circumstances the results may be precisely the opposite of those that reformers envision. Proponents see mayor-centrism as leading the way toward a more cohesive, coherent, and concentrated commitment to improve academic improvement. And the prospects for this are good when the mayor's personal style and capacities, electoral coalition, and governance regime all reinforce serious attention to public education. But the stars may not always be so nicely aligned.

Mayors come into office with issue agendas. These are shaped partly by their personal values and personalities, and partly by the commitments they have made in mobilizing the electoral coalition that propelled them into office. Once in office, mayors often adapt those agendas, partly to respond to changing events and partly to respond to the interests and priorities of other stakeholders with whom they must deal in order to build a working governance coalition. Some mayors come into office deeply committed to educational reform. Kurt Schmoke of Baltimore, Maryland, fit this description (Orr this volume). Improving education was a personal priority, but one he took to a higher level by making it a central focus of his campaign platform. More commonly, mayoral candidates are more interested in non-educational issues, or are compelled to emphasize such issues to differentiate themselves from their electoral opponents. For Schmoke's predecessor in Baltimore, W. Donald Schaefer, the identifying focus was downtown economic development. For Martin O'Malley, his successor, it was basic city services and crime. Indeed historically, for most mayors school issues have not loomed as large as personal or electoral commitments, partly because they have not been seen as falling into their realm of responsibility and partly because they have been seen as political hot potatoes safer left to others to juggle.

For most of the mayors discussed in this volume — including those like White (Cleveland), Archer (Detroit), and Williams (DC) — the incentive to take a leadership role in public school reform developed subsequent to their initial election. In those cities, and seemingly typically, the business community played an important role in convincing the mayor that this was a necessary or desirable direction in which to head. Sometimes, though, the mayors have been wary. In the District of Columbia, for example, Anthony Williams initially indicated that he thought he should concentrate on other matters. As Stone and others have argued, however, even mayors who run populist campaigns often find they must form informal alliances with the business community in order to enlist their support to get things accomplished. (Stone, 1989) When business talks, mayors listen.

This need to construct a governance regime does not mean that personal interests and electoral pressures disappear as constraining forces, however. Most mayors are motivated in large measure by their personal sense of what is right. Even if they are flexible and opportunistic, they do not have the ability to completely change their stripes. Except in rare instances, too, mayors maintain an interest in electoral office — usually looking toward reelection, although sometimes aspiring to a higher office — and that means that they are not free to forsake their original supporters unless they are confident they can reformulate a new coalition before the next election day.

When mayors have an inclination to deal with schools, and when their electoral supporters will greet or at least tolerate them diverting attention and public resources to schools instead of other issues, invitations from business and other school reform groups to grab the education baton will likely be successful. But there can be important counterpressures as well. Mayors who campaigned on other issues must worry that their supporters will feel neglected, or even betrayed. Mayors in cities with tight fiscal constraints and mobilized anti-tax constituencies must be wary of taking on a commitment that might necessitate substantial new expenditures. And any mayor facing a tough reelection battle must be concerned about taking on responsibility for problems that — even if they are aggressively and systematically attacked — may not show clear evidence of abating until well past the next election cycle.

> • *Race complicates the issue of mayor-centric structural reform. That is not because mayor-centrism, in principle, has any racially specific implications, but because the concept is being introduced into local contexts in which racially patterned interests, loyalties, perceptions, and points of institutional leverage are both sensitive and powerful.*

In each of the cities discussed in this book, political alignments on the issue of increased mayoral involvement have exhibited clear racial patterns that have been evident and troubling to local observers. That, of course, does not mean that all supporters have been white, and all opponents Black. But it does mean that traditional leaders within the predominantly white business community have tended to line up on one side, with traditional leaders within the African American community — particularly grassroots political activists and those associated with civil rights issues — have tended to line up on the opposite side. It also means that the rhetoric in which the debate was framed often conjured racial imagery — claims of white "imperialism," accusations of "plantation mentality," and charges of deliberate disenfranchisement of Blacks. Notably, the racial rhetoric and symbolism has been prominent even when the mayor who would inherit the mantle of additional power is Black. Even in a city like Boston, where Mayors Flynn and Menino employed a more gradualist approach, using their substantial political skills to build a coalition that culminated in a 70 percent vote against returning to the elected board system in the 1996 referendum (Portz, this volume; Yee forthcoming), the underlying racial cleavage was not erased, only muted.

Despite predictions that racial sentiments and interests will become less and less potent as a growing Black middle-class adopts viewpoints aligned with its new economic status, the fact remains that race continues to assert a powerful mobilizing force in American central cities. There are various reasons why this may be the case. The suburbanization of both African American professionals and working-class whites means that race and class continue to overlap in some older central cities — where a white business and young urban "gentry" that has the wherewithal to establish itself in enclave communities confront a Black population comprising those without the wherewithal to move out. The weakness of other potentially cross-cutting institutions — for example a party system sapped of vitality by the inability of Republicans, in many large cities, to generate a credible competitive threat; municipal unions that have become racially homogenous and too insular to build lasting links with a broader labor movement—also may serve to bring racial cleavages into higher relief. But probably most important is the fact that the collective racial experience has given rise to bonds of loyalty, trust, and shared suspicions that are simply more deep-seated and compelling than are acknowledged by theories based on economic determinism and material self-interest (Sigelman and Welch 1991; Kinder and Sanders 1996).

Such racial currents run especially strong in the arena of school politics because of the special place that public schools have played in the African American experience, both as a force of intellectual liberation and as a source of jobs and community development (Henig, Hula, et al. 1999; Orr 2000). African Americans won jobs as public school teachers and administrators before they were able to win elective office on school boards and before they won city council seats or captured city hall. There is a reluctance to see these valued institutions altered in ways that could conceivably weaken access.

This reluctance, it is critical to note, is not based on nostalgia alone. The mobilized electorate to which mayors are responsible differs from the electorate that selects school boards. The former tends to include more white households, those without children, and those whose children attend private schools. In addition, mayors, much more than school system leaders, are forced to structure governance regimes including white business leaders, and to weigh heavily the need to limit taxes, attract jobs, build alliances with state officials, and attract middle-class homeowners.

A case can be made—a strong and rather compelling case—that a healthy school system and a healthy city ultimately go hand-in-hand, and that, therefore, the seemingly different incentives confronting school versus city leaders exist only in the near term. But there are many ambiguities and conflicting judgments about how to realize the imagined complementarities. In the near-term—which is where politics is played out—these generate uncertainties and conflicts about priorities and sequencing: Do we attend first and foremost to building a viable economy that can support a healthy school system, or to revitalizing schools so a strong workforce can attract business?

The answer that we must "find the proper balance" begs the question of whom we can trust to do that well and fairly. And when it comes to matters of trust, the reluctance of many African Americans to cede authority to institutions over which they believe they have less control is not very different from the orientation of those favoring more formal mayoral control. Proponents of mayor-centrism argue that their position is based on objective characteristics of institutions and organizations, but at least as powerful a motivating force is the fact that they trust and believe they have the ear of the particular individuals who constitute the current cohort of mayors. Evidence of that is their unwillingness to empower mayors with whom they disagreed. Congress and the District of Columbia business community would not have dreamed of granting a stronger school governance role to Marion Barry. Michigan legislators would not do so for Coleman Young (nor, for different reasons, would New York state legislators do so for David Dinkins or Rudolph Giuliani).

> • *The premise that the fundamentally different challenges facing central cities today universally are producing a "new breed" of mayors with the desire and capacity to make school reform a centerpiece in their administrations is a shaky foundation upon which to base a major effort to perhaps permanently restructure governance institutions.*

"The impetus for turning to mayors to solve problems in urban education systems," as Kirst and Bulkley observe, "stems in part from the belief that there is a 'new breed' of mayor that can improve education and avoid past mistakes" (Kirst and Bulkley 2003). The "new, improved mayors" are believed to be pragmatic rather than ideological, managers rather than politicos, comfortable with private sector solutions as alternatives to public bureaucracies. Their style and rhetoric evoke corporate offices rather than the Civil Rights movement. The new, improved mayor has understandable appeal to those who believe that bloated public bureaucracies are a major contributing factor to the urban education crisis. The new, improved mayor is likely to stand up to unions, introduce merit pay, insist on strict performance measures and accountability, and have an open ear to market solutions such as vouchers, charter schools, or contracting out to private companies.

But formal institutional changes in governance structures are too important and too lasting to be made on the basis of personalities or short-term trends. Proponents of mayor-centrism have to be confident that this new breed of mayors is not a passing fad but is driven by broad and irreversible changes in the urban environment. Otherwise, the risk is too great that an Anthony Williams will be succeeded by a new Marion Barry, that a Michael Bloomberg will make way for a new Abe Beame, that a Dennis Archer would make way for a Coleman Young, that a Richard Daley Junior will be succeeded by Richard Daley Senior.

Certainly, cities today face some qualitatively different constraints than they did half a century ago. Changes in transportation and communications technology, coupled with the weakening of national tariff barriers, have made the movement of capital easier and faster, forcing local officials to pay more attention to their cities' economic competitiveness. These changes are here to stay.

Other factors cited as important for ushering in the new breed of mayors — such as the declining importance of federal aid, the disintegration of the traditional civil rights coalition, and new ethnic immigrant populations (Kirst and Bulkley, 2003) — may be less permanent, however, and their consequences for local mayoral styles less predictable. It remains to be seen whether the managerial style of mayoral leadership is politically viable over the longer term. While some so-called models — like Daley in Chicago, Stephen Goldsmith in Indianapolis, or Michael Bloomberg in New York — are still in the ascendancy, others previously linked to them — Kurt Schmoke in Baltimore, Edward Rendell in Philadelphia, or Henry Cisneros in San Antonio — encountered rocky political waters after initially smooth sailing. As discussed in this volume, Black mayors in particular who have taken up the mantle of mayor-centrism have experienced a phenomenon of rapid burnout. It is possible this phenomenon is idiosyncratic to the cases of White, Archer, and Schmoke, but we are inclined to think that something more is involved.

Regardless of their own race, the new breed of mayors can anticipate sniping and challenges from grassroots activists, civil rights organizations, and unions that see privatization and the language of corporate efficiency to be misguided. But for Black mayors in particular these challenges become entwined with issues of solidarity and betrayal in ways that can simultaneously increase the personal burden on the incumbent, and open the door for primary challenges from other minority candidates who paint them as "sell-outs" and seek to outflank them as a more progressive voice. Although it is too early to read the tea leaves with confidence, there is at least some evidence that this "new breed" of urban mayors may be giving way to a "new new breed" that — while not reverting completely — incorporates some elements of the earlier cohort of mayors, including greater attention to political coalition building at the community level, greater willingness to work with traditional party organizations, and a reticence to tackle issues — like schools — that present high risks of failure and controversy.

The Policy Implication of Mayor-led School Districts

City halls have been able to replace elected school boards and hire non-educators as chief executive officers (CEOs). The CEOs have reduced or eliminated budget deficits, but this is just part of the total challenge of school reform. Reconstituting inner cities schools so they can offer the same quality education as that found in suburbs will require a major systemic change. Zetlin and Lim (1998) found that the large city school districts are almost impervious to systemic change. They assert "numerous barriers arise, such as lack of commitment from the leadership or resistance to change from participants in the change process. Implementation of multiple reforms (i.e., reform of governance, curriculum, human services) adds to the complexity of the change process" (see also Squire and Reigelluth 2000). This review of six major city school systems supports their observations. The delays, misinterpretations, and confusion among city halls and school administrators demonstrate what Pressman and Wildavsky (1979) called the "complexity of joint action." When there are so many parts to a system, coordination can become a serious challenge.

The arrival of the school crisis on the mayor's agenda comes at a less-than-optimum time in the history of American cities. Many mayors of large cities are thoroughly engaged with the problems of their city's economic sustainability in light of the changing international marketplace. Most mayors took on the challenge of school reform because their constituency demanded "something be done," and state legislatures either wished to wash their hands of the issue or genuinely thought that structural changes could make the difference. To the surprise of city hall, school issues have consumed an enormous amount of the mayor's time: negotiating financial aid packages with the state legislature, dealing with internal dynamics of school board deliberations, listening to complaints about student performance, and defending the appointed CEO.

What have we learned from this review about mayor-led school reform strategies in six cities? Mayors tend to appoint loyalists to the board with the understanding that the CEO will become the key person in terms of policy and details, with the mayor adopting a supportive but relatively low-profile stance. The appointed CEO has evolved into a high-level patronage job, and no amount of mayoral rhetoric can offset that fact. Therefore, it is unlikely that an individual CEO will survive the turnover of mayors. (With the exception of Richard Daley in Chicago, several of the mayors discussed in this book decided not to run for reelection). New mayors may keep a CEO holdover during the transition, but eventually most will want to appoint their own CEO.

Mayor-centered school reform strategies seem to be most successful at improving the fiscal management of school districts. But the most frequently cited success stories, such as Chicago and Boston, were launched during a period of unusually strong and sustained national economic prosperity. Over time and under more trying conditions, the control of the school budgets may prove to be much more difficult. In turn, as was suggested in the case studies, the fiscal demands of the school system may make it difficult for mayors to satisfy their electoral and governance coalitions. The hands-off positions of Baltimore's Mayor Martin O'Malley and Cleveland's Jane Campbell's notwithstanding, the days are likely over when a mayor could blithely ride through an education crisis without suffering political repercussions. When mayors get frustrated and decide not to run for reelection (as did Kurt Schmoke, Dennis Archer and Michael White), it contributes to the marasmus and irregularity of the ongoing school reform process. Ultimately, this process may also undermine the credibility of the mayor-centric governing structure.

Recognizing that the success of mayor-centrism is contingent upon the favorable alignment of other forces does not mean that it should be jettisoned as part of the arsenal of strategies communities consider as they feel their way toward a more effective and sustained process of school reform. What it does suggest is that proposals for restructuring need to be examined in their particulars and in their local and historical context. Mayor-centrism may be worth pursuing in some places and times, but not in others.

The level of discourse about public policy in America is at times surprisingly naïve in its capacity to accommodate notions of contingency. Proponents and critics alike cross swords over whether this or that policy "works" with little pretense of specifying the conditions under which it is most likely or least likely to work, when it is likely to distract attention from other more promising approaches, or even to do harm. We seem to crave the simple guidance that comes with the language of universality. Policies should be good (i.e., worth doing) or bad (i.e., to be avoided). In other venues, for instance in medicine, our thinking is more nuanced; physicians and patients alike have come to accept the notion that the very same medical intervention might, under different circumstances, be either beneficial, harmful, or dangerously misleading because it masks some other problem.

Structural changes in school governance are major interventions. They should not be undertaken lightly. They constitute the "rules of the game" within which collective decisions are deliberated, resolved, and translated into practice. Citizens, interest groups, and political leaders need a certain degree of continuity in order to make plans, set long-term strategies, build alliances, and develop a sense of confidence and trust. Just as in a game of softball or Monopoly, a sense that the rules are always subject to revision through negotiation or assertion of power can induce anxiety and uncertainty about the fairness of the enterprise. That does not mean that the rules ought never to be changed. Times change, and so do values and expectations. Rigidity can engender dysfunction or marginalization. In professional baseball, for instance, the American League added the designated hitter to generate more scoring and fan excitement. The governance structures for local education policy are human creations; they have changed both incrementally and non-incrementally before. Should they be changed now? Our answer: "That depends."

One factor upon which the answer depends is the extent to which the existing institutions have proven incapable of meeting the challenges. We have already noted that urban education in general is falling short of what is expected and desired. We have also agreed with critics that sitting school boards often seem unable or unwilling to move beyond micromanagement and bureaucratic infighting. While that establishes the groundwork for an argument in favor of structural change, it does not suffice in itself to make the case. There is a distinction to be drawn between the failures of institutions and the failures of the individuals currently occupying key roles within those institutions. In many districts, school board elections draw mediocre candidates, spark little public notice, fail to generate an illuminating debate, and attract few voters. Episodically, communities have shown that it is possible to invigorate democracy, to spark a broad discussion of future directions and elect slates of candidates committed to reform. Such efforts at reform through school board elections do not guarantee that real reforms will follow (Henig, Hula, et al. 1999), but even when they come up short they are important exercises for raising public consciousness. Given the fact that mayor-centric reform is itself an uncertain and incomplete solution, we would argue in favor of undertaking sincere and aggressive efforts to reinvigorate traditional governance before turning to formal governance reform. Where such efforts have been tried and stymied by vested interests, a more powerful case can be made for turning to mayor-centrism than in those when it has been half-heartedly pursued and died due to civic indifference.

Another consideration is the particular historical role and symbolic meaning of local institutions. Institutions like city hall and local school systems may begin as formal structures defined by law and defended by reason, but over time they can accumulate a complex array of associations and connotations that engender more emotionally grounded reactions of loyalty, suspicion, enmity, or trust. "Sophisticated" analysts may dismiss such primitive sentiments, but decision makers who truly want to get things accomplished do so at their own risk. Whether or not a proposed governance change appears compelling when considered in the abstract, the likelihood of its being adopted, supported, and given a chance to succeed will depend in large measure on the way it is perceived in the various communities that the jurisdiction comprises. Trust and confidence in government are scarce commodities in these times, especially among some minority communities that have been ill-treated. Where elected school boards enjoy reservoirs of trust and confidence based on the particularities of local history, reformers should think at least twice before rushing to dismantle them, even when the performance of those institutions is legitimately suspect. Enlisting those loyalties in a collective endeavor to reform, instead of replace, the existing structures may be under some conditions the more sensible strategy.

Judging from our cases, the ideal organizational structure may take a responsible professional form, in which the CEO is responsible to the whole community, allowing more access to decision making. The current mayor-CEO model represents a fundamental change in the way boards and administrators relate to one another. This model is at variance with the internal organizational culture of school governance. Under the traditional elected board-superintendent model the policy stakeholders knew how to interact with the decision makers. With a new arrangement, these relationships are in flux and it will take some time to settle into a routine.

David Tyack once observed that, given the organizational culture of schools, incremental change is all that we can hope for. He counsels patience in our attempts to align policy talk with school practice. The reforms that have "stuck" to school practices were those that had modest goals. The ones that have not survived were those that overreached (Tyack 1991).

Reform of local school districts should aim to unite elected officials and professional administrators in a partnership for effective management that is adaptable to the new challenges of underachieving inner city schools. The contributors to this book agree that such a partnership is essential for true school reform.

References

Anyon, J. 1997. *Ghetto Schooling: A Political Economy of Urban Educational Reform*. New York: Teachers College Press.

Berliner, D. C., and B. J. Biddle. 1995. *The Manufactured Crisis*. New York: Longman.

Coulson, A. J. 1999. *Market Education: The Unknown History*. New Brunswick, N.J.: Transaction Publishers.

Henig, J. R. 1994. *Rethinking School Choice: Limits of the Market Metaphor*. Princeton, N.J.: Princeton University Press.

Henig, J. R., R. C. Hula, M. Orr, and D. S. Pedescleaux. 1999. *The Color of School Reform*. Princeton, N.J.: Princeton University Press.

Kinder, D. R., and L. M. Sanders. 1996. *Divided by Color: Racial Politics and Democratic Ideals*. Chicago: University of Chicago Press.

Kirst, M., and K. Bulkley. 2000. " 'New, Improved' Mayors Take Over City Schools." *Phi Delta Kappan* 80 (March): 538–46.

———. 2003. "Mayoral Takeover: The Different Directions Taken in Different Cities." In *A Race against Time: Responses to the Crisis in Urban Schooling*, ed. J. G. Cibulka and W. L. Boyd. Westport, Conn.: Greenwood Press.

Kozol, J. 1991. *Savage Inequalities: Children in America's Schools*. New York: Crown.

Lieberman, M. 1993. *Public Education: An Autopsy*. Cambridge: Harvard University Press.

March, J. G., and J. P. Olsen. 1989. *Rediscovering Institutions: The Organizational Basis of Politics*. New York: The Free Press.

Orr, M. 2000. *Black Social Capital: The Politics of School Reform in Baltimore, 1986–1998*. Lawrence: University Press of Kansas.

Rich, W. 1996. *Black Mayors and School Politics*. New York: Garland Press.

Rothstein, R. 1998. *The Way We Were?* New York: The Century Foundation.

Sigelman, L., and S. Welch. 1991. *Black Americans' Views of Racial Inequality*. Cambridge: Cambridge University Press.

Squire, K., and C. Reigelluth. 2000. "The Many Faces of Systemic Change." *Education Horizon* 78(6):143–53.

Stone, C. 1989. *Regime Politics: Governing Atlanta, 1946–1988*. Lawrence: University Press of Kansas.

Tyack, D. 1991. "Public School Reform: Policy Talk and Institutional Practice." *American Journal of Education* 100(1):1–19.

Tyack, D., and L. Cuban. 1995. *Tinkering toward Utopia: A Century of Public School Reform*. Cambridge: Harvard University Press.

Wirt, F. M., and M. W. Kirst. 2001. *The Political Dynamics of American Education*. Richmond, Calif.: McCutchan Publishing.

Wong, K. 2001. "Integrated Governance in Chicago and Birmingham (UK)." In *School Choice or Best Systems: What Improves Education?*, ed. M. C. Wang and H. J. Walberg, 161–212. Mahwah, N.J.: Lawrence Erlbaum Associates.

Yates, D. 1984. *The Ungovernable City*. Cambridge: MIT Press.

Yee, G. Forthcoming. "From Court Street to City Hall: Governance Change in the Boston Public Schools." In *A Race against Time: Responses to the Crisis in Urban Schooling*, ed. J. G. Cibulka and W. L. Boyd. Westport, Conn.: Greenwood Press.

Zetlin, Andrea G., and C. Lim. 1998. "Implementation of Systemic Reform: Restructuring Health Social Services in a Large Urban School District." *Urban Education* 33(4):516–33.

Index